SO-CDS-058

easy
CAMPING
in SOUTHERN CALIFORNIA

100 Places Anyone Can Camp This Weekend

ANN MARIE BROWN

Foghorn
Press
BOOKS BUILDING COMMUNITY™

1-57354-004-8

51295

9 781573 540049

Library of Congress ISSN Data:
May 1998
Easy Camping in Southern California
100 Places Anyone Can Camp This Weekend
First Edition
ISSN: 1099-5102

CREDITS

Managing Editor	*Donna Leverenz*
Editor	*Sherry McInroy*
Book Design, Photos	*Ann Marie Brown*
Maps	*Kirk McInroy*
Front Cover Photo	*Silver City Resort*
Back Cover Photo	*Arrowhead Pine Rose Cabins, Rhona Chavis*
Author Photo	*Nina Schuyler*

Printed in the United States of America

easy
CAMPING
in SOUTHERN CALIFORNIA

100 Places Anyone Can Camp This Weekend

ANN MARIE BROWN

Foghorn
Press
BOOKS BUILDING COMMUNITY™

CONTENTS

3—Santa Barbara & Santa Monica Mountains—page 101

4—Central Coast—page 131

5—Western Sierra—page 159

6—Eastern Sierra & Death Valley—page 217

Index—page 245

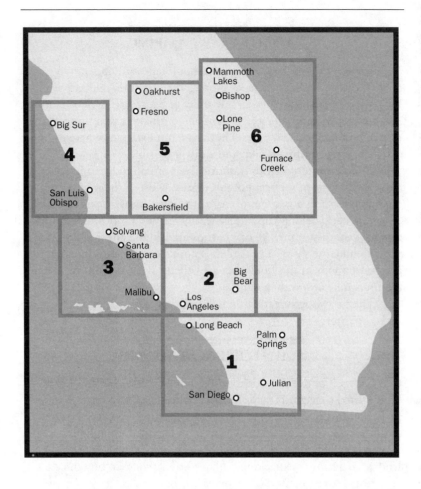

Detailed maps of each region are found on these pages:

ABOUT EASY CAMPING

Each of the "easy camps" in this book falls into one of two general categories: It is either a resort, lodge, or hotel that has cabins for rent, or it is an easy-grade, low-mileage backpacking destination. All of the easy camps are a bit out of the ordinary, a refreshing change from traditional car camping. They are set in locations where outdoor activities are plentiful, varied, and easily accessible.

The cabins range from traditional mountain lodges and cross-country ski huts to tent cabins and tepees. Most of them have cooking facilities so that you can prepare your own meals.

The backpacking trips are generally less than four miles long and have an easy grade. All of the trips are suitable for families. If you want to hike the shortest possible distance to your campsite, look for the destinations in this book that are called "Walk-in Camps." These require a hike of less than a mile.

The following information will help you plan your trip.

MAPS FOR BACKPACKING

For each of the easy backpacking trips described in this book, I have listed suggested "maps for backpacking." These include state park, national park, national forest, and commercial maps that outline the area described, as well as more detailed topographic maps that are available from the United States Geologic Survey (USGS). Under "maps for backpacking," I have noted where to buy the park or national forest maps. USGS maps can be purchased from many outdoors stores and sporting good stores, or you can contact the USGS directly. Their address is:

United States Geologic Survey, Western Distribution Branch
Box 25286 Federal Center
Denver, CO 80225
(800) 435-7627 or fax (303) 202-4693

You do not need to buy all the maps listed for each story. A single park map, national forest map, or commercial map will be sufficient for most people on an easy backpacking trip. The USGS maps are suggested only for people who wish to extensively explore the surrounding area.

QUESTIONS TO ASK WHEN RESERVING A CABIN

Wherever possible, I have tried to provide answers to these questions in the individual cabin stories that follow. But resort owners change, policies change, and times change, so it's wise to ask anyway. The best advice: Know before you go.

- How many people does the cabin accommodate, and is there any extra charge for extra people?
- Are pets allowed in the cabin?
- Does the cabin have a private bathroom and shower, or do I use a shared bathroom facility on the grounds?
- Does the cabin have electricity and heat? Should I bring flashlights and lanterns?
- Does the cabin have a fireplace or wood stove, and should I bring my own firewood?
- Does the cabin have a kitchen, and are all dishes, pots, pans, and utensils provided?
- Does the cabin have a barbecue or fire grill where I can cook outside?
- Is there a grocery store nearby, or should I bring all my own food for cooking?
- Is there a restaurant or cafe nearby?
- Does the cabin have all linens provided, or should I bring sleeping bags, pillows, and towels?
- Is the cabin a single unit or duplex-style? Is it situated very close to other cabins, so I might hear my neighbors?
- Is the cabin close to the road, so I might hear road noise?
- Does the cabin have a view?

STUFF TO TAKE ON A SHORT BACKPACKING TRIP

Every backpacker has a personal list of what to take, and what not to take, on an overnight trip in the wild. This is my list; surely you will develop your own. Note that this list is intended for a short trip of only two or three days. If you are going for a longer period of time, you'll need to bring more stuff.

- sleeping bag(s)
- sleeping bag pad(s)
- tent and all tent poles and stakes, plus rain fly

- ground tarp for under the tent
- backpack(s)
- water purification system, or bottled water *(plan on one gallon per person per day, for drinking, cooking, and other uses)*
- water bottles or canteens
- food *(more than you think you'll need)*
- clothing *(be prepared for all possible weather conditions, especially rain and cold, even in summer)*
- bear-proof storage container *(useful for raccoons and other food thieves as well as bears)*
- backpacking stove *(remember that in many places, you are not allowed to build a fire, and cold food gets boring fast)*
- fuel for your backpacking stove *(it's amazing how many people forget it, or don't bring enough)*
- pots and utensils for cooking
- dishes and utensils for eating
- maps for wherever you are going
- overnight permit or campfire permit for wherever you are going *(if required)*
- compass *(know how to use it)*
- boxes of matches in Ziploc bags *(each person carries some)*
- extra Ziploc bags in a variety of sizes *(multitude of uses, especially for food storage)*
- first-aid kit *(know how to use it)*
- hygiene and toiletry items *(toothbrush, toothpaste, comb, hair bands, small towel, etc.)*
- any necessary medications or prescriptions
- insect repellent
- plastic trowel *(for burying human waste)*
- garbage bags *(multitude of uses, including packing out your trash and emergency rain gear)*
- pocket knife *(each person carries one)*
- sunglasses
- sunscreen and lip balm
- small flashlight with fresh batteries *(each person carries one)*
- camera, film, extra battery
- fishing license and lightweight fishing equipment
- day pack for day hiking
- stuff for fun *(paperback books, a tree or wildflower guide, playing cards, binoculars, paper and pencil)*

ABOUT THE NATIONAL FOREST ADVENTURE PASS

Beginning in 1997, a fee policy was instituted in Angeles, San Bernardino, Cleveland, and Los Padres national forests, as a way of raising revenue to cover the costs of recreation on national forest land.

The policy is as follows: Any vehicle that is parked on land in Angeles, San Bernardino, Cleveland, and Los Padres national forests must display a "national forest adventure pass." Visitors are free to drive through national forest land without a pass, but if you park your car, you must have one.

Passes are available for a fee of $5 per day or $30 per year, and the same pass is valid in all four national forests. When you purchase a yearly pass, you receive an extra pass for use on a second vehicle, such as a motorcycle or trailer. Passes can be purchased at all Angeles, San Bernardino, Cleveland, and Los Padres national forest visitor centers and ranger stations. They are also available at many commercial establishments (such as grocery stores and mini-marts) located on or near national forest land.

Note that there are some gray areas to the fee policy. In some regions, such as Crystal Lake Recreation Area in Angeles National Forest or Santa Ynez Recreation Area in Los Padres National Forest, a concessionaire runs the developed services—campgrounds, picnic areas, rest rooms, etc.—and in those areas, a national forest adventure pass is not valid. You must pay a use fee directly to the concessionaire.

Following each story in this book, I have noted if a national forest adventure pass is usually required in the area described. As a general rule, areas that get the highest visitation are usually the ones where an adventure pass is required, and vehicles not displaying one will be ticketed. Typical examples are anywhere around Big Bear Lake, the Laguna Mountain Recreation Area in San Diego, the snow-play areas and trailheads of Mount Baldy, and the many trailheads along the Angeles Crest Highway.

My personal experience has shown that if you are going to take more than one hike per year or one weekend getaway per year in Angeles, San Bernardino, Cleveland, and Los Padres national forests (which cover the majority of Southern California recreation lands!), you might as well buy an annual pass and be done with it. Keep it in your glove compartment; hang it from your rear-view mirror when you park your car. That way, you'll always be prepared.

HOW TO USE THIS BOOK

This book is organized geographically, with each camp and cabin numbered from 1 to 100. Use the map on page 7 to locate the area of Southern California where you want to travel, then turn to the more detailed map of the region within each chapter. The regional maps are numbered, and the numbers correspond to the stories in each chapter.

Or you can simply scan the table of contents for the listings of easy camps, or turn to the chapter covering the region where you'd like to camp and read all of the stories in that chapter.

Each of the camps and cabins in this book is rated on a scale of 1 through 10. They have been selected for overall quality, so none of the camps received a rating lower than a 6. Although the ratings are completely subjective, they provide a marker of the relative beauty of the area, nearby recreation possibilities, and quality of facilities.

Overall Rating

① ② ③ ④ ⑤ ⑥ ⑦ ⑧ ⑨ ⑩

Poor........................Fair.............................Great

Each destination also has one or a series of graphic icons listed with it, which denote recreational activities and side-trip possibilities located at or near the cabin or camp. They are:

| Hiking | Fishing | Boating | Swimming | Surfing | Rafting |
| Kayaking | Waterskiing | Skiing | Horseback Riding | Hot Springs | Biking |

The tent icon (🏕) denotes whether or not a destination requires you to hike in carrying your own tent. Hike-in destinations such as tent cabins, tepees, or ski huts, which require a hike to reach them but do not require that you pack a tent, do not exhibit the tent icon. Lodges and cabin resorts also do not exhibit the tent icon.

INTRODUCTION

Over and over, traveling in the outdoors teaches me to be flexible and adaptable. It's a lesson for which I'm grateful, because I've found these to be critical life skills. In the outdoors, as in the rest of life, things just don't always go as you plan.

For example, in the course of researching this book, a major rainstorm on the Central Coast closed the resort where we were scheduled to stay. But a series of detours on the flooded road took us to another cabin—one I would not have found or stayed in otherwise. With a fire roaring in the fireplace and rain splashing on the windowpanes, we spent a cozy, wonderful night in a place I would have ordinarily passed by.

Another time, I spent a long and arduous night with a bear nosing around my campsite, disrupting my much-needed sleep. My food was carefully stored and "bear-proofed," but that didn't stop the big furry guy from wanting to sniff the air. When the bear finally gave up and left, I crawled out of my tent and witnessed a night sky blanketed with stars that were brilliant enough to read by. Without the bear's nosiness, I would have slept right through the show.

On another occasion, noisy neighbors in the cabin next door caused me to give up my attempt at slumber and go for a drive before dawn. I stopped my car along a desert road and was awestruck by the most incredible sunrise I've ever seen. Yet another day I drove many miles out of my way to hike a peak in the San Gabriels that I had long wanted to climb. When I arrived, I found that the trail was closed because of nearby forest fires. Sorely disappointed, I hiked to the summit of another peak instead, and near the top, I saw my first bighorn sheep. He was close-up on the trail ahead of me, bearing remarkable spiraling antlers.

There were days when it snowed in the middle of July, or rain poured down just after the day had dawned clear and blue. Sometimes giant trees fell across the road, or bridges were washed out from heavy rains. But each time, what seemed like an insurmountable difficulty turned out to be a blessing in disguise. I wound up making new friends, or discovering new places, or seeing a rare sight that I would have otherwise missed.

Kurt Vonnegut Jr. once wrote that "peculiar travel suggestions are dancing lessons from God." If you travel around Southern California and visit any or all of this book's backcountry cabins, wilderness campsites, ski huts, or guest ranches, you'll probably learn to dance. At the very least, you'll have the time of your life trying.

Ann Marie Brown

BEST CAMPS LIST

Of all the destinations in this book, here are my favorites in the following categories:

5 Best Cabins for Day-Hiking:
Knotty Pines Cabins, Idyllwild, p. 53
Grant Grove Cabins, Kings Canyon National Park, p. 184
Roads End Resort, Sequoia National Forest, p. 209
Silver City Resort, Mineral King, Sequoia National Park, p. 201
Rock Creek Lodge or Rock Creek Lakes Resort,
        Rock Creek Lake, Inyo National Forest, pp. 223 and 225

5 Best Cabins for Fishing:
Shore Acres Lodge, Big Bear Lake, p. 92
Vermilion Valley Resort, Lake Thomas A. Edison, p. 180
Bishop Creek Lodge and Parchers Resort, South Lake,
        Inyo National Forest, pp. 232 and 234
Big Rock Resort, June Lake, p. 219
Tamarack Lodge Resort, Mammoth Lakes, p. 221

5 Best Cabins for Horseback Riding:
Alisal Guest Ranch & Resort, Santa Ynez Valley, p. 105
Circle Bar B Guest Ranch, Santa Barbara, p. 108
Bonnie B Ranch, Sierra National Forest, p. 164
Rankin Ranch, Walker Basin, p. 214
Muir Trail Ranch, John Muir Wilderness, p. 182

5 Best Cabins for Water Sports:
Lake San Antonio South Shore Resort, Paso Robles, p. 147
The Forks Resort, Bass Lake, p. 162
Shaver Lake Lodge Cabins, Shaver Lake, p. 168
Wagner's Resort, Mammoth Pool Reservoir, p. 166
any of the cabin resorts at Big Bear Lake, pp. 90-95

5 Best Cabins for Downhill Skiing/Snowboarding:
Happy Bear Village Cabins, Big Bear Lake, p. 94
Mountain View Motel Cabins, Wrightwood, p. 78
Snowcrest Lodge, Angeles National Forest, p. 82
Big Rock Resort, June Lake, p. 219
Tamarack Lodge Resort, Mammoth Lakes, p. 221

5 Best Cabins for Romance:
Arrowhead Pine Rose Cabins, Twin Peaks, p. 84
Chimney Sweep Inn Cottages, Solvang, p. 103
Gorda Springs Cottages, Los Padres National Forest, p. 143
Lucia Lodge, Big Sur Coast, p. 141
Boat & Breakfast Newport, Newport Harbor, p. 29

5 Best Easy Backpack Trips in the Wilderness:
Round Valley Backpack, Mount San Jacinto State
	Wilderness, p. 55
Sheep Camp Backpack, Chumash Wilderness, p. 119
Spruce Creek Backpack, Silver Peak Wilderness, p. 145
Weaver Lake Backpack, Jennie Lakes Wilderness, p. 189
Long Lake & Bull Lake Backpack, John Muir Wilderness, p. 236

5 Best Cabins with Activities for Children:
Montecito Sequoia Lodge, Sequoia National Forest, p. 191
Rankin Ranch, Walker Basin, p. 214
Alisal Guest Ranch & Resort, Santa Ynez Valley, p. 105
Rancho Oso Cabins & Covered Wagons, Santa Barbara, p. 110
The Miramar Hotel & Resort, Montecito, p. 112

5 Best Oceanfront Cabins:
Crystal Pier Hotel Cottages, Pacific Beach, p. 38
Cayucos Vacation Rentals, Cayucos State Beach, p. 150
Clam Digger Cottages, Pismo Beach, p. 157
Gorda Springs Cottages, Los Padres National Forest, p. 143
Lucia Lodge, Big Sur Coast, p. 141

5 Best Oceanfront Camps:
Montana de Oro Backpack, Montana de Oro State Park, p. 152
Parson's Landing Backpack, Two Harbors, Catalina Island, p. 19
Echo Arch Walk-in Camp, San Onofre State Beach, p. 34
Anacapa Island Walk-in Camp, Channel Islands, p. 117
Julia Pfeiffer Burns Walk-in Camps, Julia Pfeiffer Burns
	State Park, p. 139

5 Best Walk-in Camps (walk length is one mile or less):
Two Harbors Walk-in Camp, Catalina Island, p. 21
Echo Arch Walk-in Camp, San Onofre State Beach, p. 34
Anacapa Island Walk-in Camp, Channel Islands, p. 117
Julia Pfeiffer Burns Walk-in Camps, Julia Pfeiffer Burns
     State Park, p. 139
First Falls Walk-in Camp, Inyo National Forest, p. 240

5 Most Unusual Cabins or Camps:
Boat & Breakfast Newport, Newport Harbor, p. 29
Santa Rosa Island Fly-in Overnight, Channel Islands, p. 114
Mono Hot Springs Resort, Sierra National Forest, p. 177
Pear Lake Ski Hut, Sequoia National Forest, p. 193
Oak Flat Lookout Tower, Sequoia National Forest, p. 213

4 Best Desert Cabins:
La Casa del Zorro Desert Resort, Anza-Borrego Desert
     State Park, p. 51
Mojave Rock Ranch Lodge, Joshua Tree National Park, p. 58
29 Palms Inn, Joshua Tree National Park, p. 60
Furnace Creek Ranch, Death Valley National Park, p. 242

San Diego, Orange County, & Palm Springs

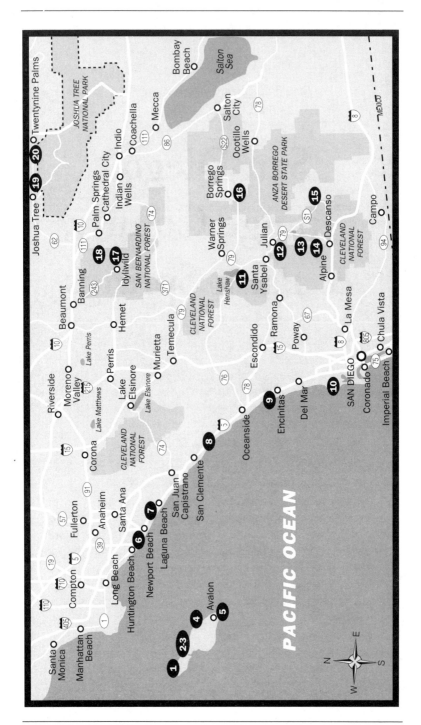

Bombay
Beach

Salton
Sea

Twentynine Palms

Joshua Tree

JOSHUA TREE
NATIONAL PARK

Mecca

Coachella

Salton
City

111

78

8

Palm Springs

Cathedral City

Indio

Indian
Wells

S22

Ocotillo
Wells

19

20

86

62

10

ANZA BORREGO
DESERT STATE PARK

Campo

111

SAN BERNARDINO
NATIONAL FOREST

18

17

243

74

Banning

Beaumont

Idyllwild

Warner
Springs

Borrego
Springs

16

Julian

79

S1

Descanso

15

94

CLEVELAND
NATIONAL
FOREST

Alpine

12

13

14

Hemet

Santa
Ysabel

11

79

Lake
Henshaw

Santa
Ysabel

CLEVELAND
NATIONAL
FOREST

371

La Mesa

Chula Vista

Temecula

Murrieta

Ramona

Poway

67

8

79

Lake Perris

10

Perris

Escondido

15

805

75

SAN DIEGO

Coronado

Imperial Beach

Riverside

Moreno
Valley

215

Lake
Elsinore

Lake Matthews

Lake Elsinore

76

78

Del Mar

10

Encinitas

9

Corona

15

CLEVELAND
NATIONAL
FOREST

74

Oceanside

5

8

91

Santa Ana

Anaheim

Fullerton

57

San Juan
Capistrano

San Clemente

7

Compton

5

39

19

710

Long Beach

Laguna Beach

Newport Beach

6

Huntington Beach

110

Avalon

4

5

405

1

Santa
Monica

Manhattan
Beach

2-3

1

PACIFIC OCEAN

N
E
S
W

1. PARSON'S LANDING BACKPACK
Two Harbors, Catalina Island

In most places, seven miles one-way would be too far to hike for an easy backpacking trip. That's because in most places, trails go uphill and downhill. But if you're backpacking to Parson's Landing Campground on Catalina Island, almost the entire seven-mile trail is flat, and smoothly surfaced as well. The seven miles whiz by in less than three hours—so quickly that you're almost sad when the hike is over, because the scenery is so good along the way.

The trip to Parson's Landing begins with a boat ride from Long Beach or San Pedro to Two Harbors on Catalina Island. If you take the express boat, you arrive in shortly over an hour, and begin hiking from the spot where the boat drops you off. Head to your right (north) down the harbor's beach, and then briefly uphill past some small cottages until you join the wide, flat, dirt road that follows the contour of the coast along the mainland side of the island. Turn right on this road (called West End Road on maps but never signed anywhere) and you're on your way.

The next five miles are about as flat as any trail could be, and about as scenic, too. You get nearly nonstop views of Catalina's rocky coastline, with one hidden cove after another appearing every half mile or so. On your right, you'll see colorful kayaks bobbing along in the sea, pelicans diving for lunch, and miles of clear emerald water—the stuff that has made this end of Catalina Island famous the world over for SCUBA diving and snorkeling. On your left, you get a close-up look at the island's foliage, which consists mostly of prickly pear cactus—more than you've probably ever seen in one place. In spring, cactus and wildflowers bloom, and at Cherry Cove (one mile out), the native cherry trees burst into color.

If you get homesick for the mainland, you can squint your eyes and just make out Long Beach and the Orange County coast, a mere blur of land some 20-plus miles away. Most people find they enjoy seeing "civilization" from this distance.

As you march along, you'll pass several private camps belonging to church and scout groups. Keep your eyes peeled after you pass the camp at Howland's Landing, 4.5 miles out, because shortly past it is a marvelous stretch of white sandy beach where you can take a break and a swim if you wish. It is marked by a couple of tall, rocky sea stacks about 150 yards offshore. An obvious spur trail leads off the main road down to the beach.

Beyond this beach, you'll pass another large camp and begin to see signs for Parson's Landing, further ahead. Keep hiking, heading inland and starting to climb a bit, then take the well-signed right fork. The trail leads up a dry, grassy ridge, and when you reach the top, you spy your destination on the other side: a beautiful rocky pocket beach. Head for it, and take your pick of six possible campsites right on the beach, each equipped with a picnic table and fire grill. Every site is reasonably private and secluded from the rest. There is only one decision left to make: Should we put up the tent or go swimming first?

When you pay for your campsite reservation at Parson's Landing, your fee includes a key for access to a locker at the campground. In the locker, you'll find bottled water (in 2.5 gallon bottles) and plenty of firewood. Other than that, you are on your own for supplies. It's a long hike back to Two Harbors, so make sure you've packed all you need. Sunscreen is a must, as well as adequate food and cooking supplies.

Aside from the fabulous beachside setting, the best thing about camping at Parson's Landing is that it gives you a perfect base from which to day-hike around the secluded northwest side of the island. Many people hike the seven-mile round-trip to Silver Peak, which

The beach at Parson's Landing Campground

offers great views. Be sure not to miss the four-mile hike to Starlight Beach, one of the most remote beaches in all of Southern California.

Facilities, reservations, fees: There are six campsites at Parson's Landing, each with a picnic table and fire grill. Bottled water and firewood are provided. Vault toilets are located near the beach. Reservations and a camping permit are required. The fee is $15 per night. Pets are not permitted.

Who to contact: Two Harbors Visitors Services, P.O. Box 5044, Two Harbors, CA 90704; (310) 510-1550. Fax (310) 510-0244.

Maps for backpacking: A trail map of Catalina Island is available for 50 cents when you pick up your camping permit. For a topographic map of the area, ask for Santa Catalina West from the USGS.

Season: Year-round; spring and fall are best.

Directions: Two companies provide ferry transportation to Two Harbors from San Pedro and Long Beach. Advance reservations are recommended. Phone Catalina Express at (310) 519-1212 or Catalina Cruises at (800) 228-2546. (Catalina Express is the faster of the two ferry services.)

2. TWO HARBORS WALK-IN CAMP
Two Harbors, Catalina Island

For the nonbelievers who think there is no unspoiled place left in Los Angeles County, we say: Board the next boat to Two Harbors on Catalina Island.

Two Harbors is the less visited northern port on Catalina, and in comparison, it makes the more famous southern port of Avalon seem like the urban jungle. While Avalon has more than 100 hotels and restaurants, Two Harbors has only one hotel (with nine rooms) and one restaurant. While Avalon has an active nightlife scene, Two Harbors rolls up its sidewalks soon after dark each evening.

But what it lacks in development, Two Harbors more than compensates for in outdoor recreation. You can rent kayaks by the hour or by the day, and paddle around the island's rocky coves. You can bring your snorkeling or SCUBA equipment (or rent some here) and go ocean swimming with colorful critters. You can hike along the island's many trails and dirt roads, or swim in the warm Pacific, or what the heck—just lie around and watch the pelicans dive into the shallow harbor waters. Good idea.

A couple of interesting and inexpensive camping options make the trip to Two Harbors easy and affordable. You can camp year-round at Two Harbors Campground, which is a mere quarter-mile walk from the pier where the boat deposits you on the island. Since the walk is so short, you can bring as much stuff as you want, including your diving or fishing gear. Camping options include traditional tent camping, or staying in the campground's tent cabins or tepees. That's right, tepees. If you choose the tent cabins or tepees, you need only bring your food, clothing, and bed linens or sleeping bags, because cots and mattresses are provided.

You'll get a clear view of Two Harbors Campground as your ferry from Los Angeles pulls into Two Harbors—the camp is off to your left along the hillside. After disembarking, simply head to your left along the coastal trail for a quarter-mile to reach the camp. (At the fork, bear right to stay on the upper trail.) If you want to leave some gear at the pier, storage lockers are provided for that purpose. If you're carrying a really big load, you can pay a few extra bucks for someone to carry it over to the campground on a large dolly. The rate is one dollar per item at regularly scheduled boat arrival times.

Two Harbors Campground itself is nothing special, just a series of campsites interspersed with the usual porta-potties, outdoor showers, fire grills and rings, and wooden shade structures. But what makes the camp extraordinary is that every single campsite has a gorgeous, unobstructed view of the ocean. Sites numbered 1 through 7 are right on the water's edge, but they are quite exposed, both to the wind and to public view. Better sites (any numbered 10 and above) are higher up on the hill, with more expansive views and more privacy.

At the very top of the campground hill, near the ranger station, are the Two Harbors tent cabins. These are the same as you find everywhere—canvas structures on wooden platforms, with cots inside and picnic tables outside. Each comes with a camp stove, lantern, and outdoor barbecue, and sleeps four to eight people. The tent cabins dutifully serve their purpose; the only thing remarkable about them is their lovely ocean views.

Slightly more fun and interesting are the Two Harbors tepees. A half-dozen large tepees are grouped together on the far side of the campground, across a little footbridge. They are spaced fairly close together, and kept separate from the rest of the camp, which makes them ideal for group camping. The tepees have foam pads inside instead of cots, and each one sleeps eight to ten people, all sharing one open space. (You have to like your fellow campers.) A camp stove, fire ring, barbecue, and lantern are provided with each tepee.

If you have your heart set on a Two Harbors vacation in a tepee or tent cabin, plan your visit for April to October. In the winter, the Two Harbors Campground remains open, but only tent sites are available. Many consider this season the finest time to camp, however, because darn near nobody is around and you get the whole island to yourself. Summer is the "busy" season at Two Harbors.

Two Harbors Campground

Facilities, reservations, fees: There are six tent cabins, six tepees, and 40 tent sites at Two Harbors Campground, each with a picnic table and fire grill. Drinking water, showers, and vault toilets are provided. Campfires are permitted. A quarter-mile walk is required to reach the campground. A general store and restaurant are available in Two Harbors. Reservations are required. Fees range from $7.50 per night for tent sites to $60 per night for tent cabins and tepees (for up to six people). Pets are not permitted.

Who to contact: Two Harbors Visitors Services, P.O. Box 5044, Two Harbors, CA 90704; (310) 510-1550. Fax (310) 510-0244.

Season: Year-round; spring and fall are best. Tent cabins and tepees are available only from April to October; tent sites are available year-round.

Directions: Two companies provide ferry transportation to Two Harbors from San Pedro and Long Beach. Advance reservations are recommended. Phone Catalina Express at (310) 519-1212 or Catalina Cruises at (800) 228-2546. (Catalina Express is the faster of the two ferry services.)

3. CATALINA CABINS AT TWO HARBORS
Two Harbors, Catalina Island

If you're well acquainted with the ways of Southern California vacationers, you know that in the winter months, most people head for the mountains to ski or else they stay home. This phenomenon has puzzled many observers, because the finest days along the coast often occur in winter, when the weather is clear, the air is crisp, the tides are more extreme, and the waves are big and full. Nonetheless, from October to March, long stretches of Southern California sand will have not a single human footprint on them.

If the beaches seem empty along the Southern California mainland in wintertime, you should see what it's like at Two Harbors on Catalina Island. Although Catalina's big city of Avalon still attracts day visitors and even some weekend overnight tourists in winter, Two Harbors gets really quiet. In fact, it gets so quiet that the mobile-home-style cottages in town, which serve as summer housing for employees in the tourism trade, are left vacant for the winter. The cottages are then made available for rent to anybody who wants an inexpensive vacation.

Inexpensive? How about 25 bucks per night for two people

Two Harbors, Catalina Island

during the week, and 40 bucks per night on the weekends? That's a downright bargain, especially considering that if it should rain during your visit, you're warm and dry with a roof over your head, instead of stuck in a campground peering out at the dripping sky through your tent flaps.

Of course, don't expect a whole lot for 25 bucks a night. The cottages are really just trailer homes, stuck in the middle of town next to the tennis courts and the children's playground. Each cottage is just large enough for two people, and you have your choice of bunk beds or a double bed. You won't have your own bathroom, but restrooms, showers, and laundry facilities are located nearby.

You will have a heater and refrigerator, and just outside the cottages is a communal kitchen area with picnic tables, barbecues, gas burners, and even a microwave. You can bring groceries from the mainland, then supplement your stock with supplies from the Two Harbors General Store, located a short walk away. Also make sure you bring your own cooking and eating utensils, as well as bedding and towels, because none are provided.

Keep in mind that if you come to Two Harbors in wintertime, you'll be on your own for planning outdoor activities. That means you won't be able to rent SCUBA gear or kayaks or mountain bikes or anything else. All of the concessionaires are gone for the winter, so you must bring your own equipment with you from the mainland.

For many people, all they need is their hiking boots, because excellent trails lead in several directions from Two Harbors. A terrific easy walk is possible across the narrowest part of the island—only a half-mile—from Two Harbors to Catalina Harbor (called Cat Harbor by the locals). At the southwest edge of Catalina Harbor, you'll spot a single bench on a hillside knoll that is the perfect place to watch the sun set.

Longer hikes are possible along the island's dirt roads to Cherry Cove and Parson's Landing. If you are smart and lucky enough to time your trip for springtime, you'll see the grove of native Catalina cherry trees blooming bright white in Cherry Cove, as well as acres of stunning wildflowers and prickly pear cactus in bloom all across the island. When you hike near the shoreline, peer down into the azure water and you'll probably see the flashes of bright red that are garibaldis, California's state saltwater fish.

Facilities, reservations, fees: There are 18 mobile-home-style house-keeping cabins at Two Harbors; each accommodates two people. Communal kitchen facilities, with gas burners and barbecues, are available outside the cabins; refrigerators are provided inside the cabins. Restrooms and showers are located nearby. Reservations are required. Fees range from $25 per night on weekdays to $40 per night on weekends. Pets are not permitted.

Who to contact: Two Harbors Visitors Services, P.O. Box 5044, Two Harbors, CA 90704; (310) 510-1550. Fax (310) 510-0244.

Season: The cabins at Two Harbors are available for rent from October to April.

Directions: Two companies provide ferry transportation to Two Harbors from San Pedro and Long Beach. Advance reservations are recommended. Phone Catalina Express at (310) 519-1212 or Catalina Cruises at (800) 228-2546. (Catalina Express is the faster of the two ferry services.)

4. CATALINA BOAT-IN CAMPS
Catalina Island's Leeward Shoreline

If you've got your own boat, or know someone who does, you're in position for the most exclusive overnight experience possible on Catalina Island. You lucky dog.

I'm talking about the boat-in beach camps along Catalina's leeward shoreline. Most people don't realize that on the southeast side of the island there are dozens of small, rugged coves, accessible only by private boat. You can't hike to them. You can't drive to them. You can't even take the small island shuttle boats to reach them. You have to have your own boat, and you have to pay five bucks per person for camping privileges. After that, you set sail for your own private cove.

The names of the places tell you how good they are: Starlight Cove, Paradise Cove, Lava Wall Beach, Gibraltar Point, and Italian Gardens, for example. There are a total of 10 coves open for camping on a space-available basis. All you need is a reservation, and you're in. Most of the coves can accommodate as many as 12 people; Paradise and Willow coves are smaller and can accommodate only six people.

Keep in mind that this is primitive camping. You get a private cove in which to moor your boat, and some island beach space for setting up your tent, but that's it in terms of amenities. You must bring all your own camping equipment, including plenty of bottled water, a backpacking stove and fuel, and a porta-potty. But since you have a boat, that's easy. You can carry as much stuff as you want to, without having to worry about squeezing it all in your backpack and schlepping it around.

The coves are all slightly different. Be forewarned that depending on recent storms and tides, there can be a lot of beach available at your cove, or only a very narrow strip of sand. Sometimes even the sand is washed away, and there is only rock, which can make it hard to find a spot to pitch your tent. (Be sure to ask about beach and weather conditions before you plan your trip.) Some of the coves are graced with a palm tree or two for shade and ambience, while others are backed against a vertical wall of prickly pear cactus and coastal scrub. You may want to pack along some kind of shade shelter, like a big beach umbrella.

When you leave your boat-in camp, make sure you pick up any trash you can find, even if it isn't yours. It's imperative to leave no trace of your visit to these secluded coves, so that others can follow you and share in a pristine island experience.

Facilities, reservations, fees: There are 10 coves available for boat-in camping at Catalina Island. No water is available; you must pack in bottled water. Reservations are required. The fee is $5 per person per night, less for children under 12. Pets are not permitted.

Who to contact: Two Harbors Visitors Services, P.O. Box 5044, Two Harbors, CA 90704; (310) 510-1550. Fax (310) 510-0244.

Season: Open year-round; winter storms can make some coves inaccessible.

Directions: Get in your boat, point it toward Santa Catalina, and steer.

5. LA PALOMA & CATALINA COTTAGES
Avalon, Catalina Island

The island of Catalina has two faces: the subdued, rustic profile of the town of Two Harbors on the north side of the island, and the bustling, metropolitan profile of the town of Avalon on the south side. If outdoor adventure is your thing, you'll find it plentiful in both places. But if you want your adventure combined with a few good restaurants and some nightlife, Avalon is the place to go.

Avalon is the city that never sleeps on Catalina. While Two Harbors has a busy season (summer) and a quiet season (winter), Avalon stays busy year-round. Even on weekdays, it's surprising how

Avalon Harbor, Catalina Island

many people are touring the streets, shops, and businesses in Avalon's downtown, and signing up for a whole variety of commercial tours and outdoor adventures. Whereas at Two Harbors you'll probably bring your own gear and plan your own itinerary, at Avalon everything is for rent or for sale. The long list of recreation possibilities includes snorkeling, SCUBA diving, sport fishing, kayaking, horseback riding, swimming, hiking, and ocean rafting. All you have to do is get on a ferry from Los Angeles and show up at the Avalon pier.

What this means, of course, is that a vacation on Avalon is not cheap. Although you can keep costs down by camping at Hermit Gulch campground just outside of town, the camp is usually a noisy, crowded Tent City, where all you can do is pray that you have good neighbors. A more civilized money-saving choice is to rent a cottage in Avalon, then cook your meals in your own kitchen instead of eating out at seafood restaurants each night. (I have friends who take a vacation in Avalon every year, and they make it more affordable by spending their days fishing, then bringing their catch home and cooking it in their rented cottage.)

Two establishments offer cottage-style accommodations in Avalon. Both are rather unremarkable, but undoubtedly you'll spend all your time outdoors anyway. La Paloma Cottages on Sunny Lane is the more charming and intimate of the two, as it is located on a side street a couple of blocks from the main drag. It has lovely outdoor flower-box gardens and landscaping. Catalina Cottages is located smack in the center of downtown about a block from the pier. The interiors of the cottages have a dormitory-like appearance, but hey, they're cheap.

Remember, this is Avalon, so your accommodations are urban in style and ambience. The cottages are packed in, one right next to the other, much like motel rooms. There are no ocean views from the cottages, although at La Paloma you can rent separate apartment units that do have views. Both Catalina Cottages and La Paloma Cottages have all the basic necessities, including fully equipped kitchens. (They expect you to wash your own dishes.) A television is found in every cottage, but you won't want to waste any time watching it. There is so much island adventuring to do.

Facilities, reservations, fees: There are eight cottages at La Paloma Cottages, plus seven apartment-style units, suitable for two to five people. All have kitchenettes, and some of the apartments have ocean views. There are nine cottages at Catalina Cottages, all with kitchens. Reservations are recommended. Fees range from $59 to $89 per night. Pets are not permitted.

Who to contact: La Paloma Cottages, Box 1505, Avalon, CA 90704; (800) 310-1505 or (310) 510-0737. Or Catalina Cottages/Hermosa Hotel, Box 646, Avalon, CA 90704; (800) 666-3383 or (310) 510-1010.

Season: Year-round, but summertime can be extremely crowded.

Directions: Several companies provide ferry transportation to Avalon from San Pedro, Long Beach, Redondo Beach, and Newport Beach. Advance reservations are recommended. Phone Catalina Express at (310) 519-1212, or Catalina Cruises at (800) 228-2546, or Catalina Passenger Service at (714) 673-5245. Transportation is also possible by plane or helicopter; phone Island Express at (310) 510-2525.

6. BOAT & BREAKFAST NEWPORT
Newport Harbor, off Highway 55 in Newport Beach

This may be the most unusual camping experience I've ever had, and I've had a few that really stretched the limits of the word "camping." But if you've ever dreamed of living on your own boat, and going to sleep to the sound of tinkling halyards on metal masts in a quiet harbor, your ship just came in. Boat and Breakfast Newport can answer your dreams.

Boat and Breakfast is a company based in Newport Beach that rents out private boats—yachts, actually—for overnight stays. In their words, you get to choose from a selection of "luxurious motor yachts or graceful sailing vessels." The boats run from 40 feet long to 75 feet long, so there's some room to move around. You won't feel like sardines packed in a can. Each yacht comes equipped with a private bath, TV and VCR, and all linens and towels.

Is this an economy vacation? Absolutely not. For two people, the tab will run anywhere between $220 and $350 per night. We rented a 41-foot yacht for four people, *La Dolce Vita,* which cost $320. With the fee divided between two couples, it was manageable, but not inexpensive. Each couple had their own stateroom (that's a bedroom for you landlubbers) and small bath. The boat also had a full galley and small dinette area, but we never used it. The four of us spent every daylight hour and some evening hours up on the aft deck, lounging around and pretending we were rich and famous. If you want to make the experience seem more like camping, you can bring your sleeping bag and spend the night "above deck," breathing in the sweet ocean air.

Since you aren't going anywhere on a Boat and Breakfast yacht, your location in the harbor is key. All of the boats have excellent views, but some are closer to the shops and restaurants, while others are farther out in the harbor. Make sure you ask plenty of questions about the location of the boat you are renting; certainly you want to be in a first-rate spot for sunsets, and if you're like me, you want to be as far away from the city as possible. The only reason I could think of to leave the yacht and head for dry land was to take an early morning walk on the lovely sands of Newport Beach.

You're only allowed to cook on board some of the yachts—the ones that have electric ranges. Even though most of the rentals have full galleys, renters aren't permitted to use the ones with propane-fueled stoves, for safety reasons. No matter—a continental breakfast is brought to your boat each morning of your stay. In addition, an Italian restaurant located in the marina will bring you dinner, room-service style, for a fee. Many people just bring their own take-out dinner, plus a bag of groceries for snacks. Evening cocktails on the aft deck usually hold an important place in the day's itinerary, so don't forget your supplies.

If you really want to blow your bank account, you can rent a Boat and Breakfast yacht and sail out of the harbor. Cruising rates are about $250 per hour, with a two-hour minimum. Some people rent yachts on the "Cruise and Snooze" program, in which you go out for a cruise for a couple hours at sunset and then return to harbor to spend the night. If you can afford it, this is probably the best possible experience.

Facilities, reservations, fees: There are 10 rental yachts at Boat and Breakfast Newport. Reservations are required. Fees range from $220 to $350 per night for two people; each additional person is $50 per night. Pets are not permitted.

Who to contact: Boat and Breakfast Newport, 3400 Via Oporto, Suite 103, Newport Beach, CA 92663; (800) BOAT-BED. Fax (714) 723-4626.

Season: Open year-round.

Directions: From Interstate 5 at Santa Ana, take Highway 55 south to Costa Mesa. Highway 55 becomes Newport Boulevard; follow it for two miles until it crosses the Pacific Coast Highway. Just beyond the Pacific Coast Highway, turn left on Via Lido. Drive about 100 yards, then turn left on Via Oporto. Boat and Breakfast Newport is located in Lido Marina Village at 3400 Via Oporto.

---

7. CRYSTAL COVE BACKPACK
Crystal Cove State Park, off Highway 1 near Corona del Mar

Crystal Cove State Park is a miraculous chunk of public land that sits smack in the middle of some of the most built-up coastline in California. When you think about how much money some developer could make by turning the park's 2,500 coastal acres into condos and townhouses, you realize how fortunate we are to have this little slice of heaven on earth, right here in Orange County.

The fact that the park even exists is the first of many marvels at Crystal Cove. Another is that on average, only 12 inches of rain fall here each year, but when you see how lush and overgrown the foliage is in the park's El Moro Canyon, you won't believe it. Although El Moro Creek flows only in the wet season, its edges are lined with oaks, sycamores, and willows, and it attracts a multitude of birds, small mammals, and butterflies.

Yet another surprise is that you can hike up El Moro Canyon to access three different backcountry environmental camps, where you can make your bed on the grasslands and live just as the Native Americans did thousands of years ago. The park's three backcountry camps have a total of 32 sites, which are open to mountain bikers as well as hikers. On fair-weather weekends you may find a few of each. The camps are rarely full, however, because most people simply don't want to make the effort it takes to reach them.

Two of the park's environmental camps are high on hillsides with ocean views—Lower Moro and Upper Moro. The third, Deer Canyon, is without views but has more trees and foliage, which provide privacy and wind protection. Any of the camps make a perfect spring backpacking trip, especially when the grasses are green and the flowers are blooming. Even in summer, the camps never get too hot, because the coastal breezes always cool things down.

It's an uphill trek to reach the camps, probably too difficult for beginners on mountain bikes but easy enough for hikers. Pick a cool day, or get an early start, because there is no shade in most of the park's backcountry—just grassy hills.

The two Moro camps are the most popular options, partly because of their ocean views and partly because of the short hike required to reach them—only two miles. For the Moro camps, walk from the ranger station parking lot back down the road toward the entrance kiosk, then pick up the dirt fire road across from the kiosk.

The fire road isn't very scenic; it curves past a trailer park. But in 10 minutes the scenery improves as you veer left on El Moro Canyon Trail and walk up the shady, tree-lined canyon. Watch for a single-track cutoff on your right that leads up to the Moro Ridge Trail and then to the camps. If you miss the single-track, you can also take the fire road signed as East Cutacross to reach Moro Ridge Trail.

Once on Moro Ridge, turn left and reach Lower Moro Camp first; Upper Moro Camp is only a quarter-mile further. From your ridgetop vantage point, the views are exceptional. In winter, be sure to scan the coast for the distinctive spouts of passing grey whales.

For Deer Canyon Camp, walk to the far end of the parking lot (beyond the ranger station) and begin hiking on No Name Ridge Trail. It's exactly three miles to the camp; the first half-mile is rocky and steep, but it quickly improves. (You can also begin hiking on the El Moro Canyon Trail, then cut over to No Name Ridge on the West Cutacross Trail.) Deer Canyon Camp is open to equestrians as well as mountain bikers and hikers, and it is sheltered by a grove of sycamores.

Each of the campgrounds has the same amenities—picnic tables and vault toilets, *c'est tout*. That means you must pack in your water (you can fill your bottles at the ranger station) and your backpacking stove; no campfires are allowed.

Morning glories, Crystal Cove State Park

The most plentiful wildlife we saw on our trip were rabbits—dozens of them—hopping along the trail in El Moro Canyon. Higher up on the hillsides, we were impressed by the huge white morning glories and nonnative purple thistles, both of which seemed to grow in unusually large sizes. The grassland flowers are glorious in springtime, but almost nonexistent by summer. With the wildflowers come the butterflies—we spotted and identified the anise swallowtail (yellow and black) and the red admiral (brown, red, and black).

When you're ready to hike out of the park's backcountry, you'll probably want to pay a visit to Crystal Cove's 3.5 miles of Pacific coastline. Beach access is available at Reef Point, Pelican Point, and Los Trancos. Reef Point is the best spot for swimming and body-surfing; Los Trancos is popular for its access to a group of historic 1930s cottages. The cottages are frequently used in Hollywood films.

Crystal Cove also has a 1,140-acre underwater park that is popular with SCUBA divers and snorkelers; park rangers can provide you with information on the best access points.

Facilities, reservations, fees: There are 32 hike-in environmental campsites at Crystal Cove State Park, divided into three different camps: Lower Moro, Upper Moro, and Deer Canyon. No water is available; you must pack in bottled water. Campfires are not permitted; bring a backpacking stove. Reservations are recommended; reserve through Parknet at (800) 444-7275 or phone the ranger station. The fee is $6 per night. Pets are not permitted.

Who to contact: Crystal Cove State Park, 8471 Pacific Coast Highway, Laguna Beach, CA 92651; (714) 494-3539. Or State Parks, Orange Coast District, (714) 848-1566.

Maps for backpacking: A free backcountry user guide map of Crystal Cove State Park is available at the visitor center. For a topographic map of the area, ask for Laguna Beach from the USGS.

Season: Open year-round; best from February to June.

Directions: From Corona del Mar, drive south on Highway 1 for three miles to the entrance to Crystal Cove State Park on the inland side of the highway. Park near the park headquarters building; you must register at headquarters before setting out for your camp.

8. ECHO ARCH WALK-IN CAMP
San Onofre State Beach, off Interstate 5 near San Clemente

If you've ever driven along the Orange County and San Diego coast, shaking your head in sadness and dismay at the urbanized state beach campgrounds along the ocean, you need to make a trip to Echo Arch. You may have never heard of it—plenty of locals haven't. You've probably never seen it, either, because unlike the other state beach campgrounds, Echo Arch is blessedly hidden from Interstate 5.

Echo Arch is the walk-in camping area at San Onofre State Beach, a park that is best known for surfing and for its famous neighbors: the San Onofre Nuclear Power Plant and Camp Pendleton. Luckily, they're not the kind of neighbors who are always coming over to borrow something. Very quickly, you'll forget they even exist.

The main oceanside campground at San Onofre State Beach is typical of others on the Southern California coast: A long strip of pavement on which RVs and tents are jam-packed, side by side, with their inhabitants drifting to sleep to the roar of the interstate instead of the roar of the ocean waves.

But if you're willing to walk a short distance, you can bypass the asphalt camping and instead spend the night at Echo Arch, on a low coastal bluff just a few yards from the beach. Echo Arch's cove is set off from the rest of the state beach; its walls form the amphitheater that gives Echo Arch its name. The only problem with the camp is that the coastal terrace it rests on is constantly eroding. Park officials have to close the camp occasionally, especially after storms, because of fear that the cliffs will tumble down on unsuspecting campers.

The walk to Echo Arch is only a quarter-mile from where you leave your car, so even if you've never carried a backpack in your life, you can make this trip. What the heck, the walk is so short, you can leave your backpack at home and just carry your stuff in grocery bags. Make sure you bring all your supplies, especially water and food, because there are only limited facilities at Echo Arch. "Limited facilities" means each campsite has a fire pit and table. Chemical toilets and an outdoor cold-water shower are located nearby. The two things you should be sure

Surfers on San Onofre State Beach

to leave at home are radios and dogs. Because this is an environmentally sensitive area, both are strictly forbidden. Dogs are allowed in certain other areas of the park, but not at Echo Arch.

Once you've set up camp, how should you spend your time? Here are three suggestions: 1) Stare at the ocean. 2) Stare at the ocean. 3) Stare at the ocean. If you keep your eyes peeled during your trip, you're likely to see dolphins or whales. When you catch sight of one of these great creatures, it makes everything seem perfect in the world. They're a thrill to watch.

If you insist on more activity, you can always surf fish, swim, walk along miles of sand, or go surfing. There are plenty of waves to go around, but the most famous ones are located at Trestles Beach. Over at Surf Beach, you'll find sand volleyball courts—usually in heavy use—and shade shelters for the sun-wary.

Facilities, reservations, fees: There are 22 walk-in campsites at Echo Arch at San Onofre State Beach. Each site can accommodate up to eight people. No water is available; you must pack in bottled water. Campfires are permitted. Reservations are recommended; phone Parknet at

(800) 444-7275. The fee is $16 per night. Pets are not permitted.

Who to contact: San Onofre State Beach, 3030 Avenida Del Presidente, San Clemente, CA 92672; (714) 492-4872.

Season: Open June 1 to October 30, depending on weather and the condition of the coastal bluffs.

Directions: From Oceanside, drive north on Interstate 5 for 21 miles. Take the Basilone Road exit, turn left (west) and drive 2.9 miles to the park entrance.

---

9. ADVENTURE IN CAMPING TRAVEL TRAILERS
San Diego Coast State Beaches, off Interstate 5 near Encinitas

Have you ever found yourself camped in a tent on a cold, windy, rainy night? You put up your rain fly, adjust your ground tarp, snuggle in with your mate, and hope it doesn't last long. Usually you can't sleep because the rain is too loud, you're too cold, and your dog keeps trying to crawl into your sleeping bag. About every half-hour, you have the nagging fear that water is seeping in somewhere. The night crawls by.

When the sun comes out the next morning, do you ever wonder if those people in RVs and travel trailers are just a hair smarter than you? You see them in the campground, cheerily cooking breakfast over a hot fire, while you yawn and dry out your socks.

Purchasing a travel trailer may be too far-fetched or high-priced for you, but renting one for your next vacation could be a pretty good idea. Adventure in Camping is a company that takes care of all the details. You call them up and reserve your choice of trailer models that range from 18 feet to 27 feet long, in floor plans that sleep two to seven people. Then best of all, you get to choose where you want to go camping along the San Diego coastline.

Your options include any of the following campgrounds: South Carlsbad State Beach, Camperland on Mission Bay, Surf and Turf RV Park, Paradise by the Sea RV Park, San Elijo State Beach, and San Onofre State Beach. Of these, South Carlsbad and San Elijo state beaches are by far the best and most popular. (San Elijo is my favorite, partly because of its beautiful beach and partly because it is located by Cardiff-by-the-Sea and Encinitas, two charming seaside towns.)

At both South Carlsbad and San Elijo, the beach is a mix of sandy stretches and smooth, cobblestone-like rocks. From the blufftop campgrounds, the beach is easily accessed by a series of wooden stairways. In addition to the usual beachside activities like surf fishing, swimming, beachwalking, and surfing, campers at South Carlsbad and San Elijo state beaches can go snorkeling or diving at an offshore reef.

Because each of these beach campgrounds is perched on a bluff about 50 feet above the ocean, you won't have much trouble finding a good place to watch the sun set. About half of the campsites overlook the water; these are the sites you want to get. The only downer: The AMTRAK train passes by both camps several times each day.

Adventure in Camping delivers your trailer to your chosen campsite, levels the trailer, and gets it set up for use. That means that when you arrive, the kitchen appliances are working, the water is running, and the toilets flush. A company representative meets you at the site to show you how to use everything and make sure you're happy. Then your host takes off and you're on your own. At the end of your stay, you just drive off in your own car, and Adventure in Camping comes to pick up the trailer.

If you want serious luxury, you can rent a trailer with all the options, like a television and VCR, microwave oven, and generator. But even the basic model comes with a full bath and a full kitchen, including all cooking and eating utensils, plus battery-run lights, hot and cold running water, and forced air heat. Is this a step up from your high-tech camp stove? You bet. The only thing that isn't provided is linens; bring your own towels and sleeping bags, or for real luxury, bring sheets, blankets, and pillows.

One more thing. For those of you who think that travel trailers are for wimps, and that you would rather "rough it," remember this: You'll have to explain that to your spouse next time you're wide awake at 2 a.m., sharing a cold, rainy night in your tent.

Facilities, reservations, fees: Rental trailers range from 18 feet to 27 feet long, in a variety of floor plans that sleep two to seven people. Reservations are required. Fees range from $129 to $198 for two nights. Rates are discounted for longer stays; there is a maximum stay of seven nights. Holiday rates are 10% higher. A $100 cleaning and damage deposit is required. Pets are permitted with a $10 fee.

Who to contact: Adventure in Camping, P.O. Box 2188, Mammoth Lakes, CA 93546; (800) 417-7771 or (760) 648-7509. Phone 9 a.m. to 5 p.m. only.

Season: Open year-round.

Directions: For San Elijo State Beach: From San Diego, drive north on Interstate 5 for 25 miles and take the Lomas Sante Fe exit. Turn west and follow Lomas Sante Fe until you reach the Pacific Coast Highway. Turn north on the Pacific Coast Highway and drive 2.5 miles to San Elijo State Beach, near Chesterfield Drive. (The beach is four miles north of Cardiff-by-the-Sea, if you are traveling on the Pacific Coast Highway.)

For South Carlsbad State Beach: From San Diego, drive north on Interstate 5 for 30 miles and take the Poinsettia exit. Turn west and follow Poinsettia to the park entrance. (The beach is five miles south of Carlsbad, if you are traveling on the Pacific Coast Highway.)

10. CRYSTAL PIER HOTEL COTTAGES
Crystal Pier, off Interstate 5 in Pacific Beach

I love the ocean more than just about anything, but I've got a big problem with it... I get seasick. Really seasick, and not just on small boats, either. I've been seasick on everything from a one-person kayak to a three-story houseboat. So while the idea of being gently rocked to sleep by the sound of the ocean waves sounds good to most people, I never thought I could stomach it. Until I spent the night at the Crystal Pier Hotel.

The Crystal Pier Hotel is not a hotel at all, but a series of side-by-side cottages perched on weather-beaten Crystal Pier in Pacific Beach. It's hard to believe there's any place left like this on the San Diego coast; the views are exquisite. You're not just looking out toward the ocean, you're on top of it. It's exactly like being on a boat on the sea, but without needing the Dramamine.

Twenty cottages were built on the pier in the 1930s, and they show their age. But six modern cottages were built at the end of the pier in the 1990s, and these have nicer amenities and a higher price tag. If you can afford it, rent one of the newer cottages; the views are better at the pier's far end and the cottages are more private. All 26 cottages have kitchenettes, which allows you to do your own cooking, if you like. You can carry your meals out to your deck and have an oceanside picnic; even the plainest food tastes fabulous in the sea air. Beware of thieving seagulls, however.

One of the little things that makes staying at the Crystal Pier unique is that each cottage comes with one parking space, so you get to drive your car out on the pier as if you own the place. Cottages also come with televisions and telephones that, while admittedly convenient, can intrude on the solitary contemplation that the nearby ocean inspires. I thought about throwing them out the window and into the Pacific Ocean, but it would have been terrible for the environment.

Although the Crystal Pier Hotel is wildly popular in summer with people looking for an oceanside vacation, our favorite time to visit is in the fall or winter. By then, all the high school and college kids are busy elsewhere, and things have quieted down in popular Pacific Beach. If you surf, swim, beachcomb, or just like to walk on the sand and gaze at the waves, you'll be in heaven. And don't forget: Because you're on a pier perched above the ocean, you can go fishing right outside your bedroom window, if you like.

Facilities, reservations, fees: There are 26 cottages at Crystal Pier Hotel, all with kitchenettes. Reservations are recommended. Fees range from $100 to $180 per night. Pets are not permitted.

Who to contact: Crystal Pier Hotel, 4500 Ocean Boulevard, San Diego, CA 92109; (800) 748-5894 or (619) 483-6983. Fax (619) 483-6811.

Season: Open year-round; least crowded in winter.

Directions: From Interstate 5 in Pacific Beach, exit at Garnet Avenue and drive west to the ocean. Crystal Pier is located at the end of Garnet Avenue.

11. LAKE HENSHAW RESORT
Cleveland National Forest, off Highway 76 near Santa Ysabel

"Take a boy fishing. Take a girl fishing, too." That's what the sign says at Lake Henshaw Resort, and it sums up the spirit of the place. True, San Diego County's Lake Henshaw is no Lake Tahoe in terms of natural beauty, but it's a great place for people who want to catch catfish or bass, then cook them up for dinner in a comfortable hillside cabin.

For those who have never heard of the place, Lake Henshaw is located near the country towns of Santa Ysabel and Julian, just a few miles from the border of Cleveland National Forest and Palomar Mountain State Park. At 2,727 feet in elevation, Lake Henshaw is more like a wide, shallow, flooded meadow than a lake; but hey, this

Cabin 15 at Lake Henshaw Resort

is San Diego—where rainfall is about as rare as baseball-size gold nuggets. Boasting nearly 25 miles of shoreline, Lake Henshaw is surprisingly large and roomy, but some people are a bit dismayed by the cows that graze along the shoreline. Like I said, it's a lot like a meadow.

The cabins at Lake Henshaw Resort are directly across the highway from the lake. They come in a variety of sizes and configurations and are spaced far enough apart to prevent you from breathing down your neighbor's neck. The studio cabin we rented was large, with plenty of room for two, plus extra beds if you want to squeeze in more people. In addition to a sleeping area and a sitting area, the cabin had a full kitchen, complete with cooking and eating utensils. A sign inside each cabin states: "Please do not clean fish or game in the cottage. Facilities for this are provided in the campground." Fair enough.

Be sure to ask for one of the upper hillside cabins, which are further away from the road. (Cabins 12 and 15 are the best of the studios.) Then wake yourself up early one morning and step outside your cabin to look at the lake. Henshaw has a habit of creating a layer of fog over its waters during the night, like a fluffy blanket to help the fish sleep. In the first hours of the morning, before the fog has a chance to burn off, the lake shimmers beautifully in the sunlight.

Because Henshaw is a private lake, a $5 lake use fee is charged whether you bring your own boat or rent one from the resort. A five-mile-per-hour speed limit is enforced on the water, and no canoes, inflatables, or boats less than 10 feet long are allowed. Lake Henshaw Resort's small store can keep you supplied with all the fishing advice and tackle you want, plus some snacks and drinks. They even have a cafe, which is basic but adequate. A popular dinner special is "All You Can Eat Catfish." For more elaborate grocery shopping or restaurant food, the town of Santa Ysabel is a mere 10 miles away, and the larger town of Julian is another seven miles beyond that.

If the fish aren't biting, plenty of other activities are possible near Lake Henshaw, including hiking on 6,140-foot Palomar Mountain, either on state park or national forest trails. The conifers on the mountain are big and beautiful, reminiscent of the Southern Sierra. Visit the famous Palomar Observatory and its Hale telescope, or the Santa Ysabel Mission. On warm days, we recommend a visit to the San Luis Rey River day-use area, a couple of miles down Highway 76, for swimming, inner tubing, and picnicking. Swimming is not permitted in Lake Henshaw.

Facilities, reservations, fees: There are 18 cabins at Lake Henshaw Resort, ranging in size from studios to two bedrooms. All have fully equipped kitchens. Reservations are recommended. Fees range from $50 to $100 per night. A private campground with RV and tent sites is also available. Boat rentals are available. A small grocery store and cafe are located at the resort. Pets are permitted with prior approval.

Who to contact: Lake Henshaw Resort, 26439 Highway 76, Santa Ysabel, CA 92070; (760) 782-3487 or (760) 782-3501.

Season: Open year-round, best in winter and spring.

Directions: From Escondido on Interstate 15, take Highway 78 east for 32 miles to Santa Ysabel. Turn left (north) on Highway 79 and drive seven miles, then turn left on Highway 76 and drive four miles to Lake Henshaw Resort on the left.

12. JULIAN BED & BREAKFAST GUILD CABINS
near Cuyamaca Rancho State Park, off Highway 79 in Julian

The mountain town of Julian is a great getaway destination that's both charming and fun, particularly if you are smart enough to visit in the off-season or during the week, when the crowds are minimal.

On weekend afternoons, there is usually a steady stream of tourists on Julian's main street, which takes away from the small-town appeal of the place. Careful timing is key for the best possible experience.

The big draw in Julian is apple season from mid-September to mid-November, when the main recreation is visiting all the bakeries and taste-testing apple pies. (Luckily, apples have a long shelf life, so if you miss the season, you can still get some pie.) I never thought I would be the kind of person who would get excited about this, but then again, I've never had apple pie as good as the pie in Julian. After a long hike in the surrounding mountains, it sure beats having another Power Bar, or a miniature box of raisins.

If mountain biking, horseback riding, fishing, and hiking interest you as much or even more than apple pie, you're in luck. Julian's the place to do all these things. If you're a less ambitious nature lover, there are activities for you, too: Just seat yourself in an open meadow and watch the autumn leaves turn red and gold.

The best way to start is with a phone call to the Julian Bed and Breakfast Guild, a group of individuals who are the keepers of 23 different cabins and country lodgings. (Make sure you state specifically that you want a cabin, because they also have other types of accommodations.) The colorful names of the cabin offerings tell you a lot about how special they are: Lutz Castle, Random Oaks Ranch, the Cabin at Strawberry Hill, Rocking Horse Inn, Coleman Creek Cabin, Shadow Mountain Ranch, and more. All the accommodations are different, but most are in a wooded or country setting, and include fireplaces, fully equipped kitchens, televisions, and VCRs. Many have jacuzzis or spas. Some are loaded with whimsy and fantasy, such as the fairy-tale-style cabins at Shadow Mountain Ranch, which include a tree house and a cabin filled with gnome carvings and figurines.

I stayed at Lutz Castle, an adobe home a few miles outside of town that looked only slightly like a castle, but felt exactly like a perfect cabin. The innkeepers were a lovely couple who did everything they could to make me feel at home, and to provide me with information about activities in Julian. After two nights at Lutz Castle and a few slices of apple pie, I never wanted to leave.

Because the Julian Bed and Breakfast Guild cabins are run like true B & Bs, you'll find that once you've checked in to your cabin, you are left in privacy. No one changes your sheets or towels each day, and you're expected to wash your dishes and leave things in order when you depart. Breakfasts are provided, but in most places this

Near the summit of Cuyamaca Peak, Cuyamaca Rancho State Park

consists of your own coffeemaker with plenty of coffee and tea, plus a few rolls or buns, fruit, and juice. If you seek a more substantial meal, you can always cook it yourself in your kitchen, or head to one of Julian's fine eateries. I heartily recommend breakfast at the Julian Cafe (out-of-this-world apple oatmeal pancakes) or any meal at the Rongbranch Cafe. In addition to good food, you'll find a warm Western ambience at all of Julian's establishments, a tribute to its rich history as a nineteenth-century gold mining town.

After you've taken care of your daily caloric needs, go burn some of them off in Julian's outdoor playland. The choice of nearby parks is wider than almost anywhere in Southern California: William Heise County Park, Cuyamaca Rancho State Park, Volcan Mountain Nature Preserve, Cleveland National Forest, and Anza Borrego Desert State Park are all within a 30-minute drive. You can hike, mountain bike, or ride your horse on hundreds of miles of trails. If you prefer something more exotic, you can rent a llama from LeeLin Llama Treks (call 1-800-LAMAPAK).

For tamer excursions, you can visit the area's wineries or the Santa Ysabel Mission. Or take an interesting tour of Eagle and High Peak Mines, Julian's hard rock gold mines which date back to 1870. Anglers should be sure to pay a visit to Lake Cuyamaca, only 12 miles away, for spring trout fishing and summer bass fishing.

Facilities, reservations, fees: There are 23 different lodgings available from the Julian Bed and Breakfast Guild. Reservations are recommended. Fees range from $60 to $200 per night, depending on season and type of accommodations. Pets are not permitted.

Who to contact: Julian Bed and Breakfast Guild, P.O. Box 1711, Julian, CA 92036; (760) 765-1555. Lutz Castle, P.O. Box 1285, Julian, CA 92036; (760) 765-0208.

Season: Open year-round. Autumn is apple season, winter sometimes brings snow, and spring and summer are best for hiking.

Directions: From San Diego, drive east on Interstate 8 for 40 miles to the Highway 79 exit. Drive north on Highway 79 for 25 miles to Julian.

From points north, drive south on Interstate 15 to Highway 76 (south of Temecula), then drive east on Highway 76 for 35 miles to its junction with Highway 79. Turn right (south) on Highway 79 and drive 14 miles to Julian.

---

13. CUYAMACA RANCHO STATE PARK CABINS
Cuyamaca Rancho State Park, off Highway 79 near Julian

Cuyamaca Rancho State Park is one of San Diego's biggest and loveliest parks, with a whopping 25,000 acres of deciduous forest, conifers, chaparral, meadows, and rocky peaks. Better yet, it's one of the few places in San Diego where the air is relatively cool and clear year-round, making it perfect for hiking in every season. In fall, you can see the plentiful black oaks do their color-changing trick, and in winter, you might even get caught in a snowstorm. (People outside of San Diego never believe this, but it's true.)

Adding to the park's delights are more than 100 miles of hiking trails, including the easy four-mile round-trip climb to the top of Stonewall Peak, elevation 5,730 feet, and the harder 5.5-mile round-trip climb to the top of Cuyamaca Peak, elevation 6,512 feet. Both offer stunning 360-degree views; from Cuyamaca Peak, you can see all the way to Mexico and the Pacific Ocean. Bikers and equestrians have miles of trails open for their pleasure, and anglers can find excellent trout and bass fishing prospects at Lake Cuyamaca.

If you want to stay in the park but don't want the traditional car camping gig, reserve one of Cuyamaca Rancho State Park's six cabins. Five of them are located at Paso Picacho Campground, and one is located at nearby Caballeros Horse Camp, suitable for equestrians traveling with horses. All of the cabins are identical, with one important exception: the Nature Den at Paso Picacho Camp. Whereas the others are newly constructed, one-room pine cabins with nothing inside but a woodburning stove and bunk beds (no mattresses or bedding), the Nature Den is a charming old stone and wood building, built in 1933 by the Civilian Conservation Corps. It has a few important luxuries, including cots, electricity, a coffeemaker, a microwave oven, and a fireplace. Just to remind

Hikers on top of Stonewall Peak

you that you're still camping, you must take a short walk to use the shared campground restroom and shower facilities.

The other cabins are very similar in style to those found at KOA campgrounds across the country. (For the uninitiated, that means they are built of pine logs and are clean and cute, but spartan.) But unlike KOA cabins, these cabins do not have electricity. The cabin named Cypress, which is near tent site number 73, is the best of the lot because it's in a secluded location up on a hill. Be sure to bring plenty of firewood (or buy it at the campground) to burn in your wood stove for heat.

If possible, reserve your stay in advance, because the cabins are popular, especially the Nature Den. Whichever one you rent, be sure to bring all your bedding, including a good sleeping bag pad or inflatable mattress. Unless you're very creative with a barbecue, you might want to bring your camp stove as well. And if you're traveling with your diamond tiara, remember: None of the cabins have locks on the doors, but you may bring your own padlock if you wish.

The park allows as many as eight people per cabin, but if you have more than four, you should bring along a tent for the extras, or be prepared to feel like sardines in a can. We found that the pine cabins are most comfortable for two people; the Nature Den can fit a few more.

Facilities, reservations, fees: There are four cabins at Paso Picacho Campground and one at Los Caballos Horse Camp. The Nature Den is located at Paso Picacho Campground. Each cabin has bunk beds that sleep four people, but no mattresses or bedding. Each cabin site has a picnic table, fire ring, barbecue, and room for a small tent. Water, restrooms, and pay showers are located nearby. The Nature Den has electricity, a microwave oven, and a coffeemaker. Reservations are recommended; phone Parknet at (800) 444-7275. Fees range from $30 to $45 per night. Pets are permitted; dogs are $1 per night. Only one car is permitted; extra vehicles are $5 per night.

Who to contact: Cuyamaca Rancho State Park, 12551 Highway 79, Descanso, CA 91916; (760) 765-0755.

Season: Open year-round. Winter sometimes brings snow.

Directions: From San Diego, drive east on Interstate 8 for 40 miles to the Highway 79 exit. Drive north on Highway 79 for 11 miles, then turn left (west) into Paso Picacho Campground.

14. CUYAMACA RANCHO BACKPACK
Cuyamaca Rancho State Park, off Highway 79 near Julian

You say you're looking for a place to go for an easy backpacking trip in San Diego County? Some place you can take your friends or family who despise long miles and steep climbs? Some place where the air is clean and you can forget your troubles for a while? I know just the place—the environmental camps at Cuyamaca Rancho State Park near Julian.

Here's some background: Cuyamaca Rancho State Park is one of San Diego County's most precious gems, a 25,000-acre outdoor wonderland that is rife with hiking, biking, and horseback riding trails. (See pages 44-45 for more information on Cuyamaca Rancho's highlights.) It's a park for all seasons, with elevations high enough to weather the San Diego summer heat. Every winter, a few inches of snow fall on the park, to the delight of cross-country skiers and snowball throwers.

The south part of the park is easily accessible from Interstate 8. There you'll find Green Valley Campground and the Sweetwater

River, the start of an easy backpacking trip to Arroyo Seco Primitive Camp. The camp is at the edge of a meadow at elevation 4,290 feet, a mere 1.5 miles from the Arroyo Seco trailhead at Green Valley, elevation 4,000 feet. That means you have a short distance to travel, and very little elevation gain. You can hike, bike, or horseback ride to the camp, following the Arroyo Seco Fire Road. At a junction with the California Riding and Hiking Trail, turn right to reach Arroyo Seco Camp in a half-mile. The best campsite at Arroyo Seco is number 3; it's the farthest off the fire road and the most private.

A popular day-hike from Arroyo Seco Camp is to continue north on Arroyo Seco Trail, then turn right on West Mesa Trail. Follow West Mesa Trail for one mile to an unmarked side trail that appears on your left, a quarter-mile after the Monument Trail comes in from the right. Follow the side trail for a few yards to the Airplane Monument, a stone bench inscribed to Colonel Marshall, whose airplane crashed here in 1922. Aside from the interesting history of the spot, the view is lovely.

A more remote camping option is possible by hiking or biking to Granite Springs Primitive Camp at 4,850 feet. This trip is substantially longer (4.5 miles instead of 1.5), and you'll be heading east instead of west. The East Mesa Fire Road travels through a variety of environs—oak woodlands, chaparral, and the high meadows of the East Mesa, where the camp is located. For the first 2.8 miles, you're mostly out in the sun and climbing, so make sure you're well supplied with water. At Oakzanita Junction, you turn left and the trail gets easier. The grade lessens, and you're sheltered in the welcome shade of pine trees.

Because the hike is longer to Granite Springs Camp, and has a greater ascent, you're more likely to have solitude there, even on weekends. However, if you're traveling with small children or first-time backpackers, I'd recommend Arroyo Seco Camp over Granite Springs Camp, especially in the summer when the trail to Granite Springs can be hot and exposed.

At both campgrounds, pit toilets and garbage cans are provided, but water is not available. (There is a spring at Granite Springs Camp, but the water has a terrible iron taste to it.) Carry in bottled water, and bring your backpacking stove and fuel for cooking; campfires are prohibited because of the high fire risk. Both camps are open to hikers, mountain bikers, and equestrians, but water for horses is available only seasonally. Also, horses must carry in their own meals, because grazing is not permitted. That means pack up the Purina Horse Chow, or leave Old Paint at home.

Facilities, reservations, fees: There are three campsites at Arroyo Seco and three campsites at Granite Springs. Each site can accommodate up to eight people. There is also one group site at each campground, which can accommodate up to 16 people. The sites are available on a first-come, first-served basis. No water is available; you must pack in bottled water. Campfires are not permitted; bring a backpacking stove. Backpackers must register and pick up a permit at park headquarters, Paso Picacho Campground kiosk, or Green Valley Campground kiosk, at least one hour before sunset. The fee is $3 per person per night. Pets are not permitted.

Who to contact: Cuyamaca Rancho State Park, 12551 Highway 79, Descanso, CA 91916; (760) 765-0755.

Maps for backpacking: Various maps of Cuyamaca Rancho State Park are available for a fee at the park visitor center. To obtain a topographic map of the area, ask for Cuyamaca Peak from the USGS.

Season: Open year-round; best from January to May.

Directions: From San Diego, drive east on Interstate 8 for 40 miles to the Highway 79 exit. Drive north on Highway 79 for seven miles, then turn left (west) at the sign for Green Valley Campground. You must register at the Green Valley Campground kiosk or park headquarters before setting out for either trail camp. Backpackers must leave their vehicles at either Green Valley Campground or Paso Picacho Campground; you may not leave a car overnight at any other park trailheads.

---

15. BLUE JAY LODGE & LAGUNA MOUNTAIN LODGE CABINS
Cleveland National Forest, off Highway S-1 on Mount Laguna

The Laguna Mountain Recreation Area is a fun-filled land of outdoor adventure within an hour's drive of downtown San Diego. Favorite activities include hiking, horseback riding, mountain biking, and as unlikely as it sounds, playing in the snow. At just shy of 6,000 feet in elevation, the Laguna Mountains are San Diego's backyard snow play area, at least during the few weeks each year when some of the white stuff sticks to the ground.

In any season, there is so much fun outdoor stuff to do in the Lagunas that you should plan to stay for a few days. Your best choice is one of two mountain lodges with cabin rentals, operated under special use permit from Cleveland National Forest. The two lodges are right across the street from each other, so their recreation offerings are identical. Just take your pick.

If you like your cabin vacation a little on the eccentric side, Blue Jay Lodge might be just the place for you. Although it looks normal enough from the outside, when you step inside the Blue Jay's restaurant and saloon, you quickly surmise that things are a little wacky. The barstools, for example, are bright red tractor seats. All manner of wagon wheels and antique farming tools hang from every inch of the ceiling and walls, interspersed with a few dozen trophy fish. The dining tables and benches are carved from giant Northwest pine trees, which must have been the size of the Empire State Building. Two stuffed bears stand on their back paws, with teeth bared and tongues wagging. Someone has put Santa hats on them.

The Blue Jay Lodge only takes cash, so come with your wallet bulging. Also, make sure you have a good supply of dishes, utensils, and cooking supplies with you, because the cabins at Blue Jay have full kitchens, but not so much as a plastic spoon. For that matter, even when we ate in the Blue Jay Lodge's restaurant, our food was served on paper plates and our coffee came in styrofoam cups. Apparently they don't have a dishwasher.

But none of this will matter after you settle in to your cabin. All of the Blue Jay's log cabins have cozy fireplaces (but bring your

Desert overlook from the Laguna Mountains

own firewood or buy it for $4). Although they are quaint one-room structures, built in the 1920s, the cabins are surprisingly large, with a separate sleeping area, kitchen/dining area, and living area. The bathrooms are tiny but serviceable, and gas heaters keep your cabin warm if your fire goes out. Our cabin had some rather funky but charming furniture, including a bed made of logs. After a good night's rest on it, we sat outside on our deck in the morning and watched the acorn woodpeckers flitting in the oak trees.

The most important thing to know about the Blue Jay Lodge is that they do not allow children or pets. Each of the cabins is for one or two adults only, and this is strictly enforced. If you have kids or pets with you, just take yourself right across the street to the Mount Laguna Lodge, where you can rent cabins ranging in size from one to three bedrooms. Some have fireplaces and/or kitchens, so be sure to ask for exactly what you want. Just like at the Blue Jay across the street, the cabins with kitchens are not equipped with utensils, dishes, pots, or pans. If you plan to cook, come prepared. If you plan to eat out, understand that there are few services in the Lagunas. Unless you're willing to drive, you're basically confined to the restaurant at Blue Jay Lodge (open for breakfast, lunch, and dinner Friday to Sunday only) and the small grocery store at Mount Laguna Lodge.

Not-to-be-missed activities in the Laguna Mountain Recreation Area include a four-mile round-trip hike to Garnet Peak, for spectacular views of the Anza-Borrego Desert. Shorter walks can be taken on the Lightning Ridge Trail, Desert View Nature Trail, and the Wooded Hill Nature Trail. All offer fine vistas. If you want more, the many hiking, riding, and equestrian trails of Cuyamaca Rancho State Park are only a short drive away.

The lodges are located next to the Forest Service's Laguna Mountain Visitor Information Station, where you can pick up maps and get all the information you need. If you're lucky enough to time your visit for when snow is on the ground, well, you won't need anybody telling you what to do with your time. Just get out there and make some snow angels.

Facilities, reservations, fees: There are four cabins at Blue Jay Lodge, each for one or two adults only. All have kitchens and fireplaces, but none have cooking or eating utensils. The lodge's cafe and saloon are open Friday through Sunday only. Reservations are recommended. Fees are $85 per night. Pets and children are not permitted.

There are 15 cabins at Mount Laguna Lodge, ranging in size from one bedroom to three bedrooms, plus motel units. Some cabins have kitchens and/or fireplaces, but none have cooking or eating utensils. A small store is available. Reservations are recommended. Fees range from $55 to $98 per night. Pets are permitted in some cabins for a $7 fee.

Special note: A national forest adventure pass is required for recreation in this area. See page 11 for details.

Who to contact: Blue Jay Lodge, Mount Laguna, CA 91948; (619) 473-8844. Mount Laguna Lodge, P.O. Box 146, Mount Laguna, CA 91948; (619) 445-2342 or (619) 473-8533. (Phone 9 a.m. to 5 p.m. only.)

Season: Open year-round. Winter sometimes brings snow.

Directions: From San Diego, drive east on Interstate 8 for 47 miles to the Highway S1/Sunrise Scenic Byway turnoff. Drive north on Highway S1 for 10 miles to the town of Mount Laguna. (From Julian, drive south on Highway 79 for six miles, then turn left and continue south on Highway S1 for 15 miles to the town of Mount Laguna.) Blue Jay Lodge is on the east side of the road; Mount Laguna Lodge is on the west side of the road.

16. LA CASA DEL ZORRO DESERT RESORT
Anza-Borrego Desert State Park, off Highway S3
near Borrego Springs

Before La Casa del Zorro, I'd never stayed in a cabin that had its own ironing board and iron. Not to mention terry bathrobes, two TV sets, a morning newspaper at the front door, and bath towels folded into fancy shapes like dinner napkins. I have to ask myself, "Is this really camping?" And the answer is: No. But if you're going to spend some time adventuring in Anza-Borrego Desert State Park, you might as well have someplace comfortable to come home to. The desert can be harsh; why rough it 24 hours a day?

The cottages at La Casa del Zorro are the antithesis of roughing it, and they offer far more privacy and intimacy than a hotel or motel. Each detached one- to four-bedroom house, or "casita" as they call them, has its own mini-kitchen (microwave oven, small refrigerator, coffeemaker, and a basic set of dishes and silverware). Some casitas have their own outdoor spa; others have fireplaces for those chilly desert nights. All of them have desert-related names, like Smoketree, Yucca, Agave, and Tamarisk.

The casitas are ideal for family vacations with young children, since parents can keep an eye on their kids but everybody has their own space. Even the one-bedroom casita is roomy, with a large separate bedroom, a bathroom and dressing area, a combination living/dining room, and a kitchenette tucked into a corner. The four-bedroom casitas have a sizable amount of property around them, plus their own swimming pools. A house this size rents for a bundle, but then again, it is large enough so that you can

Anza-Borrego Desert State Park

bring along all your aunts, uncles, and cousins. Make sure they all chip in to pay the bill.

If the kitchenettes don't match up to your culinary needs, you can rent a barbecue grill from the front desk and cook on your casita's patio, or have your meals in one of La Casa del Zorro's restaurants. The main restaurant is formal (jackets required), but the next-door lounge and pub serves a full menu of food in a casual atmosphere. (They didn't even blink at my dirty hiking boots and sweatshirt; apparently this attire is commonplace.) The food at both locations, best described as California cuisine, is first-rate. Then again, the oatmeal I cooked for breakfast in my casita wasn't bad, either, especially because I ate it on my warm, sunny patio in the middle of January.

Although most visitors use La Casa del Zorro as a base for exploring Anza-Borrego Desert State Park, some never leave the resort grounds. After all, La Casa has three swimming pools and jacuzzis, six lighted tennis courts, a fitness room, aerobics classes... you get the idea. Personally, I skipped all the "civilized" recreation and headed for the state park, which, at 600,000 acres, is one of the largest in the continental United States. Within a 30-minute drive from La Casa del Zorro, you can access several excellent trailheads, including the one at Borrego Palm Canyon Campground near the park visitor center. The Borrego Palm Canyon Trail leads to a grove of more than 800 native palm trees and a boulder-lined waterfall—a marvelous oasis in the desert. You can also head to the three trailheads at Blair Valley, where you can hike to see Native American pictographs and the remains of a 1930s desert homestead. Visitors interested in shorter walks in the park will find several easy nature trails that interpret the desert flora.

The best season to visit Anza-Borrego is unquestionably the early spring, when you can witness the spectacle of blooming desert wildflowers. Unfortunately, the "economy" rates at La Casa del Zorro are in the summer, when hikers have to limit their excursions to the early morning, before the daily sand-bake begins. From November till May, the desert has comfortable temperatures for hiking and exploring almost every day.

Facilities, reservations, fees: There are 19 casitas at La Casa del Zorro Desert Resort, ranging in size from one bedroom to four bedrooms. Motel-style accommodations are also available. Reservations are recommended. Fees range from $95 to $695 per night, depending on season and size of accommodations. Pets are not permitted.

Who to contact: La Casa del Zorro Desert Resort, 3845 Yaqui Pass Road, Borrego Springs, CA 92004-5000; (800) 824-1884 or (760) 767-5323. Fax (760) 767-4782.

Season: Open year-round; best from November to May. Spring wildflowers can be seen from March to May.

Directions: From Julian, drive east on Highway 78 for 19 miles to Highway S3/Yaqui Pass Road. Turn left (north) on Highway S3/Yaqui Pass Road and drive six miles to La Casa del Zorro Desert Resort, on the right side of the road.

17. KNOTTY PINES CABINS
San Bernardino National Forest, off Highway 243 in Idyllwild

Let's talk about the name of the town Idyllwild. The derivation is simple: First, "idyll," as in "idyllic," meaning picturesque or rustic, suggesting peace or contentment. Then "wild," as in you can still find some wilderness left there. Hooray for that.

Idyllwild is located at 5,500 feet in elevation, roughly west of Palm Springs and south of Banning, on the border of the San Jacinto Wilderness. Approaching from Interstate 10, it takes a long 25-mile drive on winding Highway 243 to reach it, but nobody complains. The road leads through San Bernardino National Forest land, at the base of 10,160-foot Newton B. Drury Peak and 10,804-foot San Jacinto Peak, so there's plenty of splendid scenery, particularly big conifers and granite walls.

Because the Idyllwild area was never developed for downhill skiing, it doesn't get anywhere near the amount of traffic as Big Bear to the north, but it does do a good business with wilderness hikers and vacation homeowners. In fact, on summer holiday weekends it can be difficult to get a wilderness permit for hiking some of the more prestigious trails in the area, including the spectacular Devil's Slide Trail to the top of 8,828-foot Tahquitz Peak.

You can make your trip easier by visiting during non-holiday periods, and by reserving a stay in one of the Knotty Pines Cabins, a group of rustic cabins that are a perfect base camp for an Idyllwild vacation. Knotty Pines is close enough to the main part of town so that you can walk to shops and restaurants if you like. If you prefer, you can rent a cabin with a fully equipped kitchen and cook all your meals in-house.

During our stay in late May, a beautiful sunny day of hiking turned into a howling rainstorm by evening, so we lit a fire in our cabin's fireplace and cozied up for the night. We enjoyed the evening in our cabin, listening to the rain patter on the roof, as much as we enjoyed the day's spectacular hiking. You'll have to pay for your firewood at Knotty Pines, but it's four bucks well spent.

While you're in Idyllwild, be sure to hike the Devil's Slide Trail. The route is 8.4 miles round-trip and offers incredible views from the fire lookout tower on top of Tahquitz Peak. A slightly easier hike is possible on the Deer Springs Trail to the overlook at Suicide Rock, providing good views of Tahquitz Peak and Idyllwild. Easiest of all is the Ernie Maxwell Scenic Trail, a good family walk through the pines and cedars. All of these trailheads are within a 15-minute drive of Knotty Pines Cabins.

For picnicking or fishing, take a drive over to pretty little Lake Fulmor on Highway 243, where you and your kids can cast a line in the water from shore. Or stop at the picnic area across the highway from Lake Fulmor at Fuller Mill Creek, where you can fish for stocked trout in springtime. Another option is to seek out the pretty waterfall on Fuller Mill Creek, just a few hundred feet from the highway on the east side.

Facilities, reservations, fees: There are eight cabins at Knotty Pines, ranging in size from studios to three bedrooms. All except one have fully equipped kitchens. Reservations are recommended. Fees range from $50 to $120 per night. Pets are permitted in some cabins for a $10 fee.

Special note: A national forest adventure pass is required for recreation in this area. See page 11 for details.

Who to contact: Knotty Pines Cabins, 54340 Pine Crest, P.O. Box 477, Idyllwild, CA 92549; (909) 659-2933.

Season: Open year-round; expect snow in winter.

Directions: From Beaumont, at the junction of Interstate 10 and Highway 60, drive east on Interstate 10 for six miles to Banning. Turn south on Highway 243, and drive 27 miles (on a very winding road) to Idyllwild. Just before you reach the village, look for a sign on the left for Knotty Pines Cabins. Turn left and drive up the driveway.

18. ROUND VALLEY BACKPACK
Mount San Jacinto State Park, via Palm Springs Aerial Tramway

The first time you ride the Palm Springs Aerial Tramway, you realize that human beings are capable of creating miracles. In just a few minutes, you are whooshed from Palm Springs' desert floor at 2,643 feet in elevation to the San Jacinto State Park and Wilderness at 8,516 feet. You do it while riding in a tram car about the size of a minivan, hooked to thin cables attached to three long-legged towers. You ride from cactus to clouds, from palms to pines, and sometimes, as in our case, from desert heat to snow flurries.

The tramway is beyond thrilling. On the 15-minute ride, you get close-up views of the mountain you are rapidly ascending, plus long-distance views of the desert you've departed. You can see all the way to the Salton Sea, 50 miles to the south. The vistas are so awesome in every direction, you don't know which way to look.

As if the tram ride alone wasn't worth the price of admission, there's more to look forward to. When your car reaches the upper tram station, you disembark, walk past the gift shop and restaurant, and head out the back of the building to the beautiful land of Mount

San Jacinto State Park. It's a shock to your senses—the air is as much as 40 degrees cooler than the desert below. You're in a forest of giant conifers, interspersed with meadows laden with corn lilies and wild-flowers.

Did you get your camping permit in advance? Good, because if you did, you're set for a perfect easy hike to Round Valley, and then an overnight stay in the Mount San Jacinto Wilderness. The trip begins by following the walkway downhill from the tram station, then continuing straight ahead, passing the Long Valley Ranger Station in a few hundred yards. Unlike day-hikers in the park, you won't need to get a wilderness permit here; the camping permit you've obtained in advance also serves as your hiking permit. Head past the ranger station, following the well-signed trail for two miles to Round Valley.

As you walk, be on the lookout for Cooper's hawks and yellow-rumped warblers, as well as black and white woodpeckers. You'll surely see the prolific work of the woodpeckers in the hole-ridden fir and pine trees. The trail is gently switchbacked and mostly shaded, roughly following the course of Long Valley Creek.

When you reach Round Valley Camp at 9,100 feet in elevation,

Trail to Round Valley dusted in snow

you must decide: Stay here or hike a half-mile further north to Tamarack Valley Camp. The camp at Tamarack Valley is smaller and often less crowded than Round Valley; both are in lovely meadowside settings. Note that whichever spot you choose, you must camp in designated state wilderness sites that are marked with brown posts. Campfires are not permitted, so bring your backpacking stove and plenty of fuel. Water is plentiful at both camps—just filter it and drink up.

If you spend the night at either of these camps, you should definitely spend the next day hiking to the top of San Jacinto Peak, at 10,804 feet in elevation. It's the second highest peak in Southern California, beaten only by Mount San Gorgonio at 11,490 feet. From Round Valley Camp, San Jacinto's summit is 3.7 miles away, making a 7.4-mile round-trip from your campsite. (Add on another mile round-trip from Tamarack Valley Camp.) The steepest part of the summit hike is the first mile from Round Valley to the junction at Wellman Divide; otherwise the grade is moderate. You're compensated for your climb with excellent vistas from Wellman Divide. Turn right (north) at the divide, then hike 2.4 miles through lodgepole pines to an intersection with the short summit trail. Turn right and hike the final quarter-mile to the top. Along the way you'll pass a stone shelter, useful for hikers who get caught in surprise storms.

While you survey the view from Mount San Jacinto, consider that John Muir called the vista from this peak "the most sublime spectacle to be found anywhere on earth." On clear days, you can see as much as 100 miles away—to the Channel Islands and parts of Mexico and Nevada—as well as the closer peaks of the San Gorgonio and San Bernardino Mountains. Besides the summit's great height, Mount San Jacinto also possesses a remarkably sharp "vertical rise"— the angle of descent or steepness from top to base. Geographers claim that the peak's vertical rise is the most sheer in all of the United States. All I can tell you is that the summit view is incredible.

Facilities, reservations, fees: There are 28 campsites at Round Valley and 12 campsites at Tamarack Valley. Water is available for filtering. Campfires are not permitted; bring a backpacking stove. A free camping permit is required from Mount San Jacinto State Park. Reserve your camping permit up to 56 days in advance by contacting Mount San Jacinto State Park and Wilderness at the address below. (Permits can be obtained by mail or in person.) There is no fee. Pets are not permitted.

The Palm Springs Aerial Tramway charges $17.65 per adult and $11.65 per child under 12 for a round-trip ticket to Mountain Station. (Phone 760-325-1391 for more information about schedules and fees.)

Who to contact: Mount San Jacinto State Park and Wilderness, P.O. Box 308, 25905 Highway 243, Idyllwild, CA 92549; (909) 659-2607.

Maps for backpacking: A hiking trail map of the San Jacinto State Park and Wilderness is available for $1 at the tramway station. For a topographic map of the area, ask for San Jacinto Peak from the USGS.

Season: The park is open year-round, but the best season for camping is from May to October, when the mountain is snow-free.

Directions: From Banning, drive 12 miles east on Interstate 10 and take the Highway 111/Palm Springs exit. Drive nine miles south on Highway 111 to Tramway Road, then turn right and drive 3.8 miles to the tramway parking area. Walk to the tram station, buy your ticket, and ride the tram to its end at Mountain Station. Walk out the back side of Mountain Station, follow the concrete path downhill, then continue straight ahead for Long Valley and Round Valley.

19. MOJAVE ROCK RANCH LODGE
near Joshua Tree National Park, off Highway 62 in Joshua Tree

My first experience at Mojave Rock Ranch Lodge was a little unworldly. First, I got terribly lost trying to find it, because I was under the false impression that it was right on Highway 62, when actually it's six miles from the main road. Then, when I finally found my way and nosed my rental car down the last stretch of dirt driveway, I thought I must be seeing things.

The place was empty. The only car in sight was an old Chevy truck that looked like it was from the 1930s, but it was in perfect condition. In a corral out front, a donkey was standing, watching me with unconcealed curiosity. (I learned later that his name is Francis, and he lives at the ranch.) A big water tank behind the corral bore the sign "Mojave Rock Ranch—Established Way Back," so I figured I must be in the right place.

I walked up to the ranch's front door, wowed by the lovely desert views surrounding the hillside house, and heard Vivaldi playing on outside speakers. Everything was landscaped with remarkable precision and beauty, using only desert plants. There were pieces of sculpture, paintings, fabulous stone work, and barrel cactus popping up in every available space. It was the most artistic and creative ranch I have ever seen, in the desert or elsewhere.

In case you haven't got the idea yet, the people who own Mojave Rock Ranch Lodge know exactly what they are doing. They have created a desert getaway that is absolutely perfect in every detail. Even if you just phone them for information, you won't believe how much stuff they send you in the mail. They want you to have a good experience at their place; they make an effort to see that you do.

The ranch is available for rent on a daily, weekly, or monthly basis. There are two facilities: the main ranch, which has two bedrooms plus a sleeping porch with a 180-degree view; and a smaller bungalow, which has two bedrooms and an exquisite koi pond and water garden. You can have as many as four people in either building; there's plenty of room for everybody. Most people stay longer than a night or two; this is the kind of place where you want to settle in for a while and pretend it's your permanent home. (It will take you several days just to check out all the varied and eclectic decor.)

A fully equipped kitchen is provided in both buildings, as well as a fireplace or wood stove, barbecue grill, and just about everything else you can think of.

Once you're settled in, you'll want to start exploring nearby Joshua Tree National Park. Since you're situated near the western end of the big park, you'll probably spend some time around Black Rock Canyon. Lucky you—it just so happens to have some of the park's nicest trails, including the six-mile round-trip hike to Warren Peak. You can also hike to Eureka Peak at 5,518 feet in elevation; although most people drive there, it's much more fun and adventurous to walk to the summit. From the west side of the park, you get great views of Mount San Jacinto and Mount San Gorgonio, both of which are snow-covered all winter.

It's also an easy jaunt to the park's west entrance station at Park Boulevard, and from there you can access the Hidden Valley Trail, Barker Dam Loop, Lost Horse Mine Trail, and Ryan Mountain Trail. All are short hikes and worth doing.

If you're staying at the ranch for more than a couple days, you should take advantage of your proximity to other parks in the area, including Mount San Jacinto State Park. Drive to Palm Springs and ride the spectacular Aerial Tramway to Mount San Jacinto, then get off the tram and hike at 8,500 feet in tall conifers and high-country beauty. There's nothing quite like the experience of walking among desert cactus in the morning, then hiking among mountain conifers in the afternoon. If you time your trip for November to April, you can probably even play in the snow.

Facilities, reservations, fees: There is one main house at Mojave Rock Ranch Lodge, with two bedrooms and a sleeping porch. A two-bedroom bungalow is also available. Both have fully equipped kitchens. Reservations are required. Fees range from $145 to $195 per night for up to four people; weekly and monthly rates are discounted. Pets are permitted, but they are not allowed inside the buildings.

Who to contact: Mojave Rock Ranch Lodge, P.O. Box 552, Joshua Tree, CA 92252; (760) 366-8455. Fax (760) 366-1996.

Season: Open year-round, but forget outdoor activities in the summer heat, except for very early in the morning.

Directions: From Banning on Interstate 10, drive east for 17 miles to the Highway 62 exit. Turn northeast on Highway 62 and drive 30 miles to the town of Joshua Tree. Turn left (north) on Sunfair Road. (If you reach Copper Mountain College on Highway 62, you've gone too far.) Drive six miles on Sunfair Road, then turn right by the wagon wheel that is signed 2015. Drive a half-mile to the lodge.

---

20. 29 PALMS INN
Joshua Tree National Park, off Highway 62 in Twentynine Palms

I never thought of myself as a desert-loving person. A mountain-loving person? Yes, of course. An ocean-loving person? Definitely. A forest-loving person? You bet. But the desert always seemed to me to be kind of... well, hot. Not to mention predominantly brown-colored. And boring.

But since my last trip to Joshua Tree National Park, I'm a changed woman. I might attribute my conversion to the fact that I visited in cool December, instead of in boiling July as I had done before. But I think it has more to do with the fact that I stayed at the 29 Palms Inn, a place that is funky, charming, and the perfect base camp for exploring the desert.

The 29 Palms Inn has been around since 1928, and has been owned by the same family for five generations. They are beyond trying to figure out how to do things right; they've got it down. Their brochure says it well: "We invite you to get lost in the desert." When you enter the main building to get your cabin key and check in, you see a carved sign that reads: "We're here in the pursuit of happiness and need all the help we can get."

In fact, there are various carved signs with quirky sayings to be found all over the grounds. Some are quite special so I won't give them away, but I'll tell you that my absolute favorite is found at the edge of the inn's property. As you drive out of the driveway, you see that the stop sign by the road is shaped like a stop sign and has the color of one, but someone has replaced the word "stop" with this message: "It's your decision."

The inn has 16 cabins, varying from adobe bungalows to old wood-frame buildings. Some of the cabins are duplexes, but they are private and quiet, with thick walls and fenced-in patios. Some units have fireplaces, some have wood stoves, and some don't have either, so be sure to ask for what you want. Only two buildings have kitchens; these are the three-bedroom "Guest House" and the one-bedroom "Irene's Historic Adobe."

Usually I don't like being without a kitchen when I travel, but at 29 Palms Inn I never missed it. In part, that's because a complimentary continental breakfast is provided each day, so I dined on fresh muffins, coffee, and juice each

Joshua Tree National Park

morning. At lunch time I was always hiking around the national park, so I had my day-pack filled with cans of tuna and crackers. And each night at dinner I was quite happy to eat at the 29 Palms Inn Restaurant, which had surprisingly delicious food served in a very friendly, casual atmosphere. I found myself looking forward to going there just so I could talk to the nice employees and eat their excellent sourdough bread.

Other charms of 29 Palms Inn include a duck pond surrounded by pomegranate trees, which is wildly popular with ducks. They quacked throughout much of the night. Near the pond is an enclosed gazebo, and hidden inside is a large jacuzzi. It's available for free to all inn guests; you just go get the key, let yourself in and have a soak, then return the key an hour later so someone else can use it. A good-sized swimming pool is located outside the inn's restaurant; it is in constant use in summer. During my visit in December, no one dared to go in it.

When you're not in your cabin, you'll be out exploring Joshua Tree National Park. The best trails close to the inn are the Fortynine

Palms Oasis Trail, the Ryan Mountain Trail, and the Lost Horse Mine Trail. Make sure you take the drive to Keys View at elevation 5,185 feet, especially if the weather is very clear, to check out the extraordinary vista. If you don't mind a longer drive, head for the south part of the park and the Cottonwood Spring area. A terrific eight-mile round-trip hike is possible from there to Lost Palms Oasis. If you don't want to hike that far, take the shorter left fork to Mastadon Peak, and scramble to the top of the rocky pinnacle.

The park visitor center is located about two miles from 29 Palms Inn on Utah Trail Road, and it's an excellent place to start your trip. The folks at the visitor center can provide you with information on all the best trailheads and destinations.

I should mention that the only thing that bothered me about my stay at 29 Palms Inn was that my cabin cost me $70 on a Thursday night, and $100 the next night, on a Friday. Apparently they do so much weekend business here, and so little business during the week, that on Friday and Saturday nights they charge 25 percent more for their accommodations. For a moment, I considered getting irritated about this, but then I decided to go sit in the jacuzzi instead. Quickly, all was forgotten.

Facilities, reservations, fees: There are 16 cabins at 29 Palms Inn, ranging in size from studios to three bedrooms. Two cabins have kitchens. A restaurant is available. Reservations are recommended. Fees range from $45 to $225 per night, depending on size of accommodations and season. Discounted rates are offered from June 15 to September 15, and midweek year-round. Pets are permitted in some cabins for a $10 fee.

Who to contact: 29 Palms Inn, 73950 Inn Avenue, Twentynine Palms, CA 92277; (760) 367-3505. Fax (760) 367-4425.

Season: Open year-round, but forget outdoor activities in the summer heat, except for very early in the morning.

Directions: From Banning on Interstate 10, drive east for 17 miles to the Highway 62 exit. Turn northeast on Highway 62 and drive 45 miles to the town of Twentynine Palms. Continue east to the far end of town and National Park Drive (one block east of Adobe Road). Turn right on National Park Drive, drive a quarter-mile and turn right on Inn Avenue. You'll enter the grounds of 29 Palms Inn immediately.

San Gabriel
&
San Bernardino
Mountains

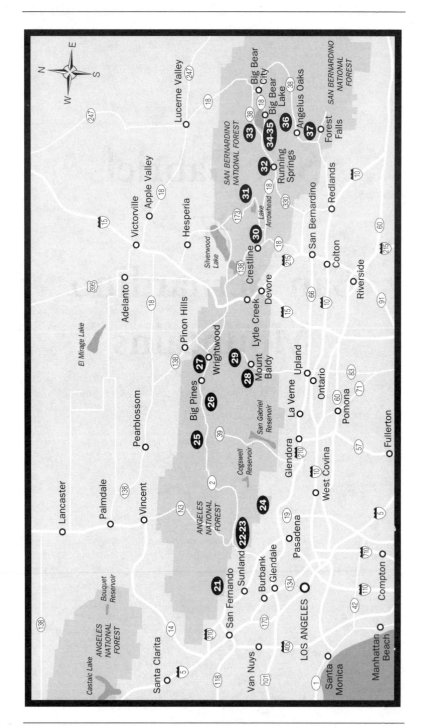

21. TRAIL CANYON/TOM LUCAS TRAIL CAMP
Angeles National Forest, off Interstate 210 near Sunland

If I lived anywhere within 50 miles of Pasadena, I'd be sure to spend a spring weekend every year at Tom Lucas Trail Camp in Trail Canyon. The canyon has a great trail, marvelous views, colorful wildflowers, a pretty waterfall, and a terrific little trail camp—which adds up to the perfect recipe for an easy spring backpacking trip.

Trail Canyon is on the western side of the San Gabriel Mountains, an area that is less visited than the more glamorous eastern side. Because the elevation is lower, the western San Gabriels are often drier and hotter than the eastern mountains. But after winter rains and for a few months in spring, the Trail Canyon Trail is neither dry nor hot. It begins with a ford, and has several more along the way, so make sure you're wearing good boots or are willing to get your feet wet. Except for the stream crossings, the Trail Canyon Trail is a breeze to follow, and it's pretty along the whole route.

After parking your car at the Trail Canyon Trailhead and strapping on your pack, follow the dirt road into a community of cabins, then continue past them, winding around the canyon. At three-quarters of a mile, where the road makes a hairpin left turn, look for the single-track trail leading off to the right, and follow it. Very shortly you'll leave the sun, chaparral, and cactus, and enter a densely shaded riparian area, thick with sycamores and alders.

As you hike deeper into the canyon, the terrain will change again. You'll leave the shade and climb back out to sparsely vegetated, exposed slopes. Count the wildflowers as you walk, both the chaparral and streamside varieties: Orange paintbrush, purple nightshade, yellow phlox, hooker's onions, scented ceanothus, tiny purple violets, sagebrush... You get a little of everything in Trail Canyon.

At 1.5 miles, after hiking steeply uphill and away from the stream, watch for a sharp left curve in the trail and then hey!—there's a waterfall up ahead. Although the falls are less than ebullient in late summer, in spring they put on a stunning show of white water, thundering down the canyon. Trail Canyon Falls spills over a smooth granite precipice in a rectangular block of water. The waterfall is about 50 feet high, and it can be as much as 15 feet wide when the stream is flowing hard.

The trail, which climbs gently but continually up to this point, suddenly goes flat after you round the curve and behold the falls. From there, it's an easy stroll to the fall's crest, then slightly past it to a point where the stream narrows enough so that you can easily rock-hop across. When you do, check out the beautiful colorful granite in the streambed. You're at the halfway point here; time to take a rest and enjoy the scenery.

Tom Lucas Trail Camp is 1.5 miles beyond the waterfall, a total of 3.5 miles from your car. You'll cross and re-cross the stream several times more, continuing your moderately uphill trek. The camp is set in the shade of alders and oaks at an elevation of 3,700 feet, near the edge of Big Cienega, a lush, meadow-like area. Its facilities are primitive—six campsites with fire grills, picnic tables, and a vault toilet, plus a hitching post in case you brought Trigger with you. You must filter your water from the stream, or boil it for five minutes, and of course, you must pack in all your food and other supplies.

So who was Tom Lucas? A famous mountain man and grizzly bear hunter from the old days. But never fear; you won't have grizzlies bothering you on your trip. Old Tom Lucas and his friends took care of that.

If you can muster the enthusiasm to leave your bucolic campsite, take a day-hike to the top of Condor Peak. Follow the Trail Canyon Trail uphill for another 1.5 miles from camp, then turn right on the Condor Peak Trail. One and a half miles of further ascent brings you near the 5,400-foot summit; you can scramble to the top and check out the clear view of Catalina Island. Wow!

Facilities, reservations, fees: There are six campsites at Tom Lucas Trail Camp. Water is available for filtering. A free campfire permit is required for overnight stays; they can be obtained at any Forest Service office. There is no fee for camping. Pets are permitted.

Special note: A national forest adventure pass is required for recreation in this area. See page 11 for details.

Who to contact: Angeles National Forest, Tujunga Ranger District, 12371 North Little Tujunga Canyon Road, San Fernando, CA 91342; (818) 899-1900. Fax (818) 896-6727.

Maps for backpacking: For a map of Angeles National Forest, send $4 to USDA-Forest Service, 630 Sansome Street, San Francisco, CA 94111. For a topographic map of the area, ask for Sunland from the USGS.

Season: Open year-round; best from December to June. Beware of high water immediately following heavy rainfall.

Directions: From Interstate 210 in Sunland, exit on Sunland Boulevard which becomes Foothill Boulevard. Drive east for one mile to Mount

Gleason Avenue. Turn left (north), drive 1.3 miles, then turn right on Big Tujunga Canyon Road. Drive 3.4 miles on Big Tujunga Road to a sign for Trail Canyon Trail on the left. Drive a quarter-mile to a fork, then bear right and drive a quarter-mile on rough road to a large parking lot. The trailhead is on the left side of the lot as you drive in.

22. COMMODORE SWITZER TRAIL CAMP
Angeles National Forest, off Highway 2 near La Cañada

An overnight backpacking trip to Commodore Switzer Trail Camp is a return to the days of the Great Hiking Era at the turn of the century, when the outdoors was fashionable, and both the elite and the masses flocked to the San Gabriel Mountains for resort vacations.

Commodore Perry Switzer built a trail resort in Arroyo Seco in 1884, long before the Angeles Crest Highway made access to this mountain area ludicrously easy. Switzer was called "Commodore" because of his talents in maneuvering his fleet of burros in rocky Arroyo Seco Canyon. Visitors would ride a half-day on mules to reach Switzer's resort from the city of Pasadena, through eight miles of wild terrain with more than 60 stream crossings. (When the Mount Lowe Railway was built in 1893, the arduous route was short-ened considerably, and Switzer's resort became even more popular.) At Switzer's, visitors were treated to a bed to sleep on, three good meals per day, and plenty of fellow-ship, all for $1.50.

Alder trees in Switzer Canyon

Like other trail resorts of that era, the camp lost business with the building of the Angeles Crest Highway and the widespread use of the automobile. Suddenly there was no point in riding a mule up Arroyo Seco when you could drive there instead, and Switzer's was abandoned in the 1930s. Today, the Commodore Switzer Trail Camp stands on the grounds of the old resort, and a pretty waterfall as well as the Switzer ruins can still be viewed.

The trail camp is an easy trip for families, best taken in spring-time when Switzer Creek is full. Summer weekdays are also a good option, but forget summer weekends, when the trailhead picnic area is crowded and noisy. From the Switzer Picnic Area parking lot, the hike to the primitive trail camp is only one mile and mostly downhill. Following the Gabrielino National Recreation Trail along Switzer Creek, you'll pass through the Switzer Picnic Area and hike down-stream on a smooth dirt trail. The route is pleasantly shaded by willows, alders, oaks, and maples—all water-loving trees. A few creek crossings are necessary, so wear waterproof boots, especially in spring. Be sure to look at the beautiful colors in the mineral-rich rock of the streambed.

In 30 minutes of hiking (or less!) you'll be at Commodore Switzer Trail Camp, elevation 2,800 feet, marked only by a few primitive sites with fire rings along the left side of the creek. There are no amenities at the camp; you're on your own for filtering water from the stream and gathering wood for your campfire. You won't know it from where you stand, but you're perched nearly on top of 50-foot Switzer Falls.

To see the waterfall, ignore the use trails that lead from the campsites, and instead cross the creek by the camp and head uphill, climbing above the canyon, still following the Gabrielino Trail. The trail passes right by Switzer Falls, affording a decent view from across the canyon. The stone building ruins you see are the remains of the Switzer chapel. Here, visitors at Switzer's camp would attend Sunday services above the waterfall.

If you're traveling with children, it's wise to be content with the view from this spot, where you can see the waterfall dropping vertically through a narrow chute in the gorge. A chain-link fence separates you from the steep dropoff into the canyon. If you insist on a closer look at Switzer Falls, a few steps further will take you to a junction where the Gabrielino Trail heads right and uphill, and the Bear Canyon Trail heads left and downhill. Take the left fork for Bear Canyon and descend steeply for one mile, being wary of the sheer dropoffs. When you reach the creek, walk a quarter-mile upstream toward Switzer Falls, but resist the temptation to climb around the lower, smaller falls to reach the large drop. There have been too many accidents here.

Should you wish to explore further, more water slides and falls can be found downstream along Bear Canyon Trail. The trout fishing is surprisingly good, and the continual roar and splash of mini-cascades along Arroyo Seco can keep you entertained for hours. (For more information on Bear Canyon, see the following story.)

Facilities, reservations, fees: There are four campsites at Commodore Switzer Trail Camp. Water is available for filtering. A free campfire permit is required for overnight stays; they can be obtained at any Forest Service office. There is no fee for camping. Pets are permitted.

Special note: A national forest adventure pass is required for recreation in this area. See page 11 for details.

Who to contact: Angeles National Forest, Arroyo Seco Ranger District, 4600 Oak Grove Drive, Flintridge, CA 91011; (818) 790-1151 or fax (818) 790-5392.

Maps for backpacking: For a map of Angeles National Forest, send $4 to USDA-Forest Service, 630 Sansome Street, San Francisco, CA 94111. A map of the San Gabriel Mountains is available for a fee from Tom Harrison Cartography, (415) 456-7940. To obtain a topographic map of the area, ask for Condor Peak and Pasadena from the USGS.

Season: Open year-round; best from February to June.

Directions: From Interstate 210 in La Cañada, take Highway 2 north and drive 9.8 miles to Switzer Picnic Area on the right. (At 9.3 miles you reach Clear Creek Information Station; bear right and reach Switzer in a half-mile.)

23. BEAR CANYON BACKPACK
Angeles National Forest, off Highway 2 near La Cañada

The Gabrielino National Recreation Trail is your ticket to visiting the waterslides, mini-cascades, and pools of spectacular Bear Canyon, then spending a night at Bear Canyon Trail Camp. It's a longer trip than the short overnighter to Commodore Switzer Trail Camp (see the preceding story), but if you have the energy for the three-mile one-way hike, the payoff is worth it.

After obtaining your campfire permit and packing up your water filter, begin hiking into Arroyo Seco Canyon from Switzer Picnic Area, which on summer weekends is usually packed with people. Never fear, you'll soon leave them behind. Head downstream through a shady canopy of willows, alders, oaks, and maples. A few creek crossings and one mile of trail brings you to Commodore Switzer Trail Camp (see the preceding story). Cross the stream by the camp and head uphill, still on the Gabrielino Trail. The route passes 50-foot Switzer Falls and the stone ruins of Switzer's camp, a popular trail camp from the turn of the century.

A few steps beyond the falls is a junction where Gabrielino Trail heads right and uphill, and Bear Canyon Trail heads left and downhill. Enjoy the lofty view down Arroyo Seco Canyon at this junction, then bear left and descend steeply down into Bear Canyon for one mile. The walls of the creek gorge are impressively steep; the trail is even carved out of rock in places. When you reach the canyon bottom of Bear Creek, continue along the stream for another mile to Bear Canyon Trail Camp, passing many waterslides and crystal-clear pools along the way.

Bear Canyon Trail Camp is much like its neighbor at Switzer's— primitive but serviceable. A few fire grills and flat sites for tents can be found on the right side of the creek. Big cone spruce and oaks keep the stream cool and shady. Trout fishing in the creek is fair year-round, but best in spring. Swimming is first-rate in summer.

If you are staying at Bear Canyon, remember that your hike was largely downhill on your way in to camp. While you're splashing around in the creek, be sure to save some energy for the hike back to your car. Luckily, your pack will be empty for the return trip. Your heart, on the other hand, will be full of happy memories.

Facilities, reservations, fees: There are five campsites at Bear Canyon Camp. Water is available for filtering. A free campfire permit is required for overnight stays; they can be obtained at any Forest Service office. There is no fee for camping. Pets are permitted.

Special note: A national forest adventure pass is required for recreation in this area. See page 11 for details.

Who to contact: Angeles National Forest, Arroyo Seco Ranger District, 4600 Oak Grove Drive, Flintridge, CA 91011; (818) 790-1151 or fax (818) 790-5392.

Maps for backpacking: For a map of Angeles National Forest, send $4 to USDA-Forest Service, 630 Sansome Street, San Francisco, CA 94111. A map of the San Gabriel Mountains is available for a fee from Tom Harrison Cartography, (415) 456-7940. To obtain a topographic map of the area, ask for Condor Peak and Pasadena from the USGS.

Season: Open year-round; best from February to June.

Directions: From Interstate 210 in La Cañada, take Highway 2 north and drive 9.8 miles to Switzer Picnic Area on the right. (At 9.3 miles you reach Clear Creek Information Station; bear right and reach Switzer in a half-mile.)

24. SPRUCE GROVE & HOEGEE'S TRAIL CAMPS
Angeles National Forest, off Interstate 210 near Arcadia

Because of is its proximity to where thousands of people live and work in Pasadena and Arcadia, Big Santa Anita Canyon is probably the easiest hiking and backpacking destination in all of Angeles National Forest. Rather than having to drive the Angeles Crest Highway to reach your trailhead, you simply head to the "city side" of the mountains at Chantry Flat. You can be hiking within a few minutes of leaving your desk job.

Check dam in Big Santa Anita Canyon

The canyon is not the high mountains by any stretch of the imagination, but it's overflowing with foliage and provides a short, simple, and sweet escape from urban life. Pack up your water filter, pick up a campfire permit at the ranger station, and start hiking on the Gabrielino National Recreation Trail from Chantry Flat, elevation 2,200 feet. Your destination is Spruce Grove Trail Camp, four miles away. The camp can be crowded on summer weekends, but you're likely to have the place to yourself during the week.

The trail is paved for the first six-tenths mile heading downhill, but when you reach the canyon bottom, you leave the pavement behind. Immediately you'll hear the sound of streaming water—it comes from the combined rushing of Big Santa Anita Creek, Winter Creek, and the flow of water over man-made debris dams. Although the small dams mar the natural beauty of the canyon, they also make an oddly pretty sight, forming small waterfalls every few hundred yards.

If you're wondering about the cute little cabins in the canyon, they are all that remains of Roberts Camp, a popular trail resort from the early 1900s. At present, they are leased as summer homes. (Since there is no road into the canyon, residents get supplies to their cabins the old-fashioned way—by horse pack train.)

You'll cross Roberts Footbridge by the first of the cabins, then bear right on the dirt pathway. In a half-mile, you'll reach a trail junction where you can continue straight to Sturtevant Falls (worth the side trip in spring), or take a hard left turn to climb out of the canyon. (There is also a middle trail, but it's not a good path if you're carrying a backpack—it's too steep.)

Turn left on the Gabrielino Trail and head for Cascade Picnic Area, where you rejoin the babbling stream. This is a lovely spot for a rest; when you're refreshed, continue along the trail for less than a mile to Spruce Grove Trail Camp, elevation 3,100 feet. There, in the shade of giant-sized big cone spruce trees, plus normal-sized laurel, maple, and oak trees, are six perfect campsites with picnic tables and fire grills.

A second backpacking option in Big Santa Anita Canyon, with shorter mileage and less elevation change, is to hike to Hoegee's Trail Camp, 2.3 miles from Chantry Flat. Follow the Gabrielino Trail to the end of the pavement at Roberts Footbridge, but after crossing the bridge, head to your left instead of right. You'll be leaving the Gabrielino Trail and following the Lower Winter Creek Trail, climbing moderately past summer cabins in the shade of a lush, mixed forest.

Because your destination is only 2.3 miles from where you left your car, the trail to Hoegee's Camp may be a better backpacking option if you have young children in tow. The camp is also larger and more popular—it has 16 sites with picnic tables and fire grills. It is perched on the shady southern bank of Winter Creek, where you can filter your water.

Like nearby Commodore Switzer's Trail Camp, Hoegee's Trail Camp is built by the ruins of an old trail resort from the Great Hiking Era at the turn of the century. You can still see overgrown ivy and stone remains from the days when hundreds of people would stop here at Hoegee's Resort as they hiked up Mount Wilson.

If you like, you can make a loop hike out of your overnight trip to Hoegee's, by returning to Chantry Flat on the Upper Winter Creek Trail, a quarter-mile upstream from the camp. Taking Upper Winter Creek Trail for your return is only a slightly longer walk than the Lower Winter Creek Trail, and a pleasant variation.

Facilities, reservations, fees: There are six campsites at Spruce Grove Trail Camp and 16 campsites at Hoegee's Trail Camp. Water is available for filtering. A free campfire permit is required for overnight stays; they can be obtained at any Forest Service office. There is no fee for camping. Pets are permitted.

Special note: A national forest adventure pass is required for recreation in this area. See page 11 for details.

Who to contact: Angeles National Forest, Arroyo Seco Ranger District, 4600 Oak Grove Drive, Flintridge, CA 91011; (818) 790-1151 or fax (818) 790-5392.

Maps for backpacking: For a map of Angeles National Forest, send $4 to USDA-Forest Service, 630 Sansome Street, San Francisco, CA 94111. A map of the San Gabriel Mountains is available for a fee from Tom Harrison Cartography, (415) 456-7940. To obtain a topographic map of the area, ask for Mount Wilson from the USGS.

Season: Open year-round; creek crossings may be impassable after heavy rain.

Directions: From Interstate 210 in Pasadena, drive seven miles east to Arcadia. Exit on Santa Anita Avenue and drive six miles north to the road's end at Chantry Flat. The Gabrielino Trail begins across the road from the first parking area.

25. COOPER CANYON BACKPACK
Angeles National Forest, off Highway 2 near Mount Waterman

After the snow has melted, here's a first-rate reason to make the 34-mile drive to the summit of Mount Waterman: A visit to Cooper Canyon Falls, and an overnight stay at Cooper Canyon Trail Camp. The best thing about the camp and the waterfall, besides the fact that they're set in a gorgeous, high elevation forest, is that they are just far enough away so that they don't get heavily visited. But the hike to camp is only three miles one-way, easy enough for even children to make the trip, while carrying their own sleeping bags. All you need is your water purifier and a pack full of food, and you're set to go.

Start off from Buckhorn Campground, an hour's drive from La Cañada, at the trailhead for the Burkhardt Trail. Your elevation is 6,400 feet, so the scenery is pretty and the air is cool and clean right from the start. Although you'll see small waterfalls and swimming holes along Buckhorn Creek within a quarter-mile of the camp, the real treasure is two miles away at Cooper Canyon and Little Rock Creek. The hike is mostly downhill, through a dense forest of big firs, cedars, and pines. There's almost no undergrowth in these woods—just conifers and big rocks. It feels like you're in the southern Sierra Nevada, but no, this is the San Gabriels.

The Burkhardt Trail laterals along the canyon slopes, high above Buckhorn Creek, then makes a left turn into Cooper Canyon, and traces a long switchback downhill. Look for a group of five young cedar trees, an unusual set of quintuplets, growing together near a tiny stream crossing. At 1.75 miles from Buckhorn Campground, you'll reach a junction with the Pacific Crest Trail and Silver Moccasin Trail. A sign points to Cooper Canyon Camp to the left, but before you go there, head to the right for one-tenth mile to check out Cooper Canyon Falls.

Burkhardt Trail from Buckhorn Campground to Cooper Canyon

In minutes you'll hear the waterfall, which drops just below the trail's edge. Take off your backpack and make use of the rope that's in place to help you clamber down to the falls' base. You can stand on an island of boulders and enjoy the wide, noisy, 35-foot plunge of water. Be sure to get here early in the year, when the stream flow is in full force. Swimming in the falls' big pool is tempting, but let me warn you: It's icy cold.

When you're ready to head to camp, lift your pack back on your shoulders and walk 1.2 miles westward and uphill on the Pacific Crest Trail, passing your junction with the Burkhardt Trail. Once you reach the large campground, you'll have some jobs to do: Choose a campsite. Start gathering wood for your fire. Set up your tent. Filter water from the stream. Spend some time admiring this fine camp.

Fire grills, picnic tables, and a vault toilet are provided at Cooper Canyon—the place is set up for when the Boy Scouts come marching through on their ritual hike on the Silver Moccasin Trail. (The 53-mile Silver Moccasin Trail, which has been making scouts out of boys since the 1940s, follows the same route as the Pacific Crest Trail in this section.)

Several shorter hikes are possible from camp: You can head west on the Pacific Crest Trail to Cloudburst Summit, or east past Cooper Canyon Falls to Little Rock Creek. Small trout can be found here; occasionally one or two will accept an invitation to dinner. There is no formal trail along Little Rock Creek, but most anglers make their way by rockhopping.

Another option is to take the left fork shortly after Cooper Canyon Falls, putting you back on the Burkhardt Trail, this time heading north and climbing 3.5 miles to Burkhardt Saddle. The hike isn't easy but the scenery is enthralling; they don't call this Pleasant View Ridge for nothing. From the 7,000-foot saddle, you can look deep into the abyss of the Devil's Punchbowl, and stare at miles and miles of desert from your conifer-shaded perch.

Facilities, reservations, fees: There are 20 campsites at Cooper Canyon Camp. Water is available for filtering. A free campfire permit is required for overnight stays; they can be obtained at any Forest Service office. There is no fee for camping. Pets are permitted.

Special note: A national forest adventure pass is required for recreation in this area. See page 11 for details.

Who to contact: Angeles National Forest, Arroyo Seco Ranger District, 4600 Oak Grove Drive, Flintridge, CA 91011; (818) 790-1151. Fax (818) 790-5392.

Maps for backpacking: For a map of Angeles National Forest, send $4 to USDA-Forest Service, 630 Sansome Street, San Francisco, CA 94111. A map of the San Gabriel Mountains is available for a fee from Tom Harrison Cartography, (415) 456-7940. For a topographic map of the area, ask for Waterman Mountain from the USGS.

Season: Open whenever the trail is snow-free, usually late April to November.

Directions: From Interstate 210 in La Cañada, take Highway 2 north and drive 34 miles to Buckhorn Camp on the left. (It's 1.5 miles past the Mount Waterman ski lift, just beyond Cloudburst Summit.) The Burkhardt Trail starts at the far end of the camp near the restrooms (bear left at site 18).

26. LITTLE JIMMY TRAIL CAMP
Angeles National Forest, off Highway 2 near Islip Saddle

The first time I hiked to Little Jimmy Trail Camp, I was so tuckered out from a week of climbing peaks in the San Gabriel Mountains, I almost skipped the short side trip from the camp to Islip Summit. I had been on top of taller mountains in the previous few days, and I figured the view couldn't be any better than what I'd already seen.

Luckily a rest and a snack at Little Jimmy Camp restored my energy, and I set off for the peak of 8,250-foot Mount Islip. Once there, I learned my lesson: The best views aren't always from the tallest summits. Mount Islip's vista is a stunner, worth saving your last Power Bar for.

The peak is a short day-hike from Little Jimmy Trail Camp, a large Forest Service camp that's an easy two-mile trek from the Islip Saddle Trailhead on Highway 2. The Little Jimmy Trail (also the Pacific Crest Trail here) begins across the highway from the large Pacific Crest Trail parking area. The first half-mile of the route climbs and is completely exposed, but your reward for enduring it is that just before you enter the forest, you get a nice view to the south over the San Gabriel Mountains. Keep heading gently up, up, and up, now in the shade, and cross a dirt service road at one mile from the trailhead. After the first mile, the trail goes flatter, and if you look over your left shoulder, you can see the desert around Palmdale and Lancaster.

Little Jimmy Trail Camp is surprisingly large and developed, with dozens of sites, picnic tables, fire grills, and even a few vault toilets and garbage cans, although they ask you to pack out your own trash anyway. Because the camp can be serviced via a dirt road, it has many amenities that you don't usually get when backpacking. The camp does not have piped water, however, but that's no problem because there's a reliable spring a quarter-mile to the southeast. Just follow the Pacific Crest Trail to reach it.

Fire lookout tower remains on Islip Summit

Remember that the San Gabriels are in bear country (just black bears, the grizzlies are long gone), so store all your food high in a tree away from sleeping areas, or carry a bear-proof food canister.

Here's an insider's tip: Don't just throw down your stuff and set up your tent in any of the main campsites without first checking out the more private sites that are only 100 yards away, along the Mount Islip Trail. Locate the signed Mount Islip Trail at the far end of camp; follow it uphill for a very short distance. Three campsites are perched near the edge of a cliff with a spectacular view of the desert, plus far more privacy than at the main camp. Someone has built a log wind shelter, because the spot is more exposed than the shady, tree-lined main camp. If there's a pack of Boy Scouts staying in the main camp, this could be a very sweet alternative place to spend the night.

Don't miss out on the trail to Islip's summit. After passing the three isolated campsites, just keep heading steadily uphill. In a quarter-mile, you'll come out to a ridgeline and great views of the mountains and valleys below. Then you simply follow the ridgeline, with an easy grade and views all the way. That spot of blue down there is Crystal Lake.

At a signed fork, turn right for the peak, walking less than a quarter-mile uphill. You'll find the remains of a stone cabin (an old Forest Service lookout tower), and stunning 360-degree views. Islip's summit is very pointy and has little surface area, so when you're on top, you're really on top.

Facilities, reservations, fees: There are 30 campsites at Little Jimmy Trail Camp. Water is available for filtering. A free campfire permit is required for overnight stays; they can be obtained at any Forest Service office. There is no fee for camping. Pets are permitted.

Special note: A national forest adventure pass is required for recreation in this area. See page 11 for details.

Who to contact: Angeles National Forest, Arroyo Seco Ranger District, 4600 Oak Grove Drive, Flintridge, CA 91011; (818) 790-1151 or fax (818) 790-5392.

Maps for backpacking: For a map of Angeles National Forest, send $4 to USDA-Forest Service, 630 Sansome Street, San Francisco, CA 94111. A map of the San Gabriel Mountains is available for a fee from Tom Harrison Cartography, (415) 456-7940. To obtain a topographic map of the area, ask for Crystal Lake from the USGS.

Season: Open whenever the trail is snow-free, usually late April to November.

Directions: From Interstate 210 in La Cañada, take Highway 2 northeast and drive 42 miles to Islip Saddle. (If you are coming from Highway 138 near Phelan or Piñon Hills, take Highway 2 west for 25 miles to Islip Saddle, which is 15 miles west of Big Pines.)

27. MOUNTAIN VIEW MOTEL CABINS
near Angeles National Forest, off Highway 2 in Wrightwood

It's December in Los Angeles, and somehow you just can't conjure up the feeling of Christmas amid the crowded malls, Santa Claus bikinis, and palm trees dressed in twinkling lights. Get in your car, wave good-bye to it all, and take the one-hour drive to Wrightwood, a snowy mountain town that knows how to do winter right.

Book yourself a cabin at the Mountain View Motel. They've got units with and without jacuzzi tubs, fireplaces, wood-burning stoves, and kitchens, so you can get one that is right for you. Make sure you've brought your warm clothes, because the elevation is 6,000 feet, so it can get mighty chilly up here. Take a stroll around the town (population 3,300) and look at all the decorated houses and shops. Then take your pick from the ski resorts in nearby Big Pines—Ski Sunrise or Mountain High Resorts—and make a few runs down the mountain. Snowboarding and skiing both are popular, and Mountain High offers lighted night skiing till 10 p.m. daily. If it's a poor year for snow, don't fret—they make their own white stuff if they have to.

If wintertime isn't your cup of tea, the other seasons are also fine at the Mountain View Motel. Their rates go down after ski season ends, so you can save a few bucks by coming in spring, summer, or fall. At those times, the big attraction in the Wrightwood area is hiking in the San Gabriel Mountains, with dozens of trailheads located within a 30-minute drive of your cabin. The elevation is high enough here so that it is rarely too hot in summer, and the air is always fresh and clean—free of the valley smog. If you want an easy stroll, there are three nature trails just five minutes' away in Big Pines, near the Forest Service Visitor Center. If you seek more of an adventure, there's the classic climb to the peak of Mount Baden-Powell, starting from either the Vincent Gap or Dawson Saddle trailheads on Highway 2.

You can even do some fishing in the Big Pines area, at little Jackson Lake along the Big Pines Highway (Road N4). The Department of Fish and Game keeps the lake stocked with trout all summer; you just drive up to the picnic area and fish from shore. If you've always wanted to try your hand at gold prospecting, Big Rock Creek is the place, just a few miles down Highway 2.

If you're the kind who prefers not to wander far from your cozy cabin, the Mountain View Motel makes it easy for you. Right on their premises is the Mountain View Bird Sanctuary, a small fenced garden oasis for birds. The motel owners are trying to establish the little town of Wrightwood as a center for birdwatchers across the state.

After two stays in Mountain View Motel's cabins, one in summer and one in winter, I recommend it wholeheartedly. On both trips, I had only one small complaint: They charge five bucks for firewood, and of course you will buy it. Who wants to have a fireplace but no wood to burn?

Facilities, reservations, fees: There are 10 cabins at Mountain View Motel, ranging in size from one to three bedrooms. Some have kitchens and jacuzzis; all have fireplaces or wood-burning stoves. Reservations are recommended. Fees range from $69 to $149 per night. Pets are not permitted.

Skiing at Big Pines near Wrightwood

Special note: A national forest adventure pass is required for recreation in this area. See page 11 for details.

Who to contact: Mountain View Motel Cabins, P.O. Box 458, 1054 State Highway 2, Wrightwood, CA 92397; (760) 249-3553.

Season: Open year-round; expect snow in winter.

Directions: From Interstate 10 at Ontario, drive east for seven miles and take Interstate 15 north. Drive north on Interstate 15 for 22 miles to Highway 138, then go west on Highway 138 for nine miles to the Highway 2 cutoff. Go west on Highway 2 for five miles to Wrightwood; Mountain View Motel is on the right as you drive through town.

28. MOUNT BALDY LODGE
Angeles National Forest, off Interstate 10 near Ontario

Maybe I'm just nostalgic, but Mount Baldy is one of my favorite peaks in California and the Mount Baldy Lodge is one of my favorite places to go. When I was a college student in Claremont, we'd head to Mount Baldy at the first sign of snow in November or December. Often we'd stop our cars as soon as we drove into the white stuff, just for the sheer joy of throwing snowballs at each other in Southern California. Other times, and in other seasons, we'd drive up to our favorite trailhead at Ice House Canyon, and hike in the conifers amid cool, clean mountain air. It was such a sweet, revitalizing shock to our smog-ridden Los Angeles Basin lungs.

We also passed many happy summer evenings at the Mount Baldy Lodge, having dinner and dancing to live bands. Years later, I finally stayed overnight at the Mount Baldy Lodge cabins. Most of the night, I found myself wondering how I could have spent so much of my life at the place without ever having stayed there. We had cabin number 8, which has a huge stone fireplace—the walk-in kind, one of the best I've ever seen. The bed was placed in a tiny alcove, separated somewhat from the main living area, which made it especially cozy.

All the cabins are old and rustic, with fine woodworking and details, but with modern conveniences like electric heaters. Although they are right next to the lodge restaurant and Mount Baldy Road, there is surprisingly little noise. After 9 p.m. or so, few people drive up the mountain. You might want to plan your trip for a weeknight, however, because if a band is playing at the lodge on Friday or Saturday night, you'll have to wait for them to quit before you can get some sleep. On the other hand, you could always dance till you drop, then retire to your cozy cabin.

On the down side, there are no kitchens in the cabins, but you can get your meals at the lodge restaurant or at the nearby Buckhorn Lodge. On the up side, you wake up and you're in a mountain wonderland, just a half-hour from sprawling suburbs and smog but oh, so far away. In minutes you can drive up the hill to the Mount Baldy ski lift, or if the mountain is snow-free, you can head for hiking adventures at any number of nearby trailheads. An easy hike is 1.7 miles one way on the Bear Canyon Trail from Mount Baldy Village to Bear Flats. A longer, more challenging trip is to take the Icehouse Canyon Trail to the Three T's Trail, where you can pay a visit to three peaks: Thunder, Timber and Telegraph. The Mount Baldy Ranger Station is right in town, ready to answer all your questions.

Facilities, reservations, fees: There are four studio cabins at Mount Baldy Lodge, each with a fireplace. There are no kitchen facilities. The restaurant at Mount Baldy Lodge is open for lunch and dinner daily and breakfast on Sundays only. Reservations are recommended. Fees range from $65 to $75 per night. Pets are not permitted.

Special note: A national forest adventure pass is required for recreation in this area. See page 11 for details.

Who to contact: Mount Baldy Lodge, Mount Baldy, CA 91759; (909) 982-1115.

Season: Open year-round; expect snow in winter.

Directions: From Interstate 10 at Ontario, exit on Mountain Avenue and drive north for six miles until Mountain Avenue joins Shinn Road. Bear left on Shinn Road and continue to Mount Baldy Road. Bear right and drive 5.5 miles north on Mount Baldy Road to Mount Baldy Village. Mount Baldy Lodge is on the right side of the road.

29. SNOWCREST LODGE
Angeles National Forest, off Interstate 10 near Ontario

As I write this, I'm watching the snowflakes fall vertically and sometimes sideways outside my cabin window at Snowcrest Lodge on Mount Baldy. The wind is howling and the white stuff is falling fast; they are expecting two feet today. With any luck at all, we'll be snowed in and won't be able to leave for a week. Good thing we have plenty of firewood.

We knew we were going to have a good time at Snowcrest when we drove up and were greeted first by a tail-wagging black Labrador, then by the lodge manager. He talked to us like we were old friends, which is apparently the norm here. Their advertising motto is "We have that 'Honey, we're home' feeling... No strangers here." Sure enough, all three people we dealt with at the lodge went out of their way to be friendly to us, and I never let on that I was writing a guide book.

The main lodge building has a cafe and bar, which looks exactly like a mountain lodge cafe should look. Various stuffed animal heads hang from the walls, including a very impressive moose head. A display of full-bodied stuffed animals, including a wolf, a coyote, and a bobcat, are remarkably lifelike. The stone fireplace is large enough to pitch a tent in. The dining room is immense, with an assortment of mismatched furniture. It's the kind of place where you would feel ridiculous wearing a suit and tie. Thank goodness.

There are six cabins at Snowcrest, and the best ones are the larger cabins that come with kitchens. (Bring your own utensils, pots, and pans—none are provided.) If you're on a budget, the smaller cabins are 20 bucks cheaper, but you won't be able to cook. Although the larger cabins are built of stone and cute as can be, the smaller ones are duplexes, and a bit shabby. However, even the small cabins have a separate living room and bedroom, so there's some room to move around. All of the cabins have big stone fireplaces, heaters, bathrooms, and comfortable beds, which is really all you need anyway.

The main reason people come to Snowcrest Lodge is because it's only a half-mile from the Mount Baldy Ski Lift. You wake up in the morning, have some breakfast at the restaurant or make your own in your cabin, and then a few minutes later you are riding the chairlift uphill. Sound easy? It is.

Snowcrest Lodge and the ski lift are located at 6,500 feet in elevation. The Mount Baldy Ski Lift's first chair takes you to 7,800 feet (The Notch Restaurant is located there), and the second and third chair take you to 8,800 feet. Most winters, there is plenty of snow up this high, but the ski resort also makes snow to supplement it. Snowboarders and skiers share the slopes, which are rarely crowded.

Another great activity for late winter and spring is hiking to San Antonio Falls, an 80-foot waterfall that drops in three tiers. The trailhead is only a quarter-mile up the road from the cabins at Snowcrest Lodge, so you could easily walk there. The hike itself is easy, following the ski lift maintenance road gently uphill for three-quarters of a mile to a sharp curve in the road, where the big waterfall pours. When it's running, you can't miss it. The best time to see it flow is just when the snow starts melting.

Ice House Canyon on Mount Baldy

Very fit hikers can continue past the waterfall for another six miles to the peak of Mount Baldy at 10,064 feet. This is one of the greatest hikes in all of Southern California, a 13-mile epic trip that all serious outdoor lovers should take. If you go too early in the season, you'll need to carry ice axes and crampons and know how to use them. It's easier to wait until the snow is gone; then the only requirements are full water bottles, some snacks, and plenty of energy. Views from the peak of Baldy are extraordinary, taking in a panorama of desert, city, ocean, and even the southern Sierra Nevada.

There are plenty of tamer activities to be sampled on Mount Baldy. Kids love to visit the town's trout pools, where you can pay a couple of bucks to toss a line in the water. No fishing license is required. Snowcrest Lodge has its own Olympic-sized swimming pool, great for lounging in the sun or playing in the water. In winter, some folks bring their trash can lids or boogie boards up to the mountain, and spend all afternoon sledding down the hillsides.

Facilities, reservations, fees: There are six cabins at Snowcrest Lodge, ranging in size from one to two bedrooms, some with kitchens. Cooking and eating utensils are not provided. Reservations are recommended. Fees range from $75 to $95 per night. Pets are permitted with a $20 refundable deposit.

Special note: A national forest adventure pass is required for recreation in this area. See page 11 for details.

Who to contact: Snowcrest Lodge, P.O. Box 383, Mount Baldy, CA 91759; (909) 985-3012.

Season: Open year-round; expect snow in winter.

Directions: From Interstate 10 at Ontario, exit on Mountain Avenue and drive north for six miles till Mountain Avenue joins Shinn Road. Bear left on Shinn Road and continue to Mount Baldy Road. Bear right and drive nine miles north on Mount Baldy Road, past Mount Baldy Village, to Snowcrest Lodge on the left side of the road.

30. ARROWHEAD PINE ROSE CABINS
near Lake Arrowhead, off Highway 189 in Twin Peaks

There are folks who are in the cabin business, and there are folks who are in the cabin business and know how to do it right. The folks who run Arrowhead Pine Rose Cabins are in the latter category.

First, they have a great location: near lakes Gregory, Silverwood, and Arrowhead in the San Bernardino Mountains. Next, they do everything they can to make your stay extraordinary. Instead of just basic, cookie-cutter cabins and cottages, the owners have made

Arrowhead Pine Rose Cabins into individual hand-crafted master-pieces. Each one is different, although they all have kitchens and most have fireplaces. You can tell by the way these cabins are decorated that the owners believe in going the extra mile.

We stayed in "Rustic Romance," which has an open-beamed ceiling, a beautiful stone fireplace, and perfectly coordinated linens, rugs, lamp shades, and hand-painted detailing on the walls. The centerpiece of the room is a jacuzzi with—get this—a natural stone waterfall. The shower stall is also lined with stone. If this sounds a bit too Las Vegas for you, let me emphasize that the overall effect is tasteful, subtle, and rustic, not splashy.

On the porches outside most of the cabins are big willow chairs, where you can while away the hours watching the birds or reading a book. If you want more activity, the cabin owners have built an outdoor, playground-sized checkerboard, using tree stumps for pieces. Too much trouble to move those stumps around? You can borrow all kinds of boards games from the front desk, or play badminton, croquet, or horseshoes on the grounds. On warm days, you can take a swim in the heated outdoor pool.

If you can tear yourself away from Arrowhead Pine Rose Cabins, you'll want to take advantage of all the outdoor recreation in the area. In the winter, skiing at Snow Valley and Green Valley is the major draw. Ice skating on the year-round rink in nearby Blue Jay is also popular.

Summertime is the season for waterskiing, boating, and fishing on the area's lakes. Although many visitors are disappointed by the lack of public access to Lake Arrowhead, there are two good alternatives: big Lake Silverwood or little Lake Gregory. Silverwood is a huge reservoir that is popular for waterskiing, and Lake Gregory is a family-oriented place with swimming beaches, a water slide, and rental boats. Trout fishing is good in both lakes.

Facilities, reservations, fees: There are 15 cabins at Arrowhead Pine Rose, ranging in size from studios to five bedrooms. All have fully equipped kitchens. Reservations are recommended. Fees range from $50 to $325 per night, with a two-night minimum stay on weekends. Pets are permitted in some cabins with prior approval.

Special note: A national forest adventure pass is required for recreation in this area. See page 11 for details.

Who to contact: Arrowhead Pine Rose Cabins, 25994 Highway 189, P.O. Box 31, Twin Peaks, CA 92391; (909) 337-2341 or (800) 429-PINE. Fax (909) 337-0258.

Cabin 11 at Arrowhead Pine Rose Cabins

Season: Open year-round; expect snow in winter.

Directions: From Interstate 10 near San Bernardino, take the Waterman Avenue exit. Drive north on Waterman Avenue for five miles to Highway 18, then drive north and then east on Highway 18 for 15 miles to the Lake Gregory/Twin Peaks turnoff on the left. (Look for the closed Cliffhanger Restaurant.) Turn left, then turn right almost immediately on Highway 189. Take Highway 189 east for two miles to Twin Peaks. Arrowhead Pine Rose Cabins is on the left side of the road, at the intersection of Highway 189 and Grandview Road.

31. SADDLEBACK INN COTTAGES
Lake Arrowhead, off Highway 173 near Lake Arrowhead Village

Lake Arrowhead is a tough nut to crack. The mile-high lake is undoubtedly one of Southern California's most beautiful bodies of water, yet gaining access to it is darn near impossible. Almost every inch of its shoreline is private property, neatly lined with the vacation homes of the ultra-wealthy. Even though the lake is located in San Bernardino National Forest on public land, the public has never felt too welcome there.

This explains why you should know about the cottages at Saddleback Inn. Located across the highway from the lake and the town of Lake Arrowhead Village, the cottages at Saddleback Inn are your chance to get close to Lake Arrowhead. Lakefront property they aren't, but around here, "lake-near" is as good as it gets.

When you first drive up, Saddleback Inn just looks like a typical, nice, old-style hotel. But what isn't obvious is that behind the main hotel building are nearly a dozen private cottages, tucked into the conifers. They are small—mostly one-bedroom in size—but many have luxuries like whirlpool tubs and gas fireplaces. Our favorites are numbers 24 and 36 (named "Sooner" and "Maple Leaf") because they are the most private. For families who need something larger than a one-bedroom cottage, the Saddleback Inn also has two- and three-bedroom suites, which sleep up to seven people.

How you spend your time at Lake Arrowhead depends on what season it is. In winter, the big draw is downhill skiing and snow-boarding at the nearby Green Valley and Snow Valley ski areas in Running Springs. If those runs aren't treacherous enough for you, you can head a few miles further east to the ski areas at Big Bear Lake: Snow Summit and Bear Mountain. The town of Blue Jay has a year-round ice skating rink, where hopeful Olympians and wobbly-ankled skaters alike glide away the hours.

In summer, most vacationers want to get out on Lake Arrow-head, and the only way to do this is to take a commercial tour, unless you know somebody with a boat who lives on the lake. (No public boat launching is permitted.) Fishing and waterskiing tours are popular, and the McKenzie Waterski School offers lessons for neophytes, or plain old boat rides for those uninterested in water-skiing. You can even take a cruise on the *Arrowhead Queen,* a 60-seat paddlewheeler out of Lake Arrowhead Village.

Hiking in San Bernardino National Forest is also excellent. The best trail near Lake Arrowhead is the Pacific Crest Trail at Deep Creek; the trailhead is only a short drive from Saddleback Inn. Another popular option is the short but steep hike to Deep Creek Hot Springs, where you can soak in one of several pools alongside the creek. The Arrowhead Ranger District of San Bernardino National Forest can provide you with maps and updated information.

There's only one down side to a stay at Saddleback Inn at Lake Arrowhead: None of the cottages have full kitchens, although they do have refrigerators and coffeemakers. You'll have to rest your culinary talents for a while, and eat someone else's cooking. The inn has an excellent full restaurant and bar, and the restaurants and shops of Lake Arrowhead Village are a few steps away.

Facilities, reservations, fees: There are eight one-bedroom cottages at Saddleback Inn, plus six one-bedroom suites, one two-bedroom suite, and one three-bedroom suite. None of the cottages have kitchens. Hotel rooms are also available. Reservations are recommended. Fees range from $90 to $140 per night on weekdays and $110 to $300 per night on weekends. Pets are not permitted.

Who to contact: Saddleback Inn, P.O. Box 1890, 300 South State Highway 173, Lake Arrowhead, CA 92352; (800) 858-3334 or (909) 336-3571. Fax (909) 337-4277.

Season: Open year-round; expect snow in winter.

Directions: From Interstate 10 near San Bernardino, take the Waterman Avenue exit. Drive north on Waterman Avenue for five miles to Highway 18, then drive north and then east on Highway 18 for 19 miles to the Highway 173/Lake Arrowhead cutoff on the left. Drive two miles to Lake Arrowhead Village and Saddleback Inn on the right.

32. GREEN VALLEY LAKE COZY CABINS
San Bernardino National Forest, off Highway 18
near Running Springs

One of the best reasons to spend a cabin vacation at Green Valley Lake is because most other people will be somewhere else. Sure, the scenery is beautiful, the lake has good fishing, and there are miles of trails to explore in San Bernardino National Forest. But that's true of many places in the nearby area, most notably Big Bear Lake and Arrowhead Lake. The crowds are assembled at those other places; it's just you and a few others at Green Valley Lake.

The lake and the town are located at 7,200 feet, midway between Big Bear and Arrowhead in the San Bernardino Mountains. All the important elements are in place: cool mountain air, big conifers, pretty lake for fishing and boating, and more than 50 rental cabins to choose from. The cabins are privately owned; Green Valley Lake Cozy Cabins manages them and rents them out. Since they are private homes, they have all the amenities you probably have in your own house: fully equipped kitchens, fireplaces or wood-burning stoves, televisions, stereos, microwaves, coffeemakers, etc. Blankets and pillows are provided in each cabin, but you are supposed to bring your own sheets, pillowcases, and towels, and paper products like toilet paper and paper towels.

When you make your reservation, ask for exactly the kind of cabin that you want. The offerings vary from one-bedroom bungalows in the forest to five-bedroom mini-mansions on the lake. Some are large enough to accommodate as many as 16 people comfortably. A two-night minimum stay is required, and you must clean up the cabin before you leave or forfeit your cleaning deposit. Most people stay for a week; the fee for seven nights is a real bargain at around $450 for a cabin that sleeps four to six people.

After you arrive at Green Valley Lake, take your pick from a huge selection of outdoor activities. In winter, the Green Valley Cross Country Ski Area is open just down the road by Green Valley Campground. It has numerous one-way and loop trails, including the advanced trail "Snowslide" that leads all the way to Fawnskin at Big Bear Lake. Also open is the small, family-run downhill skiing area right across from the lake, Ski Green Valley. It's popular with snowboarders and beginning skiers. More advanced skiers and snowboarders head for the long downhill runs at Snow Valley Ski Area, six miles away on Highway 18.

In summer, anglers rent a rowboat and row around the edges of Green Valley Lake, or fish with bait from shoreline. Trout are planted regularly in spring and summer. No motorized boats are allowed on the small lake, so it is always quiet and serene. Hikers can find a few short trails near Green Valley Campground and Green Valley Cross Country Ski Area, or they can drive down Camp Road and Meadow Lane to the Little Green Valley YMCA Camp. From there, hike the Little Green Valley Trail into Snow Valley. The trail is four miles one-way, nearly flat, and passes some large and glorious stands of big pines and cedars.

Mountain bikers can cruise around almost anywhere in San Bernardino National Forest, but many head straight for Snow Valley Ski Area, which becomes a mountain bike park in summer. You know the drill: You take the lift up the mountain, then ride downhill like a maniac. It's fun.

Facilities, reservations, fees: There are 55 vacation rental cabins at Green Valley Lake Cozy Cabins, ranging in size from one bedroom to five bedrooms, all with fully equipped kitchens. Reservations are required; a two-night minimum stay is required. Fees range from $80 to $200 per night; weekly rates are discounted; a $100 refundable cleaning deposit is required. Pets are permitted in some cabins with prior approval.

Special note: A national forest adventure pass is required for recreation in this area. See page 11 for details.

Who to contact: Green Valley Lake Cozy Cabins, P.O. Box 8345, Green Valley Lake, CA 92341; (909) 867-5335.

Season: Open year-round; expect snow in winter.

Directions: From Interstate 10 at Redlands, drive north on Highway 30 for five miles to the Highway 330 exit. Drive north on Highway 330 for 13 miles to Running Springs. Turn east on Highway 18 and drive four miles to Green Valley Lake Road. Turn north on Green Valley Lake Road and drive three miles. The rental office is located at 33231 Green Valley Lake Road; check in there to get your keys and directions to your cabin.

33. QUAIL COVE CABINS
Big Bear Lake, off Highway 38 in Fawnskin

Quail Cove Cabins has a whole lot going for it, but probably the thing we like best is that it's located on the far edge of Big Bear Lake in the small town of Fawnskin, not the big town of Big Bear Lake. On weekends, it can be difficult to find a quiet place in Big Bear Lake, but Fawnskin is always quiet. From your Quail Cove Cabin, the only sound you'll hear is the lake lapping near your doorstep. Now that's my idea of a cabin vacation.

Two of the lodge's green and white cabins are so close to the lake that you could cast a line out your bedroom window, although we don't recommend it. If you really want a "lakeside" vacation, reserve cabin number 1 or 2. Both are studios that sleep only two people, with full kitchens, fireplaces, and queen beds. Cabin number 2 has the prettiest view, both of the lake and the ski slopes. If you have a larger party, reserve cabin number 5 or 6; the latter can accommodate as many as eight people. You can do all your own cooking in your fully equipped kitchen, or head for the multitude of restaurants in Big Bear.

Luckily for mountain bikers, Quail Cove is situated right across the highway from the Grout Bay Trailhead. The dirt roads leading from here to Butler Peak Lookout make a great 14-mile round-trip bike ride, with terrific views from the 8,400-foot peak. For hikers, the Castle Rock Trail is also close by (see page 92), as is the uphill romp to Bertha Peak on the Cougar Crest Trail. The Big Bear Ranger

Station is located three miles east of Fawnskin on Highway 38; get updated trail information there.

Anglers can fish right from the cabin property by casting or bait-dunking in the lake or the creek, or rent a motor boat at Gray's Landing, only a half-mile away. In addition to fishing boats, you can rent jet skis, waterski boats, and the like.

Then again, you can just do nothing. It's so quiet here in Fawnskin, you may decide just to sit on your cabin's porch and listen to the water lapping at the shore.

Facilities, reservations, fees: There are six cabins at Quail Cove, all with fully equipped kitchens. Reservations are recommended. Fees range from $79 to $169 per night. Pets are permitted; $10 fee per night.

Special note: A national forest adventure pass is required for recreation in this area. See page 11 for details.

Who to contact: Quail Cove, P.O. Box 117, 39117 North Shore Drive, Fawnskin, CA 92333; (800) 595-2683.

Season: Open year-round; expect snow in winter.

Directions: From Interstate 10 at Redlands, drive north on Highway 30 for five miles to the Highway 330 exit. Drive north on Highway 330 for 13 miles to Running Springs. Turn east on Highway 18 and drive 14 miles to the Highway 18 and Highway 38 fork at Big Bear Lake. Bear left on Highway 38 (Northshore Drive), and drive three miles to Quail Cove, on the right side of the road.

Quail Cove Cabins on the shore of Big Bear Lake

34. SHORE ACRES LODGE
Big Bear Lake, off Highway 18 near Big Bear Village

There are so many lodging options at Big Bear Lake, including cabin rentals instead of ordinary motel rooms, that it's hard to know which is the best place to stay. I've stayed at nearly a dozen of them, and it's still hard for me to decide which places to recommend. But one place I can endorse wholeheartedly is Shore Acres Lodge, particularly for people visiting Big Bear Lake with children in tow.

Shore Acres Lodge has 11 cabins for rent, but it also manages a huge list of private vacation homes in the nearby area. If you rent one of the latter, you get full use of all the resort's facilities, but you're away from the hubbub of the lodge and its guests. You get to choose the kind of vacation experience you want to have.

The 11 cabins on the resort's premises are cozy and comfortable. Although they are nestled in tall pine trees, many have lake views. All of them have fully equipped kitchens, plus barbecues on their decks, and most have fireplaces. A pool and spa are available for lodge guests, plus a children's playground and a private boat dock.

Fishing is excellent at Lagunita Point and Gibraltar Point, a few hundred yards from the lodge. Many people simply drop in a line from shore, but the best success is had by trolling. You can rent boats at nearby Holloway's Marina. A full list of water recreation activities are available on Big Bear Lake; see the story on page 94 for more information. The same is true for skiing and other snow activities in winter.

In summer, if you can leave your beach chair at the lake's edge (or the poolside) for an afternoon, several excellent hiking trails are located nearby. An easy half-mile trail leads to the Champion Lodgepole Pine, a 400-year-old tree with a circumference of 20 feet. It stands 112 feet tall, and since it's a lodgepole, it's the straightest 112 feet of lumber you'll ever see. A slightly more difficult trail leads to Castle Rock from a turn in the highway near Boulder Bay. This is a pleasant climb through granite boulders and ponderosa pines to reach increasingly larger boulders, the largest of which is Castle Rock. As you climb, keep turning around to check out the views of Big Bear Lake. On our trip in April, we had a few snow flurries drop on us as we hiked this trail, and the vista from on top of the big rocks was breathtaking.

Looking out over Big Bear Lake from the Castle Rock Trail

Facilities, reservations, fees: There are 11 cabins at Shore Acres Lodge, plus numerous private vacation rentals, ranging in size from one bedroom to five bedrooms. All cabins have fully equipped kitchens. Reservations are recommended. Fees range from $80 to $180 per night; summer rates are discounted. Pets are permitted; $5 fee per night.

Special note: A national forest adventure pass is required for recreation in this area. See page 11 for details.

Who to contact: Shore Acres Lodge, 40090 Lakeview Drive, P.O. Box 110410, Big Bear, CA 92315; (800) 524-6600 or (909) BIG-BEAR. Fax (909) 866-1580.

Season: Open year-round; expect snow in winter.

Directions: From Interstate 10 at Redlands, drive north on Highway 30 for five miles to the Highway 330 exit. Drive north on Highway 330 for 13 miles to Running Springs. Turn east on Highway 18 and drive 14 miles to the Highway 18 and Highway 38 fork at Big Bear Lake. Stay right on Highway 18, and continue 3.5 miles toward the village of Big Bear Lake. A half-mile before you reach the village, turn left on Lakeview Drive, and drive three-quarters of a mile to Shore Acres Lodge.

35. HAPPY BEAR VILLAGE CABINS
Big Bear Lake, off Highway 18 in Big Bear Village

If you've never been to Big Bear before, you may be a little put off on your first visit when you realize that almost everything in the town has the word "bear" worked into its title. The cabins at Happy Bear Village are no exception, but you'll quickly get over the extreme cuteness of it all when you see what a fine vacation cabin you have, and how much fun awaits you in Big Bear.

To begin with, Happy Bear's cabins have something you don't always get in a rental cabin—space. I rented the studio-sized cottage, but found it to be unusually large inside, with more than plenty of room for two people. The full kitchen had a table large enough for sitting down and eating breakfast, the bed was king-sized, and the big fireplace made the whole place warm and cozy. I was surprised to find a coffeemaker, microwave, and toaster in addition to the usual pots, pans, and dishes in the kitchen. On cool evenings, the resort owners will sell you either Duraflame logs or real wood for your fire, depending on your pyrotechnical skills.

The owners of Happy Bear Village run a tight and tidy ship, so the outdoor pool and jacuzzi are well cared for and there are plenty of flowers planted around the cabins in summer. Many people never get to see or enjoy them, however, because most people come to Big Bear in the middle of winter. Skiing and snowboarding top the list of tourist recreation, with two large resorts located near the lake: Bear Mountain and Snow Summit. More unusual snow activities include dog sled rides in the meadows around Big Bear, and the Alpine Slide at Magic Mountain, where you can go inner-tubing down a ski hill or try out the bobsled track. Cross-country skiing and snowshoeing are also popular.

Summer rates are much lower than winter rates at Happy Bear Village, and in the rest of Big Bear, so don't neglect to make a warm-weather visit. In summer, Snow Summit ski resort turns into a mountain bike park; mountain bike rentals are available all over town. You can take a dinner or brunch cruise on Big Bear Lake aboard the *Big Bear Queen,* or rent your own boat at one of the lake's marinas. Fishing is excellent in Big Bear Lake, and although shore fishing is popular, most people do better by trolling.

You want more? No problem. There are miles and miles of

hiking trails in San Bernardino National Forest, some beginning right at the lake's edge, as well as two stables that rent horses for riding. Waterskiing, jet skiing, and windsurfing are all possible on the lake, with several marinas renting equipment and even providing lessons. Then there are the tamer pursuits, like golf and tennis, but who has time for the tamer pursuits?

There's one more thing to know when planning your trip to Big Bear and Happy Bear Village: Big Bear is a crowd scene on weekends, but barely stays alive during the week. Because of its proximity to Los Angeles and other major Southland cities, most people drive up here on Friday night and leave on Sunday night; few people stay for a full week. If you want the whole lake and the town to yourself, visit on a weekday, especially midweek.

Facilities, reservations, fees: There are 10 cabins at Happy Bear Village, all with fully equipped kitchens and fireplaces. Reservations are recommended. Fees range from $60 to $100 per night. Summer rates are lower than winter rates; weekdays cost less than weekends. Pets are not permitted.

Special note: A national forest adventure pass is required for recreation in this area. See page 11 for details.

Who to contact: Happy Bear Village/Smoketree Resort, 40210 Big Bear Boulevard, P.O. Box 2801, Big Bear Lake, CA 92315; (909) 866-2350 or (909) 866-2415.

Season: Open year-round; expect snow in winter.

Directions: From Interstate 10 at Redlands, drive north on Highway 30 for five miles to the Highway 330 exit. Drive north on Highway 330 for 13 miles to Running Springs. Turn east on Highway 18 and drive 14 miles to the Highway 18 and Highway 38 fork at Big Bear Lake. Stay right on Highway 18, and continue four miles to the village of Big Bear Lake. Highway 18 becomes Big Bear Boulevard; Happy Bear Village is at number 40210 on the left side of the road.

36. SEVEN OAKS MOUNTAIN CABINS
San Bernardino National Forest, off Highway 38 near Angelus Oaks

Everybody in Southern California knows about Big Bear Lake, and almost everybody in Southern California knows about the Falls Recreation Area, where Big Falls tumbles down the mountainside. But in between those two stellar destinations is a place that almost nobody knows about—Seven Oaks Mountain Cabins.

Unlike the nearby Angelus Oaks Cabins (see story on page 98), Seven Oaks Cabins are hidden, situated three miles off the main highway. Plenty of people driving the famous Rim of the World Highway in San Bernardino National Forest cruise right by the cute cabins at Angelus Oaks. They slam on their brakes, pull in, and decide to spend the night. But at Seven Oaks that almost never happens; you just don't find it by accident.

There are only six cabins at Seven Oaks, so you don't have to worry about sharing your vacation with the masses. The cabins have fully equipped kitchens, but no phones or television sets. There's nothing else on this stretch of road but the cabins and the main lodge building, so if you want nightlife, you're probably going to have to make your own, or go somewhere else.

Of course, who cares about nightlife when you have a complete array of national forest adventures to look forward to? First on my list is always a visit to Big Falls, Southern California's largest year-round waterfall at more than 500 feet. In a good snow year, you can bring your sleds and snowman-making supplies to the snow-play area around Big Falls, then let loose. Earlier in the year, usually in late summer, that same area is excellent for blackberry picking. Fill up your berry baskets and then go bake a pie in your Seven Oaks cabin kitchenette.

Jenks Lake, on the Rim of the World Highway near Angelus Oaks

The Santa Ana River runs right through the Seven Oaks cabin grounds, and provides excellent stream fishing prospects. The river in these parts is typically about 10 to 15 feet across and a foot deep—a perfect fishing creek. It is stocked with rainbow trout every other week in spring and summer.

Anglers can also head for little Jenks Lake, which is pretty year-round but especially scenic in early spring when the surrounding mountains are still snow-covered. The biggest peak you see in the background is Mount San Gorgonio, the tallest mountain in Southern California at 11,490 feet. The lake isn't stocked until May each year, but it's worth visiting any time.

Be sure to check out the numerous hiking and mountain biking trails in the area. If you aren't up for hiking the 14-mile round-trip to the top of Mount San Gorgonio on the Vivian Creek Trail, you can find plenty of shorter options nearby. Don't miss the Ponderosa Vista Nature Trail and the Whispering Pines Trail, which are conveniently located right across the highway from each other. You can walk both of them in just over an hour, while getting a good lesson in the natural and human history of the area.

The South Fork, Forsee Creek, and Aspen Grove trailheads (all near Jenks Lake) head into the San Gorgonio Wilderness. Note that even day-hikers need a wilderness permit to enter the area; that's how they keep the crowds from getting out of hand. In summer or autumn, be sure to walk at least the first section of the Aspen Grove Trail, which leads to one of the very few aspen groves to be found this far south in California. Just the drive to the trailhead is worth the trip; it provides fabulous views of the surrounding mountains and valleys.

If you're not feeling so ambitious, you can always just hang out at the lodge at Seven Oaks. The place is rustic, as in not the slightest bit fancy, but it's the kind of place where you can play pool or ping pong and exchange a few stories with the lodge owners, who are really nice people.

Facilities, reservations, fees: There are six cabins at Seven Oaks Mountain Cabins, all with fully equipped kitchenettes, patios, gas heaters, and barbecues. Reservations are recommended. The fee is $70 per night for two people. Pets are permitted; $5 fee per day.

Special note: A national forest adventure pass is required for recreation in this area. See page 11 for details.

Who to contact: Seven Oaks Mountain Cabins, 40700 Seven Oaks Road, Angelus Oaks, CA 92305; (909) 794-1277.

Season: Open year-round; expect snow in winter.

Directions: From Interstate 10 just west of Redlands, take the Alabama Avenue exit. Turn north on Alabama and drive to the third stop sign. Turn right (east) on Lugonia Avenue, which will become Highway 38. Drive 25 miles on Highway 38 to Angelus Oaks, then continue six more miles on Highway 38 to the left turnoff for Seven Oaks and Glass Road. Turn left and drive three miles (keeping to the left at all junctions). Seven Oaks Mountain Cabins is on the right side of the road.

37. THE LODGE AT ANGELUS OAKS
San Bernardino National Forest, off Highway 38 in Angelus Oaks

The cabins at Angelus Oaks Lodge are the embodiment of rustic and cozy—the kind of vacation place that makes you want to say good-bye to "civilized life" forever. For starters, they're in a first-rate location, on the Rim of the World Highway halfway between Big Bear Lake and the Falls Recreation Area. You have two of San Bernardino National Forest's premier recreation spots within a few minutes' drive of your cabin, but you're not stuck in the middle of town with a whole bunch of tourists.

The possibilities for outdoor adventures are endless, and change with each passing season. Most winters, the snow falls thick and fast for at least a few weeks, which opens up all kinds of possibilities for snow play. In spring, summer, and fall, hiking is spectacular in the national forest and the San Gorgonio Wilderness. Trails range from very easy ones for families—like the half-mile walk to Big Falls, Southern California's largest year-round waterfall—to very difficult ones, like the 14-mile round-trip ascent of Mount San Gorgonio, Southern California's tallest peak at 11,490 feet.

Families enjoy a fishing trip to nearby Jenks Lake, where you can stand on the shoreline and cast for stocked trout. Experienced anglers drive down the Middle Control Road from Angelus Oaks to Forest Service Road 1N09. From there, they can access Bear Creek, a wild trout area on a tributary stream to the Santa Ana River. The limit is two fish, with a minimum length of eight inches or larger. Only artificial lures or flies with barbless hooks can be used in Bear Creek.

However you decide to spend your days, you'll end each one by returning home to your Angelus Oaks cabin. The cabins are minimalist, but adequate. They're small, the paint's peeling, but, hey, we're

Rustic cabin at The Lodge at Angelus Oaks

camping. You can make dinner in your own kitchen, or barbecue outside your cabin, or head for the restaurant a mile down the road. Evenings can be spent in the main lodge, playing pool or listening to somebody play the lodge organ, or looking through the telescope at the stars. We found the main lodge to be so cozy—like an old Canadian hunting lodge right out of a movie set—that we spent almost every evening there, playing board games in front of the fire.

Facilities, reservations, fees: There are eight cabins at The Lodge at Angelus Oaks. Reservations are recommended. Fees range from $50 to $100 per night. Pets are permitted with prior approval.

Special note: A national forest adventure pass is required for recreation in this area. See page 11 for details.

Who to contact: The Lodge at Angelus Oaks, 37825 Highway 38, Angelus Oaks, CA 92305; (909) 794-9523.

Season: Open year-round; expect snow in winter.

Directions: From Interstate 10 just west of Redlands, take the Alabama Avenue exit. Turn north on Alabama and drive to the third stop sign. Turn right (east) on Lugonia Avenue, which will become Highway 38. Drive 25 miles on Highway 38 to Angelus Oaks. The Lodge at Angelus Oaks is on the right side of the road.

MORE CABIN RENTALS IN BIG BEAR, ARROWHEAD, & RUNNING SPRINGS:

Bear Manor Cabins, 40393 Big Bear Boulevard, Big Bear Lake, CA 92315; (909) 866-6800 or (800) 472-BEAR.

Castle Wood Cottages, 547 Main Street, P.O. Box 1746, Big Bear Lake, CA 92315; (909) 866-2720.

The Forrester Homes, 38850 Newberry Street, Cherry Valley, CA 92223; (909) 845-1004 or (800) 587-5576.

Sleepy Hollow Cabins, 24033 Lake Drive, Crestline, CA 92325; (909) 338-2718.

Bear Claw Cabins, 586 Main Street, Big Bear Lake, CA 92315; (909) 866-7633.

Grey Squirrel Resort, P.O. Box 5404, Big Bear Lake, CA 92315; (909) 866-4335.

Frontier Lodge, 40472 Big Bear Boulevard, Big Bear Lake, CA 92315; (800) 457-6401.

Giant Oaks Motel and Cabins, 32180 Hilltop Boulevard, Running Springs, CA 92382; (909) 867-2231 or (800) 786-1689.

Santa Barbara
&
Santa Monica
Mountains

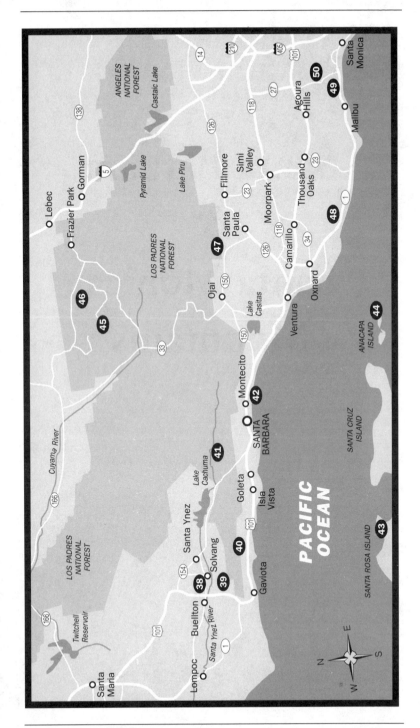

38. CHIMNEY SWEEP INN COTTAGES
near Los Padres National Forest, off Highway 246 in Solvang

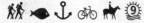

Every now and then when I'm out field-testing cabins, I stay in one that is nicer and more appealing than the house I live in. That's what happened at the Chimney Sweep Inn's cottages in Solvang, and I knew it from the moment I stepped inside.

First, some background: Solvang is a popular tourist town northwest of Santa Barbara and south of Santa Maria. Its Danish heritage is its appeal, and an incredible amount of Danish architecture and culture presides in the town. When you first lay eyes on it, you see immediately that it's like no place else in Southern California. Most people find Solvang to be charming and picturesque, although some say it's the Danish Disneyland of Central California. Take your pick.

What I like about Solvang, besides its proliferation of tasty bakeries, is that it is perfectly situated for an outdoor vacation in the Santa Ynez Mountains. Within a few miles of the town are Los Padres National Forest, La Purisima Mission State Historic Park, Lake Cachuma, Nojoqui Falls County Park, and Gaviota State Park. All of these are perfectly suited for day-trip adventures, and a cottage at the Chimney Sweep Inn in Solvang is the perfect base camp.

But a "camp" this is not. The Chimney Sweep Inn has six cottages, all beautifully appointed, as well as a manicured garden with a tiny stream, goldfish, and footbridges. We stayed in the Dawn Treader, which is a two-story cottage with a large bedroom upstairs, and a living room, dining area, and small kitchen downstairs. What made it nicer than my own house? More than a few features: It had two fireplaces—one upstairs in the bedroom and one downstairs in the living room, two bathrooms with unusual antique fixtures, and French doors that opened to a small patio and private jacuzzi.

But these are just the bold strokes. The real beauty of the place lies in the details, such as the hand-painted tile work, the wide-plank pine floors, and the ambient lighting. I must confess that what impressed me the most was the automatic drapes in the bedroom—you just push a button above the bed and the drapes open or close.

All of this comes with a price, of course. The cottages range from $155 to $275 per night, but this includes a bottle of wine or sparkling cider and a continental breakfast (plenty of Danish pastries, since this is Solvang). Our cottage was easily big enough for a family

Hiking at Gaviota State Park near Solvang

of four; all that was needed was a rollaway bed, which the inn will provide. If you like, you can save money on your trip by cooking some or all of your meals in your cottage.

An incredible amount of imagination has gone into the cottages' construction and decoration. All of them are named after, and modeled around, C.S. Lewis' books, *The Chronicles of Narnia.* When you enter the garden behind the main inn, you pass through an iron gate inscribed "Land of Narnia." Our cottage had some fascinating architectural details, including a large wooden front door suitable for a Viking, giant-sized beams, and carved banister posts on the stairway. Much of this was resurrected from an old mansion in Europe, then shipped over and incorporated into the cottage decor. Miscellaneous bits and pieces were salvaged from an old bank in the Midwest, including a teller cage which is used as the bed headboard. The most compelling element is a gold lion's head painted in the tilework above the fireplace. It took us a while to figure out that it was Aslan, the lion from *The Chronicles of Narnia.*

It wasn't easy to leave this great cottage, but we pushed ourselves out the door to go see the 80-foot waterfall at Nojoqui Falls County Park (six miles south on U.S. 101) and to hike to the hot springs and Gaviota Peak at Gaviota State Park (nine miles south on U.S. 101). Another good side trip is to head west on Highway 246 for 16 miles to La Purisima Mission State Historic Park, where you can visit the historic mission and then hike around its lovely grounds. The 2.5-mile Las Zanjas and El Camino Loop is a good introductory walk. Be sure to take the short, steep side trail to Vista de la Cruz, where you'll find a cross on a hillside and a sweeping view of the Pacific.

If you're hankering for higher mountains, take the drive up Figueroa Mountain Road (from Solvang's neighboring town, Los Olivos) to the Pino Alto Trail located near the peak. The elevation is 4,600 feet, and you'll actually find yourself walking in the shade of conifers. The view from the Figueroa Lookout Tower site is truly memorable.

Longer hikes are possible on the slopes of Figueroa Mountain; an excellent trail for first-timers is the Davy Brown Trail. You can begin hiking from Davy Brown Campground or the trailhead on Figueroa Mountain Road.

Facilities, reservations, fees: There are six cottages at Chimney Sweep Inn, with full kitchens, fireplaces, and private spas, plus eight lodge rooms and suites. Reservations are recommended. Fees range from $155 to $275 per night for cottages, $70 to $110 per night for lodge rooms, and $115 to $185 per night for suites. Pets are not permitted.

Special note: A national forest adventure pass is required for recreation in this area. See page 11 for details.

Who to contact: Chimney Sweep Inn, 1564 Copenhagen Drive, Solvang, CA 93463; (800) 824-6444 or (805) 688-2111. Fax (805) 688-8824.

Season: Open year-round.

Directions: From Santa Barbara, drive north on U.S. 101 for 40 miles to the Buellton/Highway 246 exit. Drive east on Highway 246 for three miles to Solvang, then turn right on 5th Street. In one block, turn left on Copenhagen Drive, and drive two-tenths of a mile to Chimney Sweep Inn on the right.

39. ALISAL GUEST RANCH & RESORT
Santa Ynez Valley, off Highway 246 near Solvang

One thing is for certain: No one will complain that there's nothing to do when they visit the Alisal Guest Ranch and Resort. Sure, the main attraction is horseback riding, but if you tire of it (or if your butt gets too sore), you can always go hiking, mountain biking, fishing, windsurfing, or swimming; or play golf or tennis, or visit the historic Santa Ynez Mission, or even take your kids to the Alisal's petting zoo.

Okay, one other thing is certain: You can't stay at the Alisal Guest Ranch unless you've saved up a fair number of pennies.

The 10,000-acre ranch and resort is a family vacation center in the Santa Ynez Valley. This lovely winery-filled valley, northwest of Santa Barbara near the Danish tourist town of Solvang, is home to a few famous wealthy folks like Michael Jackson and Jane Fonda, as well as plenty of other people you've never heard of, but who have serious bucks at their disposal. So it figures that a guest ranch here caters to a big-budget crowd.

However, there are ways to make it affordable. First, you rent a cottage at the resort, and bring your family with you. All of the cottages look like individual ranch houses with covered porches on the outside, and have one or two large rooms on the inside, with high-beamed ceilings, fireplaces, refrigerators, and coffeemakers. You pay a hefty nightly fee for two adults only, but you can add on your children or an additional adult for very little. (That's what makes the Alisal affordable for families but more expensive for couples.) A huge range of children's and teenagers' activities are offered in the summer, ranging from horseback riding lessons to arts and crafts.

There are no kitchens in the cottages; that's because the resort operates on a modified American Plan—breakfast and dinner are included in your room rate. Typical of a guest ranch, meals are a big deal here, with plentiful portions and a wide menu. You may gain a few pounds during your stay. And get this: Men are supposed to wear jackets to dinner. What? This is supposed to be camping? Well, it's not really, but the food is a heck of a lot better.

Couples with no kids, take heart: A popular option at the Alisal is to take advantage of the "round-up vacation package" that is available from November through March (holidays excluded). The two-night package includes horseback riding, fishing, tennis, and golf for two people, plus all meals and accommodations. The rate is almost half what it is during the summer at the Alisal. The round-up package is also available on weekdays only in September, October, April, and May. During those months, you must begin your visit on a Sunday or Wednesday night.

One of the most interesting programs at the Alisal is its fly-fishing school. The ranch has its own spring-fed 90-acre lake, which is used for windsurfing and canoeing as well as flyfishing lessons. If you sign up for the school, you get to stay at the ranch for four days and learn fly techniques, knots, tackle, and fly-casting skills. Both beginning and experienced flyfishing enthusiasts are welcome; the classes are kept small so that the instructor can provide plenty of individual attention. The complete flyfishing school package includes three days of lessons, resort accommodations for four days and three nights, three huge meals per day including wine with dinner, and use of a flyfishing rod and reel for instruction. It also includes unlimited golf, tennis, and horseback riding, so you can bring a friend with you who isn't into flyfishing. The cost for this program for two people is currently $1,550, which includes taxes and tips. When you add it all up—two people, three nights, all your meals, plus flyfishing lessons, horseback riding, golf, etc.—you realize that this is actually an excellent deal.

If you tire of catching bass and bluegill at the resort's lake, you can always head for Lake Cachuma, a 20-minute drive away, where 150,000 rainbow trout are planted each year. Bass, catfish, crappie, and perch are also plentiful. Boat rentals are available. From November through February, you can take a two-hour "eagle cruise" on the lake with a park naturalist. With any luck, you'll see an American bald eagle, but if not, you'll definitely see some of Lake Cachuma's more than 200 species of resident and migratory birds.

Facilities, reservations, fees: There are 73 cottages at Alisal Guest Ranch. Reservations are required. Regular fees range from $325 to $375 per night for two people, which includes breakfast and dinner each day; additional people are $65 per night, $40 per night for children under six. Reduced fees are available on the "round-up vacation package" from September through May. Pets are not permitted.

Who to contact: Alisal Guest Ranch and Resort, 1054 Alisal Road, Solvang, CA 93463; (805) 688-6411 or (800) 425-4725. Fax (805) 688-2510.

Season: Open year-round; summer and spring break can be crowded.

Directions: From Santa Barbara, drive north on U.S. 101 for 40 miles to Buellton and take the Solvang/Highway 246 exit. Drive east on Highway 246 for four miles through Solvang, then turn right on Alisal Road. Drive 3.5 miles on Alisal Road, past the golf course, to the Alisal Guest Ranch on the left.

40. CIRCLE BAR B GUEST RANCH
near Refugio State Beach, off U.S. 101 near Santa Barbara

Circle Bar B Guest Ranch is one of the best and most interesting places in Southern California for a cabin vacation. It's a study in contrasts—part horse ranch, part upscale hotel, part outdoor resort, and part dinner theater. Can any place be all these things and do each of them well? Circle Bar B Guest Ranch does.

The drive in to Circle Bar B tells you a lot about the place. The minute you pull off Highway 101 on to Refugio Road, you see you're on to something good. The road narrows and snakes its way through a lush canyon, crossing Refugio Creek half a dozen times on its 3.5-mile route to the ranch. In winter, it can be so lush and green in this canyon that you might think you're somewhere in the tropics, not in Southern California.

As you get close to the ranch, you start seeing horses—lots of them. They're across the creek, grazing in the pasture or hanging out in their stalls, hoping someone will come by and give them an apple. When you turn in at the ranch's entrance sign, you enter what looks like a small Western village. In addition to the ranch office and a large swimming pool, there are several Western-style cottages, horse corrals, and even a brightly painted, false-front building with a sign reading "Blacksmith Shop."

Blacksmith shop at Circle Bar B Guest Ranch

What caught my eye was the deeply carved canyon that curves behind the ranch, lined with tall, chaparral-covered hillsides. It turns out that's where the ranch's riding trails go. If you reserve a horse at Circle Bar B, you'll get to explore the many secrets of that canyon and the hundred of acres of coastal hills surrounding it.

The cabins at Circle Bar B Guest Ranch are modern and beautifully decorated. Ours was a large studio with a huge bed, a wood-burning stove, and a separate bathroom. It was remarkably inviting and cozy. Also available are larger cabins, which include a small refrigerator, but none of the units come with kitchens. That's because the price for one night's stay at Circle Bar B includes three meals. The meals are hearty; the only thing missing is wine or beer. The ranch does not have a liquor license, so they suggest that you bring your own if you want any.

Most people ride horses while staying at the ranch; guided rides are offered every morning and afternoon. The fee is $25 for a 90-minute ride. Each day's destination is a little different, but most likely you'll be treated to ridgetop views of the ocean and Channel Islands, and maybe explore a hidden canyon where a narrow waterfall cascades down a sandstone cliff. If horses don't interest you, you can hike on the ranch's property instead, or drive three miles down Refugio Road to Refugio State Beach, where you can swim, surf, or surf fish. The ranch also has its own swimming pool and hot tub.

Most surprising of the ranch's offerings are its comedy theater performances on Friday and Saturday evenings in summer; tickets are $11 per person. These performances have become so popular in the local area that they frequently sell out. Guests come from all over Santa Barbara County to enjoy an outdoor tri-tip barbecue at the ranch and then enter the barn to watch the evening's play. If you are staying at the ranch on a summer weekend, don't miss the show; it's a real treat.

Facilities, reservations, fees: There are 14 cabins at Circle Bar B Guest Ranch, all with fireplaces. Ranch rooms are also available. Kitchen facilities are not provided; three meals per day are included in the price of your stay. Reservations are required. Fees range from $185 to $225 per night for two people, including meals. Each additional adult is $75 per night; additional children are $60 per night. Pets are not permitted.

Who to contact: Circle Bar B Guest Ranch, 1800 Refugio Road, Goleta, CA 93117; (805) 968-1113.

Season: Open year-round.

Directions: From Santa Barbara, drive north on U.S. 101 for 18 miles and take the Refugio State Beach exit. Turn right (north) and drive 3.5 miles on Refugio Road to the Circle Bar B Ranch.

41. RANCHO OSO CABINS & COVERED WAGONS
Santa Ynez Recreation Area, off U.S. 101 near Santa Barbara

Did you ever want to spend the night the way the Western pioneers did, in one of a group of covered wagons drawn into a safe, tight circle? Well, start calling out "Westward ho!" because here's your chance.

At Rancho Oso Campground in Santa Barbara's Santa Ynez Recreation Area, you can live out your pioneer fantasy in a rented covered wagon (minus the oxen), or stay in one of five Western-style cabins. Although Rancho Oso is one of the Thousand Trails chain of membership-style campgrounds, their cabins and covered wagons are open to the public for rental without having to pay membership fees.

The covered wagons look a lot like the real thing, except that on the inside of each one are four simple cots, not your entire family's belongings as you ride the dusty trail to the wild West. The five cute cabins are lined up in a row so they look like the main street of an old Western village, complete with false fronts and clapboard siding. Each one has a hitching post out front and a name plate; generally people vie to stay in the one marked "Saloon." As a rule, children tend to prefer camping in the covered wagons, while adults usually prefer the electric heat and privacy of the little cabins. The cabins have small beds inside, a step up from the wagons' meager cots. Bring your own bedding and towels for both the wagons and cabins. Also, note that the cabins are very small. Although they are supposed to accommodate four people, more than two will be a crowd.

Before you sign up for a visit, make sure you understand that Rancho Oso is mainly an RV park, so there will be plenty of motor homes sharing the ranch with you. However, the RVs have their own camping area and it's across a seasonal creek, on the far side of the horse pasture from the cabins and covered wagons. They go their way, you go yours. The cabins and covered wagons have the nicest location on the ranch, because they are surrounded on three sides by green meadows and grazing horses. Make sure you pack a few extra carrots for Trigger and his friends.

Rancho Oso is a private landholding in Los Padres National Forest. Its present-day 300 acres are what is left of an 1845 Spanish land grant. Still standing from the old days are an original adobe building and jailhouse. The Santa Ynez River runs along one side of

Horses in the corral at Rancho Oso

the ranch, and is accessible for fishing and swimming. Most people rent horses and go for guided rides when they visit Rancho Oso (or they bring their own horse and ride solo). You can venture off on your own two feet if you prefer, hiking the many trails of the Santa Ynez Recreation Area. My personal favorite is the hilly Aliso Canyon Loop Trail, which begins at nearby Sage Hill Campground. Check out the spring wildflowers from February to May.

One more item: If you like to fish or waterski, you'll want to spend at least one day on a boat at Lake Cachuma, only 12 miles away. (See the story on the Alisal Guest Ranch and Resort on pages 105-107 for more information on Lake Cachuma.)

Facilities, reservations, fees: There are five one-room cabins at Rancho Oso, plus 10 covered wagons. Trailers and RVs are also available for rent. Kitchen facilities are not provided, but barbecue grills are available. Horses are available for guided trail rides. Reservations are required. Fees range from $27 per night for covered wagons to $36 per night for cabins; each can accommodate four people. Pets are permitted in the covered wagons, but not in the cabins.

Who to contact: Rancho Oso, 3750 Paradise Road, Santa Barbara, CA 93105; (805) 683-5686. Fax (805) 683-5111.

Special note: A $4 entrance fee is charged on Paradise Road beyond the entrance to the Santa Ynez Recreation Area. In this area of Los Padres National Forest, a national forest adventure pass is not valid; instead you must pay an entrance fee to the concessionaire.

Season: Open year-round.

Directions: From U.S. 101 in Santa Barbara, take Highway 154 north for 11 miles to the Paradise Road turnoff on the right. Turn right on Paradise Road and drive 5.5 miles to the sign for Rancho Oso on the right. Turn right and drive 1.5 miles to the entrance kiosk; the cabins and covered wagons are located a quarter-mile beyond the kiosk.

42. THE MIRAMAR HOTEL & RESORT
Montecito, off U.S. 101 near Santa Barbara

Anyone who has ever driven south of Santa Barbara on U.S. 101 knows the cheerful blue-and-white buildings of the Miramar Hotel, a Montecito area fixture since the turn of the century. In its present-day form, the Miramar bears the countenance of something midway between a roadside motel and a private resort, yet it maintains its 100-year-old reputation as a well-loved vacation spot for families and beach lovers.

Unlike the nearby Montecito resorts at the Biltmore Hotel and San Ysidro Ranch, the Miramar is relatively affordable and comfortably casual. In part, that's because of its drawbacks: It's situated too close to the freeway, and the Southern Pacific railway runs right through the middle of its grounds. (When the railway was completed in 1901, the Miramar was used as a passenger stop.) Even so, when you can rent a cottage within walking distance of the beach and still come home with some change in your pocket, you're willing to put up with a few inconveniences.

Make sure you know what you're getting when you make your reservations, however; the resort's accommodations vary widely. The Miramar has several cottages that are right next to the freeway, and these won't make for a peaceful, outdoorsy vacation. Other cottages are located in the center of the 15-acre complex, without ocean views but with easy access to the beach. At the ocean's edge are pricey townhouse-style accommodations, which the Miramar calls "suites." These units are by far the most scenic, and, like the other cottages, they come with fully equipped kitchens. But they are not separate units—you'll share exterior walls with your neighbors.

If you opt for the oceanfront suites, forget what I said about coming home with some change in your pocket—they cost more than double what the cottages without views cost. Are they worth the big bucks? Probably. Remember that you are getting oceanfront property in Montecito, one of the most elite towns in Southern California. Cuddled up in your seaside suite at night, the only sounds you'll hear are the churning ocean waves, despite the proximity of the freeway to the resort. In the morning, you get a million-dollar ocean view, while the inland cottages get a view of the parking lot, or maybe the train tracks.

If you opt for the more affordable inland cottages, you'll find that they range in size from one to four bedrooms, and most have kitchenettes and fireplaces. A major downer is that all of the accommodations have telephones, and even worse, cable television. We suggest you move the TV into the bathroom and hide the phone under the bed.

The primary reason the Miramar has remained so popular for more than a century is its beach. The coastline in Santa Barbara County is considered by many to be the finest in all of California. The geography of the land faces south, not west as in most of the state; this creates a microclimate of exceptionally mild weather similar to that of the French Riviera. Although the Miramar Resort has its own restaurant, tennis courts, two swimming pools, fitness facilities, and even a railroad car that serves as a cafe, the beach is where you'll spend all your time. Surfing, swimming, and surf fishing are popular, as well as traipsing along the sand, especially when the tide is low and beachcombing is good. You can walk to the west for

Surfers on the beach at the Miramar Hotel and Resort

about a mile to the Biltmore Hotel, passing Hammonds Beach, a famous surfing spot. Or walk to the east for a couple of miles to Lookout County Park.

The resort can provide you with sunbathing necessities—umbrellas, back rests, mats—or even rent you a bicycle for exploring the area. If you tire of endless days of sun, sea, and sand, you can drive to either the Cold Springs Trailhead or the San Ysidro Trailhead of Los Padres National Forest (both located within five miles of the resort) and hike in Montecito's shady mountain canyons. However, unless the fog moves in and stays too long, it's unlikely you'll be willing to stray from the ocean's edge.

Facilities, reservations, fees: There are 48 cottages at Miramar Hotel and Resort, plus 24 oceanfront suites. Motel rooms and a restaurant are also available. Reservations are recommended. Fees range from $140 to $360 per night. Pets are not permitted.

Who to contact: Miramar Hotel and Resort, P.O. Box 429, Santa Barbara, CA 93102; (805) 969-2203 or (800) 322-6983. Fax (805) 969-3163.

Season: Open year-round.

Directions: From Santa Barbara on U.S. 101, drive south for three miles to Montecito. Take the San Ysidro Road exit south; the Miramar is right alongside the highway on the south side. (If you are coming from Los Angeles, drive 85 miles north on U.S. 101 to the San Ysidro Road exit.)

43. SANTA ROSA ISLAND FLY-IN OVERNIGHT
Santa Rosa Island, Channel Islands National Park

If you're tired of long drives to the Sierra, if you're weary of freeway traffic on the way to Big Bear, and if you get seasick on the Catalina ferry, I've got the perfect easy trip for you. This is the classiest way to go camping—in your own chartered plane.

No kidding. You can fly in to Santa Rosa Island, the second largest of the Channel Islands, then camp on the island for up to seven days. How do you do it? By phoning Channel Islands Aviation, the authorized concessionaire to Channel Islands National Park. They will whisk you off to the island from either Santa Barbara or Camarillo airports.

The plane ride lasts a mere 25 minutes each way. That's right, 25 minutes in a little plane to get to an island that takes four hours to reach by boat. Airfare is currently only $150 per person round-trip. Passage by boat costs about $80, so if you add in the cost of your time, it's not much more expensive to fly.

If the trip still seems pricey to you, think about it—it's not as if you're going to spend any more money once you're on Santa Rosa Island. There's nothing to spend it on. In fact, you might as well burn all your cash before you come, because out here on the island, your most valuable currency might be your mocha-flavored Power Bars, which you can trade for somebody else's freeze-dried lasagna.

Santa Rosa Island is nearly 15 miles long and 10 miles wide, and all of the island is accessible for hiking. (There is no ranger escort required, as on some of the Channel Islands.) It has a beautiful three-mile-long beach near the campground, complete with sand dunes, plus a nearby forest of Torrey pines, just like in San Diego. The eastern tip of Santa Rosa Island is a unique freshwater coastal marsh, one of the largest in the Channel Islands. Nearly 200 bird species are found on Santa Rosa. They are attracted to the coastal marsh, as well as to the extensive grasslands that cover most of the island.

Most hikers climb to the top of Black Mountain at 1,298 feet in elevation, although cross-country mountaineers ascend Soledad Peak at 1,574 feet. Wear your hiking boots even for short hikes—the island's terrain is steep. You can also fish from the island's shores; just pack along your surf fishing gear and California fishing license.

However you plan to spend your time, make sure you've brought plenty of clothes for layering. Because Santa Rosa is one of the outer Channel Islands, it's often extremely windy.

The island's campground is located at Water Canyon off Bechers Bay, on the northeast side of the island. A trail leads from the harbor and ranger station to the campground, and then five miles beyond it to East Point. Since the landing strip is located close to the campground, you need to carry your gear only a short distance. (Campers traveling by boat must hike 1.5 miles; campers traveling by plane hike only about a quarter-mile.)

The camp has 15 sites, with a maximum of 50 people allowed in the entire campground. If you time your trip for weekdays in summer, you'll have little chance of having 49 neighbors. Any time before Memorial Day or after Labor Day is also an excellent time to visit; the weather tends to be less foggy during these periods, and the crowds are nonexistent.

Another element that makes this trip easy is that Santa Rosa Island's campground is the only one of the five Channel Islands'

Channel Islands' coastal bluffs

campgrounds that has potable water. Although some people choose to bring their own water anyway, you don't need to. Plus, what luxury—they even have solar-heated showers. You will need to bring your backpacking stove, however, because no fires are permitted.

Like the rest of the island, the campground is very grassy, with no natural shade. Each campsite has a windbreak and a picnic table; pit toilets are close by. Remember that you will have to pack out all of your trash, so bring garbage bags.

Facilities, reservations, fees: There are 15 campsites on Santa Rosa Island, which can accommodate a total of 50 people. Potable water is available at the campground. Campfires are not permitted; bring a backpacking stove. Reservations and a camping permit are required; phone (800) 365-CAMP to reserve a campsite ($2.50 reservation fee). Campsites are free, but a fee is charged for transportation to the island via Channel Islands Aviation, an authorized concessionaire to Channel Islands National Park. Phone Channel Islands Aviation at the number below for rates and departure information. The current cost is $150 per person for an overnight trip. Pets are not permitted. (You can also take a boat to Santa Rosa Island; phone Island Packers at (805) 642-7688 or (805) 642-1393 for information and reservations.)

Who to contact: Channel Islands National Park, 1901 Spinnaker Drive, Ventura, CA 93001; (805) 658-5700 or (805) 658-5711. Or phone Channel Islands Aviation at (805) 987-1301 for information and reservations.

Maps for backpacking: A free map of Channel Islands National Park is available from park headquarters. For a topographic map of the area, ask for Santa Rosa Island North, South, East, and West from the USGS.

Season: Open year-round; best in fall and spring.

Directions: Channel Islands Aviation provides air transportation to Santa Rosa Island from either Santa Barbara or Camarillo airports. Advance reservations are required. Phone Channel Islands Aviation at (805) 987-1301 for information and reservations.

44. ANACAPA ISLAND WALK-IN CAMP
East Anacapa Island, Channel Islands National Park

Anacapa Island is the closest Channel Island to the mainland at only 12 miles from Port Hueneme. That means the boat ride takes only an hour and a half, as opposed to the five hours it takes to reach San Miguel Island, the Channel Island furthest from the mainland.

Because of its proximity, you get to spend most of your Anacapa vacation hiking, snorkeling, swimming, and camping, rather than bobbing up and down on a boat out at sea. Easy? Yeah, this is easy. And best of all, after all the day visitors leave, just you and a few other folks will be camping on an island in the Pacific. The sunset hour, after the last boat leaves, and the first few hours of the next morning, before the first boat arrives, are pure heaven.

Here's how you plan an overnight getaway to Anacapa Island: First, choose the dates you want to travel and make your boat reservations with Island Packers, the park's transportation concessionaire. After you've secured your passage, call (800) 365-CAMP to get your camping reservation for Anacapa. (You have to get your boat passage before your camping reservation; the former is actually more difficult to get.)

Then, start packing your gear. Since the accessible part of the island is very small, you probably won't stay for more than a night or two. The most important thing you must bring is water; there is none at the campground. Your camp stove will also serve you well, because no campfires are allowed on the island. Plan on dressing in layers. The weather can be foggy, cool, windy, sunny, hot, or all of the above in one day.

Anacapa Island is actually three tiny volcanic islets, connected by submerged reefs, and the boat drops you off on the easternmost one.

After you disembark, your first task is to climb up the 154 stairsteps that cling to the island's cliffs. Make sure you don't pack too much gear, because it could require dozens of trips back and forth to carry all your stuff. Island Packers, the ferry service, insists that no single item of your luggage weigh more than 40 pounds; this rule will serve you well when you have to haul everything up those stairs.

Once you ascend the cliffs, the campground is only a half-mile hike away. It's a small camp, with only seven sites, accommodating a maximum of 30 people. (On summer weekends the camp can feel cramped; plan your visit for a weekday if possible.) The camp has picnic tables and pit toilets—nothing fancy here—and you must carry out your own trash.

While you're on Anacapa, you'll certainly hike the 1.5-mile East Anacapa Loop Trail, which tours the entire eastern islet. The trail's main highlights are two overlooks at Inspiration Point and Cathedral Cove, where you can look down on seals and sea lions on the rocks below. (You'll probably hear their lonesome barking during the night.) There are millions of opportunities for birdwatching; bring your binoculars to identify the sea birds. Where you can see over the edge of the rocky cliffs, you'll spot some of the island's 130 sea caves.

Although fall usually brings the best weather to Anacapa Island, many visitors like to make the trip in April or May. Spring wild-flowers are superb, including the giant coreopsis, which looks like a yellow daisy on steroids. The eight-foot-tall flowers reportedly bloom so brightly that they can sometimes be seen on the mainland, 12 miles away.

Be sure to bring your swimsuit to Anacapa. Although the island's beaches are inaccessible because its perimeter cliffs are hundreds of feet high, on calm days you can swim at the landing cove. Snorkeling is also popular.

Facilities, reservations, fees: There are seven primitive campsites on East Anacapa Island, which can accommodate a total of 30 people. No water is available; you must pack in bottled water. Campfires are not permitted; bring a backpacking stove. Reservations and a camping permit are required; phone (800) 365-CAMP to reserve a campsite ($2.50 reservation fee). Campsites are free, but a fee is charged for transportation to the island via Island Packers, the authorized concessionaire to Channel Islands National Park. Phone Island Packers at the number below for rates and departure information. The current cost is $48 per person for an overnight trip. Pets are not permitted.

Who to contact: Channel Islands National Park, 1901 Spinnaker Drive, Ventura, CA 93001; (805) 658-5700 or (805) 658-5711. Or Island

Packers at (805) 642-7688 or (805) 642-1393 for information and reservations.

Maps for backpacking: A free map of Channel Islands National Park is available from park headquarters or the Anacapa Island visitor center. For a topographic map of the area, ask for Anacapa Island from the USGS.

Season: Open year-round; best in fall and spring. Fall has the least fog; spring features the giant coreopsis bloom.

Directions: Island Packers provides boat transportation to Anacapa Island from Ventura Harbor and Oxnard (Channel Islands Harbor). Advance reservations are required. Phone Island Packers at (805) 642-7688 or (805) 642-1393 for information and reservations.

45. SHEEP CAMP BACKPACK
Chumash Wilderness, off Interstate 5 near Frazier Park

An overnight backpacking trip in the Chumash Wilderness promises the possibility of seeing a magnificent condor fly overhead, and a visit to Mount Pinos, the highest point in Los Padres National Forest at 8,831 feet. It's only a 2.5-mile hike to reach your overnight camp in the wilderness, and get this—it's downhill most of the way. Sound good? It is good; start packing.

The Chumash Wilderness is a small wilderness area, only 38,000 acres, but with some of the highest and most rugged terrain in Los Padres National Forest. The easiest way to approach it is from Interstate 5 at Frazier Park. A 20-mile drive off the interstate takes you into the forest and up the slopes of Mount Pinos; the trailhead for your camp is at the mountain's peak.

It's a culture shock—one minute you're driving 80 miles per hour on the interstate; an hour later you're walking in the wilderness, where no mechanized vehicles can ever go. Feel better? We did too.

From the summit of Mount Pinos, the Vincent Tumamait Trail runs for five miles to Mount Abel, elevation 8,286 feet (also called Mount Cerro Noroeste). Because your trailhead is at Mount Pinos' summit, you have to tear yourself away from the view to start your hike. The peak's vista takes in the Sespe, Dick Smith, San Rafael, and Chumash wilderness areas, plus the San Joaquin Valley, the Sespe River Valley, and yes—there it is—the crest of the Sierra Nevada. How about a round of applause?

To get to your camp, follow the Vincent Tumamait Trail for only two miles, heading downhill at first and then up Sawmill Mountain, to the North Fork Trail junction. This will be your only climb and your only junction on the way to camp.

Bear left on the North Fork Trail and walk a half-mile to Sheep Camp, then choose a campsite under the Jeffrey pines and set up your tent. You will have crossed a tiny stream with a spring box a few hundred feet before the camp; this is where you can pump and filter your water.

The camp is in conifer country, with the mountain covered in snow a good part of the year. The trees are remarkable in this wilderness—white firs and Jeffrey pines are giant-sized and look like they have lived through much. At their bases grow several shrubs typical of the Sierra: snowberry, gooseberry, lupine, and buckwheat.

Sheep Camp has only four campsites, spaced about 75 yards apart, so it's always peaceful and private. Because this is a wilderness area, the campsites are primitive, with only a fire grill, a flat spot for your tent, and a few logs to sit on. The best site is the fourth one, furthest down the trail from the spring. It sits on a ridge with a spectacular view of the canyon below.

Keep in mind that black bears also love Mount Pinos, so hang your food from one of several ropes in the trees or plan on losing it. You're also likely to see dozens of lodgepole chipmunks scurrying around; don't give the cute little guys any handouts.

After a peaceful night in camp, take a day-hike back to the Vincent Tumamait Trail junction, then follow that trail to Mount Abel. As you hike, keep scanning the skies for giant condors, many of whom nest in the nearby condor sanctuary. The condor has a nine-foot wingspan and an average weight of 20 pounds, so if you see one, you won't mistake it for anything else. The local Chumash Indians considered the condor to be a sacred bird. To them, it symbolized the balance of power in all living things.

Facilities, reservations, fees: There are four campsites at Sheep Camp, each with a fire grill. Water is available for filtering. Campfires are permitted. No reservations or permits are necessary. There is no fee for camping. Pets are permitted.

Special note: A national forest adventure pass is required for recreation in this area. See page 11 for details.

Who to contact: Los Padres National Forest, Mount Pinos Ranger District, 34580 Lockwood Valley Road, Frazier Park, CA 93225; (805) 245-3731 or fax (805) 245-1526.

Maps for backpacking: For a map of Los Padres National Forest, send $4 to USDA-Forest Service, 630 Sansome Street, San Francisco, CA 94111. For a topographic map of the area, ask for Sawmill Mountain from the USGS.

Season: Open year-round; the road is sometimes closed in winter.

Directions: From Los Angeles, drive north on Interstate 5 through the San Fernando Valley to Gorman. Just beyond Gorman, take the Frazier Park/Mount Pinos exit and turn west. Drive 12 miles on Frazier Mountain Park Road, which will become Cuddy Valley Road. At 12 miles, bear left on Mount Pinos Highway and drive nine miles to the road on the left signed for Mount Pinos Summit. Turn left and drive 1.8 miles to the summit parking area (stay left at the fork).

46. PINE MOUNTAIN CLUB CABINS
Los Padres National Forest, off Interstate 5 near Mount Pinos

Are there any surprises left in the Southern California Great Outdoors? Judging from an informal poll I took at three outdoor stores in Los Angeles, I'd say there are, because not one of the 60 or so people I spoke to had ever been to Mount Pinos or Pine Mountain Club.

Mount Pinos? That's right. Make sure you say it correctly; it's not "Mount Piños" as you might expect, but Mount Pinos, as in pine trees. There are plenty of those on the mountain—large beautiful forests of them, arguably best seen when they are crowned with snow. That's right, snow. At 8,831 feet, Mount Pinos is the tallest mountain in Los Padres National Forest, and it gets a fair share of snowfall every winter. The snow may not hang around for months, but when it arrives, it provides excellent cross-country skiing, snowshoeing, and snow play.

Mount Pinos is accessed from the unlikely town of Frazier Park on Interstate 5, just south of Grapevine. You drive west of Frazier Park's giant truck stop for 12 miles, and suddenly you've left the interstate life behind and entered a different world. A right turnoff on Mil Potrero Highway takes you through six miles of Los Padres National Forest to the small town of Pine Mountain Club, where numerous cabin rentals are available.

The cabin you will rent is someone's private vacation home, so you'll find that it is large enough for four to eight people, and it will

Little hiker on the summit of Mount Pinos

have a fully equipped kitchen, linens, a television, a VCR, and all the modern conveniences. All of the rental cabins have fireplaces or wood stoves, and firewood is often provided by the owner. Some cabins have views, some allow pets, some allow smoking, and so on, so make sure you request exactly what you want.

After you get settled in your cabin, head back to the main road to drive the remaining few miles to the top of Mount Pinos. If there is snow, you'll find many areas on Mount Pinos that are open for cross-country skiing and snowshoeing. If there is no snow, numerous hiking trails are available on the mountain, including the Vincent Tumamait Trail from Mount Pinos' summit, detailed in the story on page 119. Even if you don't hike, a drive to the summit provides an awesome view that extends all the way to the San Joaquin Valley and the peaks of the Sierra Nevada. While you look around, be sure to watch for giant condors soaring in the sky; they are often seen on the edge of the Chumash Wilderness.

Another popular hiking trail is the Cedar Creek Trail, which leads from Thorn Meadows Campground off Lockwood Valley Road in nearby Lake of the Woods. The drive to the trailhead will take a little less than an hour; get an early start so you'll have plenty of time to hike the nine-mile round-trip to the Fishbowls along Piru Creek. In summer, the sandstone pools are popular swimming holes.

Several local hikes are possible right in Pine Mountain Club, including a short waterfall trail that begins at the end of Woodland Drive. The nice folks at Mountain Properties Vacation Rentals can supply you with a street map and a list of trails and trailheads.

Facilities, reservations, fees: There are 28 cabins and private homes for rent in Pine Mountain Center. An inn with motel rooms is also available. Reservations are required. Fees range from $80 to $135 per night, depending on the size of cabin and accommodations. Most cabins sleep four to eight people. Weekly rentals are available at discounted rates. Pets are permitted in some cabins; you must get advance permission to bring your pet.

Special note: A national forest adventure pass is required for recreation in this area. See page 11 for details.

Who to contact: Mountain Properties Vacation Rentals, 16229 Pine Valley Lane, P.O. Box 6675, Pine Mountain Club, CA 93222; (805) 242-2500 or (805) 242-2517.

Season: Open year-round.

Directions: From Los Angeles, drive north on Interstate 5 through the San Fernando Valley to Gorman. Just beyond Gorman, take the Frazier Park/Mount Pinos exit and turn west. Drive 12 miles on Frazier Mountain Park Road, which will become Cuddy Valley Road. At 12 miles, turn right on Mil Potrero Highway and drive six miles to Pine Mountain Club. Turn left at the gas station in town, across from the golf course, and enter the shopping center. Drive 50 yards on Pine Circle. Mountain Properties is located in the shopping center at the intersection of Pine Circle and Pine Valley Lane.

47. SANTA PAULA CANYON BACKPACK
Los Padres National Forest, off Highway 150 near Ojai

You can convince almost anyone to hike three miles, especially if you promise them a waterfall and a cold dip in a stream when they finish. That's why it's easy to assemble your friends for the short backpacking trip to Santa Paula Canyon, where they can set up their tent just a few hundred feet from the sandstone gorge of Santa Paula Creek.

Here's what you should know: What starts out rather pedestrian gets much, much better as you hike along the Santa Paula Canyon Trail. That's because the first mile of the route is mostly on pavement, meandering around the grounds of Thomas Aquinas College and a private ranch and oil-drilling operation. The pavement seems to go on forever, but at last, you're on a real trail in the real outdoors. Have patience.

Once you're on the "real" trail, you'll head deep into Santa Paula Canyon, following Santa Paula Creek and crossing it twice. (After the first crossing, be sure to head to the right; some people lose the trail here.) In spring, you could almost call this waterway the Santa Paula River, but by summer, it's a tame and pretty stream. The trees are dense and shady along the route, and the wildflowers are sublime. On our trip in April, we saw and smelled a ton of ceanothus, plus purple nightshade, yellow phlox, sweet peas, lupine, hooker's onions, and more. Butterflies frequent this canyon.

After the second creek crossing at two miles out, get ready for your first climb on the trail, as you follow a wide dirt road up and around Hill 1989. Following the ascent, the trail drops down to a grassy flat surrounded by big cone spruce. This is your destination— Big Cone Camp. It has six sites with fire rings, so take your pick of the sites. The best of the lot is at the far edge of the camp, on your left; it's a few yards away from the other sites. What makes it the best? Besides the privacy, it's the only site that has a partial view of one of the waterfalls on Santa Paula Creek.

A short distance from the camp, the trail continues steeply down to Santa Paula Creek, to a stretch of stream that locals call "The Punchbowls." A series of waterfalls and sandstone plunge pools make

Primitive campsite at Santa Paula Canyon

this a swimmer's delight, but exercise caution if the stream is high.

Remember that this is primitive camping, and the only amenities provided are a few fire rings and some rocks to sit on. You need to boil or filter your water, pack out all your trash (bring an extra bag to pack out any other trash you might find), and have some way to prepare your food. When we visited, my sister and I dined on pasta with sun-dried tomatoes cooked on our backpacking stove. The only other campers at Big Cone Camp were three teenagers; they carried in an entire cooler full of canned foods and drinks. To each his own.

Facilities, reservations, fees: There are six campsites at Santa Paula Canyon. Water is available for filtering. Campfires are permitted. No reservations or permits are necessary. There is no fee for camping. Pets are permitted.

Special note: A national forest adventure pass is required for recreation in this area. See page 11 for details.

Who to contact: Los Padres National Forest, Ojai Ranger District, 1190 East Ojai Avenue, Ojai, CA 93023; (805) 646-4348 or fax (805) 646-0484.

Maps for backpacking: For a map of Los Padres National Forest, send $4 to USDA-Forest Service, 630 Sansome Street, San Francisco, CA 94111. For a topographic map of the area, ask for Santa Paula Peak from the USGS.

Season: Open year-round.

Directions: From Ojai, at the junction of highways 33 and 150, drive east on Highway 150 for 11.5 miles to Thomas Aquinas College on the left (look for iron gates and stone buildings). Drive 100 yards further to the parking pullout on the right side of the road, just beyond the highway bridge over Santa Paula Creek. Park there and walk back across the bridge to the paved road on the right side of the college.

48. LA JOLLA CANYON BACKPACK
Point Mugu State Park, off Highway 1 near Oxnard

Of all the parks in the Santa Monica Mountains, Point Mugu State Park wins hands down. Maybe it's because Point Mugu is further north on the highway, closer to Oxnard than it is to Los Angeles, or maybe it's the park's proximity to the ocean, but this place seems more wild, and more pristine, than the others. Things are just plain better at Point Mugu.

The park has an excellent hike-in camp, accessible via an easy two-mile hike from the Ray Miller state park trailhead on Highway 1, near Thornhill Broome State Beach. There are two trails at the Ray Miller Trailhead in La Jolla Canyon, so make sure you take the right one, which is the wide dirt road signed as La Jolla Canyon Trail. You hike through a wide-open valley, which is continually freshened by cool ocean breezes blowing up the canyon.

Cross La Jolla Creek, then at eight-tenths of a mile from the trailhead, you'll reach a small waterfall at a second stream crossing. It's a good place to set down your pack and take a rest before heading deeper into La Jolla Canyon. When you proceed, you'll find that the canyon gets steeper, narrower, and rockier. Hidden amid the chaparral are rock caves that were once used by Native Americans for religious ceremonies.

Stay straight at the first fork, but at 1.5 miles, take the left fork signed for the campground. The trail flattens out and brings you to an area of native grasses, which looks something like a savannah. Six thousand years ago, this was the home of a tribe of Native Americans called the Oak Grove People. Today the La Jolla Canyon Campground is located there, shortly beyond a cattail-bordered pond. Blue and orange dragonflies and red-winged blackbirds congregate by the water. (There is also a large group camp nearby; you'll want to head for the smaller family camping area to the left.)

Piped water and restrooms are provided at the camp, so you don't need to carry bottled water or worry about whether or not your purifier is going to work. You will need to bring a backpacking stove and fuel, because campfires are not allowed at the camp.

Pick your campsite from the 12 sites available. The coastal chaparral is high enough to give you some privacy; the sites are located on the edge of the grassland but still in the taller chaparral. Then consider how you want to spend your time. In spring, there is plenty to see, most notably the grassland wildflowers. In late winter, you may be witness to an even more colorful event: Monarch butterflies who winter in this park begin to mate and leave for their return migration to Canada and the northern United States. The monarchs cluster in neighboring Sycamore Canyon in Point Mugu State Park.

Several hiking trails continue from the camp; the best option is to follow the La Jolla Canyon Loop Trail, taking the fire road westward until it turns to single-track. Then either bear left to stay on the three-mile La Jolla Canyon Loop, or bear right to make a longer loop on the Mugu Peak Trail. The latter path circles Mugu Peak, elevation

La Jolla Canyon Trail heading up to the hike-in camp

1,266 feet, and will return you back to the La Jolla Canyon Loop Trail, adding only two miles to your trip. Views of Point Mugu and the Pacific coast are outstanding.

Facilities, reservations, fees: There are 12 campsites at La Jolla Canyon Campground. Sites are available on a first-come, first-served basis and can accommodate as many as eight people. A hike-in group campground is also available. Backpackers must register at the ranger station at Sycamore Canyon Campground or at La Jolla Cove at least one hour before sunset. Potable water is available at the camp. Campfires are not permitted; bring a backpacking stove. The fee is $3 per person per night. Pets are not permitted.

Who to contact: Point Mugu State Park, 9000 Pacific Coast Highway, Malibu, CA 90265; (805) 488-5223 or State Parks, Angeles District, 1925 Los Virgenes Road, Calabasas, CA 91302; (818) 880-0350.

Maps for backpacking: A trail map is available for $1 from the ranger kiosk at Sycamore Canyon Campground, one mile south of the Ray Miller Trailhead on Highway 1. A map of the Santa Monica Mountains is available for a fee from Tom Harrison Cartography, (415) 456-7940. For a topographic map of the area, ask for Point Mugu from the USGS.

Season: Open year-round; the best months are February through June.

Directions: From U.S. 101 in Camarillo, take the Los Posas Road exit and drive south through Oxnard. Follow Los Posas Road for eight miles to Highway 1, then turn south on Highway 1. Drive five miles to the La Jolla Canyon trailhead parking area on the left, across from Thornhill

Broome State Beach. (Alternatively, from Highway 1 in Malibu, drive west on Highway 1 for 22 miles to the La Jolla Canyon trailhead parking area on the right.)

49. TOPANGA RANCH MOTEL CABINS
near the Santa Monica Mountains, off Highway 1 in Malibu

Let's just say right away that the cabins at Topanga Ranch Motel are nothing fancy. After all, what can you expect for sixty bucks a night in pricey Malibu? Not a whole heck of a lot. However, if you want to take advantage of all the great outdoor adventures of the Malibu coast and the Santa Monica Mountains, a stay at the Topanga Ranch cabins can give you the chance to do so and still go home with some change in your pocket.

The cabins were built in the 1920s and are showing their age, but have been painted a cheerful red and white on the outside. They are spacious enough for a couple or a small family, and their fully equipped kitchens will give you the option to cook your meals at home. Although the furniture is not exactly fashionable, remember: You're supposed to be camping.

The cabins are arranged motel-style, lined up in a row in the parking lot, with the busy Pacific Coast Highway not far away. Nonetheless, we managed to get a good night's sleep, and heard much less traffic noise than we feared. The silver lining to having the PCH close by is that on its far side is the ocean, which means you are never more than walking distance from the beach. Just throw your surfboard over your shoulder and look both ways before you cross.

If hiking is your bag, the Santa Monica Mountains National Recreation Area awaits, as well as more than a dozen state and county parks in the immediate area. Take your pick from the trail offerings at Point Mugu State Park, Leo Carrillo State Beach, Charmlee Natural Area, Malibu Creek State Park, Solstice Canyon Park, and Topanga State Park. There are enough parks and trails within a half-hour drive of Malibu to keep you busy for a whole summer.

Honestly, though, most people come to Malibu for one reason, and that's the beach. Don't forget your bathing suit and towel.

Facilities, reservations, fees: There are 14 cottages at Topanga Ranch Motel, some with kitchens. Reservations are recommended. Fees range from $50 to $120 per night. Small pets are permitted.

Who to contact: Topanga Ranch Motel, 18711 Pacific Coast Highway, Malibu, CA 90265; (800) 200-0019 or (310) 456-5486.

Season: Open year-round.

Directions: From Santa Monica, drive north on Highway 1 for six miles to Malibu. Look for the Topanga Ranch Motel on the east side of the road, just north of the junction with Topanga Canyon Boulevard.

50. MUSCH TRAIL BACKPACK
Topanga State Park, off Highway 1 near Santa Monica

The hike to Topanga State Park's trail camp at Musch Ranch is so short and so easy, it almost seems criminal. It's a simple and pretty walk that is only one mile in length, which begs the question: Is it fair and just to call this walk in the park a backpacking trip?

Be your own judge and jury as you take the uphill trek from the Trippet Ranch trailhead at Topanga State Park to Musch Trail Camp at 1,500 feet. The path is simple: Follow the paved road from the eastern edge of the parking lot for about 100 yards to the single-track Musch Trail, then turn right. Shortly you'll have the company of shady oak, bay, and sycamore trees, as well as hundreds of ferns alongside a small stream. In a few minutes of hiking, you'll leave this behind and head onto sunny chaparral-covered slopes, then spy a grove of eucalyptus trees up ahead. This is the location of Musch Trail Camp, previously the location of Musch Ranch.

Piped water, restrooms, and picnic tables are provided at the camp, which once again calls into question whether or not we can fairly call this backpacking. Well, at least they don't have a snack bar. You have to carry in and cook your own food, and since campfires are not allowed, you have to do it on your backpacking stove. Now that's roughing it.

After a good night's sleep in camp, you'll be ready for a morning hike. Less than a mile beyond Musch Trail Camp on the Musch Trail is Eagle Junction. From there you can turn left and head for Topanga State Park's most notable feature, sandstone Eagle Rock. Hike up its back side and explore the tiny caves and hollows in the smooth sandstone outcrop. Most surprising are the 360-degree views from the valley to the ocean; Eagle Rock's elevation is only 1,950 feet, but this close to the coast, it seems a whole lot higher. The rock's sandstone is millions of years old, which gives you something to think about while you are sitting on top of it.

From Eagle Rock, you can continue hiking in a loop, heading further east to Hub Junction, a four-way intersection. At the junction, turn right and take a side-trip to Temescal Peak at 2,036 feet, or simply loop back to Eagle Junction via Eagle Springs. Practice naming the chaparral plants as you hike: White sage, chamise, yucca, poison oak, elderberry, and chia, among others. Watch for roadrunners scurrying among them.

Another popular hike from the Trippet Ranch trailhead is to follow the Eagle Springs Fire Road for a half-mile, then turn right on the Santa Ynez Canyon Trail. This single-track path will lead you deep into a shady, flower-filled canyon. A mile and a half from Trippet Ranch, look for a tributary stream coming in on your left, and follow the trail alongside it for a half-mile to a lovely sandstone waterfall. In the spring, you'll find tall, orange tiger lilies growing near the stream banks in Santa Ynez Canyon.

Facilities, reservations, fees: There are eight primitive campsites at Musch Trail Camp, available on a first-come, first-served basis. Potable water is available at the camp. Campfires are not permitted; bring a backpacking stove. The fee is $3 per person per night. Pets are not permitted.

Who to contact: Topanga State Park, 20825 Entrada Road, Topanga, CA 90290; (310) 455-2465. Or State Parks, Angeles District, 1925 Los Virgenes Road, Calabasas, CA 91302; (818) 880-0350.

Maps for backpacking: A map of the Santa Monica Mountains is available for a fee from Tom Harrison Cartography, (415) 456-7940. For a topographic map of the area, ask for Topanga from the USGS.

Season: Open year-round. Best months are February to June.

Directions: From Santa Monica, drive north on Highway 1 and turn right on Topanga Canyon Boulevard. Drive 4.7 miles to Entrada Road, then turn right and drive one mile to the park entrance at Trippet Ranch. The Musch trailhead is at the far side of the parking lot.

Central Coast

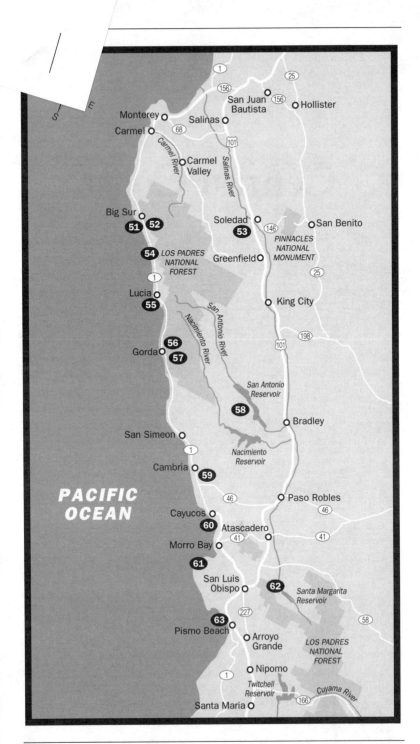

PACIFIC
OCEAN

Monterey
Carmel
Carmel Valley
Salinas
San Juan Bautista
Hollister
Big Sur **51** **52**
Soledad **53**
San Benito
54 LOS PADRES NATIONAL FOREST
Greenfield
PINNACLES NATIONAL MONUMENT
Lucia **55**
King City
Gorda **56** **57**
San Antonio Reservoir
58
Bradley
San Simeon
Nacimiento Reservoir
Cambria **59**
Paso Robles
Cayucos
60 Atascadero
Morro Bay
61
San Luis Obispo
62 Santa Margarita Reservoir
63
Pismo Beach
Arroyo Grande
LOS PADRES NATIONAL FOREST
Nipomo
Twitchell Reservoir
Cuyama River
Santa Maria

51. BIG SUR CAMPGROUND & CABINS
near Pfeiffer Big Sur State Park, off Highway 1 in Big Sur

Why do people come to this private campground in Big Sur, when Pfeiffer Big Sur State Park is practically across the road? Two reasons: One, the camp is located right on the Big Sur River, at a lovely bend where you can swim, fish, or just watch the water roll by. And two, the people who run Big Sur Campground and Cabins are some of the nicest people I've come across in the cabin business. They want people to have a good time, and they do their best to make it happen. An attitude like that attracts business.

You have several options for accommodations at Big Sur Campground and Cabins. Besides regular tent and RV sites, the camp has 12 cabins, all with fireplaces, and four tent cabins available in summer only. The tent cabins are an excellent inexpensive camping option, but remember that they are minimalist in nature: You have to use a public bathhouse and do your cooking over a barbecue or backpacking stove. Your dog can stay with you in the tent cabins for a $10 fee per night; pets are not allowed in the other cabins.

The 12 regular cabins are all slightly different. Many people prefer the three A-frame cabins, which have full kitchens, bathrooms, fireplaces, and an upper loft that serves as an extra bedroom. These can house four to six people, but they are not directly on the Big Sur River. The rest of the cabins are spread out in the big redwoods on the south side of the campground, with numbers 101 and 102 right at the river's edge. These two are the choice options. All of the cabins are fun to stay in, because you're never more than a few steps away from the water. Each cabin has its own bathroom, and most of the units have fully equipped kitchens. There is even an option for campers on a budget: Cabin 65 is a duplex unit, and costs a few less bucks.

Besides fishing and swimming in the Big Sur River, a favorite activity here is to rent an inner tube from the camp managers and float around all day. If you need more exercise, all of the trails of Big Sur await you. (See the stories on pages 134 and 139 for trail descriptions). Ocean access is also possible nearby, either to the north at Andrew Molera State Park, or to the south at Pfeiffer Beach. To reach Pfeiffer Beach, drive three miles south on Highway 1 to the Sycamore Canyon Road turnoff on the right. Turn right and drive two miles to the beach.

Facilities, reservations, fees: There are 12 cabins at Big Sur Campground and Cabins, plus four tent cabins (available from May to September only), and numerous RV and tent sites. Reservations are recommended. Fees range from $88 to $140 per night for regular cabins and $44 per night for tent cabins. Pets are not permitted except in tent cabins and tent and RV campsites; $10 fee per night.

Who to contact: Big Sur Campground and Cabins, Highway 1, Big Sur, CA 93920; (408) 667-2322.

Season: Open year-round.

Directions: From San Luis Obispo, drive north on U.S. 101 for 24 miles to the Highway 46 West exit near Templeton. Turn west on Highway 46 and drive 23 miles to Highway 1. Turn north on Highway 1 and drive 75 miles to Big Sur. (Plan on 2.5 hours for these last 75 miles.) Big Sur Campground and Cabins will be on your left, shortly beyond Pfeiffer Big Sur State Park.

52. BIG SUR LODGE CABINS
Pfeiffer Big Sur State Park, off Highway 1 in Big Sur

I was a little disappointed by Pfeiffer Big Sur State Park the first time I visited. It was a Saturday in summer, the place was crawling with tourists, and I couldn't seem to find a moment's peace among the giant redwood trees. I didn't hang around long; instead I got back in my car and headed for the quieter trails of the Ventana Wilderness.

Then I got smart. The next time, I planned my trip carefully, and my visit to Pfeiffer Big Sur State Park was a perfect redwood fantasy. Instead of staying in the park's crowded car campground, I booked a cabin at the Big Sur Lodge. Instead of visiting on a summer weekend, I showed up March. And instead of hiking at midday, I was out of bed early every morning to explore the park's trails. Often I saw no one else until 10 a.m. or so, even on the most popular paths.

That's the way a trip to Pfeiffer Big Sur State Park should be, and all you have to do is play it smart. Start by making your cabin reservation. If possible, book a cabin with both a fireplace and a kitchen; it doesn't cost much more than a standard unit, and it's great to have a fireplace in the misty, damp redwoods. All of the cabins have decks or balconies, and none of them have phones, televisions, radios, or any other fluff.

If you don't want to cook, pay a few bucks less for a cabin without a kitchen and have your meals at the Trail's Head Cafe, the lodge's beautiful dining room. It has big picture windows that look out on the ferns and red-woods. The food is casual, delicious, and surprisingly affordable.

Pfeiffer Big Sur State Park's showpiece trail is the 1.6-mile Pfeiffer Falls and Valley View Loop, which begins near the park nature center. You hike up Redwood Creek's canyon, crossing the stream on little foot-bridges, until you reach 60-foot Pfeiffer Falls,

Redwood Creek, Pfeiffer Big Sur State Park

which streams down a vertical rock face. Then you backtrack a short distance and pick up the Valley View Trail, which climbs above the canyon to a wide overlook of the Big Sur Valley and Point Sur.

Another excellent view hike, and one that is less traveled, is the Buzzards Roost Trail. It begins near the park's bridge over the Big Sur River. A healthy two-mile climb brings you to Buzzards Roost Overlook, with wide vistas of the Pacific Ocean and Big Sur Gorge. Have a snack or some lunch while you're there, then head back downhill for a two-mile return.

If you want to explore outside Pfeiffer Big Sur, Andrew Molera State Park is just four miles north on Highway 1. Families like to take the easy walk from the parking lot to Molera Point, where you can look down on a large colony of sea lions. Along the way, check out Cooper Cabin, the oldest structure still standing on the Big Sur coast, built in 1861. Many longer hikes are possible by linking together the park's trails.

Facilities, reservations, fees: There are 61 cabins at Big Sur Lodge, ranging in sizes that can accommodate two to six people. Some cabins have kitchenettes and/or fireplaces. A restaurant and general store are available. Reservations are recommended. Fees range from $79 to $179 per night. Pets are not permitted.

Who to contact: Big Sur Lodge Cabins, Pfeiffer Big Sur State Park, P.O. Box 190, Big Sur, CA 93920; (408) 667-3100 or (800) 424-4787.

Season: Open year-round.

Directions: From San Luis Obispo, drive north on U.S. 101 for 24 miles to the Highway 46 West exit near Templeton. Turn west on Highway 46 and drive 23 miles to Highway 1. Turn north on Highway 1 and drive 75 miles to Big Sur. (Plan on 2.5 hours for these last 75 miles.) Pfeiffer Big Sur State Park will be on your right.

53. PARAISO HOT SPRINGS
near Pinnacles National Monument, off U.S. 101 near Soledad

There aren't too many places left in California like Paraiso Hot Springs. It's historic, it's funky, it's completely unpretentious, and if you're looking for a room at the Ritz, you won't find it here. But if you like soaking in natural mineral springs, hiking in a wide variety of landscapes, and maybe tasting some of Monterey County's wines, you'll like Paraiso Hot Springs.

The drive to the resort tells you a lot about the place. You leave U.S. 101 and head for the countryside, first winding through deep green vegetable fields and then through fertile vineyards. Six miles on a back road takes you into the foothills of the Santa Lucia Mountains. When you round a curve and leave the county-maintained road, you enter the resort under the swaying fronds of palm trees.

Not just ordinary palm trees, either. A grouping of remarkably tall royal palms towers over the more common date palms that ring the Olympic-sized swimming pool. The effect is strangely tropical. In the midst of the palms stand some picturesque Victorian buildings, a bit worn at the edges but still elegant. Off to one side are a few double-wide mobile homes. Away on a sheltered hillside, a group of small cabins are nestled in oak and pine trees.

You can choose between these various accommodations when you stay at Paraiso. We chose the hillside cabins, which are extremely spartan but serve their purpose. They are very small, one-room cabins; inside each one is squeezed a double bed, a small kitchenette and dining table, a dresser, and an overstuffed chair. Don't plan on practicing your country line dancing inside.

Luckily the cabins have little back decks where you can sit and listen to the birds during the day and the frogs at night. After an evening rain followed by clearing skies, we saw one heck of a star show from our deck.

We didn't complain about having to walk 50 feet to the communal bath house for restrooms and showers, but we did take exception to the fact that our "kitchenette" had only a hot plate and tiny refrigerator. It seemed a little skimpy considering the price of the cabin.

Barbecue grills are found in the grassy area amid the cabins; you are welcome to cook on them, but you are not permitted to barbecue on your cabin deck. Because the resort has burned to the ground twice in its history, the owners are very concerned about fire.

Most people spend their days at Paraiso's huge outdoor swimming pool and its neighboring warm mineral pool, which are kept at 80 and 100 degrees Fahrenheit, respectively. For an additional $5 fee, you can access the enclosed hot bath area, or the historic hot springs pools that are in the old bathhouse area. These are two tile tubs that were in use in the 1800s; they are kept at 102 and 108 degrees Fahrenheit.

If you are planning to stay for more than a night at Paraiso, you'll probably want a full kitchen and/or larger accommodations. That means you must pay almost twice as much for either a cottage or mobile home. The cottages range in size from one room to large two-story houses, and each has its own bathroom; these are the best options for a large family. The mobile homes are less expensive but less charming; still, they have all the amenities you need.

Another great accommodation option is the resort's large yurt, which is hidden from view behind the campground and main lodge buildings. The yurt has its own private yard, a separate kitchen and bathroom, and it is completely furnished with rugs, mattresses, a wood-burning fireplace, and even a stereo system. (If you've never seen one, a yurt is a large canvas tepee or tent, which is set on a wooden platform. It is several steps up in quality from a typical tent cabin, because it has a door and windows, and it looks more like a real house on the inside.) Paraiso's yurt is particularly nice because it is off by itself, away from the rest of the resort. A hiking trail leads from the yurt area into the canyon beyond.

While you're at Paraiso, be sure to visit the Soledad Mission, just down the road a mile. It's a sweet little church in a tranquil setting. Also, check out the great old photographs of turn-of-the-century

Paraiso Hot Springs, which are hanging on the main lodge walls. You'll see that the resort's palm trees and many of the Victorian buildings look much the same as they did 100 years ago. Only the people look different.

If you stay at Paraiso long enough to tire of soaking in hot mineral water, a great day-trip is possible to the western side of Pinnacles National Monument. (Drive through the town of Soledad and follow Highway 146 for 12 miles until it ends.) A

Hiking trail in Pinnacles National Monument

terrific introductory hike is the 2.4-mile Balconies Caves Loop; a more challenging trek is the 8.8-mile Pinnacles High Peaks Loop. Both are walks you won't soon forget, due to the fascinating geology and flora of the park. Don't forget a flashlight for visiting the caves.

Facilities, reservations, fees: There are 10 one-room cabins at Paraiso Hot Springs, all with small kitchenettes. Restrooms and showers are located nearby. There are also six mobile homes, eight cottages, and one large yurt, all with full kitchens and bathrooms. Reservations are recommended. Fees range from $110 to $285 per night for two people; additional persons are $55 to $140 per night. Credit cards are not accepted. Pets are permitted; $15 fee per night.

Who to contact: Paraiso Hot Springs, Soledad, CA 93960; (408) 678-2882.

Season: Open year-round.

Directions: From San Luis Obispo, drive north on U.S. 101 for 100 miles to the Arroyo Seco Road exit, seven miles north of Greenfield. (If you reach the Soledad exit, you've driven one mile too far north.) Head west on Arroyo Seco Road for three miles, then bear right on Paraiso Road. Drive five miles on Paraiso Road to the resort entrance.

54. JULIA PFEIFFER BURNS WALK-IN CAMPS
Julia Pfeiffer Burns State Park, off Highway 1 near Big Sur

There are two state parks in Big Sur within 10 miles of each other, bearing similar names, similar addresses, and similar scenery, and many people get them confused. Julia Pfeiffer Burns is the small, little-developed state park with great hiking trails, big redwoods, and the famous waterfall that drops to the beach, McWay Falls. Pfeiffer Big Sur is the much larger state park with a campground, lodge, and restaurant, plus great hiking trails, big redwoods, and a small inland waterfall, Pfeiffer Falls.

They're easy to confuse. Except that if you're traveling north on Highway 1 from San Simeon, you reach Julia Pfeiffer Burns State Park 10 miles before you reach larger Pfeiffer Big Sur State Park. After you reach the first park, you might not want to go anywhere else. Luckily, even though Julia Pfeiffer Burns is small and doesn't have the range of accommodations that Pfeiffer Big Sur State Park has, it has something that may appeal to you more: Two walk-in, environmental campsites.

An environmental campsite is one that you must reach by hiking. This isn't car camping; everything must be carried in on foot, including your drinking water. It's just like backpacking except that the distance is short; you only need to hike a half-mile from where you park your car. This makes your camping trip fool-proof; if you forget anything in your car, you just walk back and fetch it. If your six-year-old decides he isn't going to carry his own sleeping bag, and your pack is full, you can make more than one trip.

What makes environmental camping at Julia Pfeiffer Burns extra special is the location of the campsites. They are placed so that they offer spectacular views of the rugged Big Sur Coast, but because they are in a grove of sturdy cypress trees, they are mostly protected from the wind. Plus, there are only two sites, so you won't be sharing the natural beauty of the land with hundreds of other campers.

Each site has a storage cabinet for keeping your food away from the local critters, a vault toilet, and a fire pit for cooking. Unless you're pretty handy with a campfire, you might want to bring your backpacking stove, or resign yourself to eating hot dogs and marshmallows off sharpened sticks. Also, be sure to bring plenty of warm clothes, because the weather can be foggy, damp, or chilly at any time

McWay Falls, Julia Pfeiffer Burns State Park

of year—even in July. Park rules say you may have as many as eight people at your campsite, but this place is so special and serene that you'll probably want your group to be smaller.

While you're at Julia Pfeiffer Burns, of course you will visit its famous waterfall, McWay Falls, which plunges dramatically to the sea. You can't see the falls from your campsite, but they are only a short walk away. In addition, be sure to hike the park's Ewoldsen Trail, my favorite trail in Big Sur, for a good aerobic climb with gorgeous redwoods, streams, and ferns.

Another excellent trip is to drive north on Highway 1 for about two miles to a curve in the highway and a trail sign for Partington Point and the Tan Bark Trail. Park in the pullout alongside the highway, then hike the short dirt road down to the ocean at Partington Point. Experienced SCUBA divers enter the waters here to explore the diversity of caves, canyons, and natural undersea bridges. An entry permit is required for SCUBA diving; hikers can just walk down the road, find a rock to sit on, and enjoy the above-the-water spectacle.

Facilities, reservations, fees: There are two walk-in campsites at Julia Pfeiffer Burns State Park. No water is available; you must pack in bottled water. Campfires are permitted. Reservations are required; phone Parknet at (800) 444-7275. Fees range from $14 to $16 per night. Pets are not permitted.

Maps for backpacking: A map of Julia Pfeiffer Burns State Park is available for $1 at Pfeiffer Big Sur State Park, nine miles north on Highway 1. For a topographic map of the area, ask for Partington Ridge from the USGS.

Who to contact: Julia Pfeiffer Burns State Park c/o Pfeiffer Big Sur State Park, Big Sur, CA 93920; (408) 667-2315.

Season: Open year-round.

Directions: From San Luis Obispo, drive north on U.S. 101 for 24 miles to the Highway 46 West exit near Templeton. Turn west on Highway 46 and drive 23 miles to Highway 1. Turn north on Highway 1 and drive 70 miles to Julia Pfeiffer Burns State Park on the right. (Plan on nearly two hours for those last 70 miles.)

---

55. LUCIA LODGE
Los Padres National Forest, off Highway 1 near Big Sur

If you've driven Highway 1 along the spectacular Big Sur Coast, you've seen it: Lucia Lodge, clinging precariously to the cliffs.

The thing is, I must have driven by a dozen times before I finally stopped in and found out the place has cabins. I was always too busy gaping at the view and trying to keep my car on the road.

The 50-year-old cabins at Lucia Lodge are perched 500 feet above Lucia Bay, on steep cliffs that descend with wild abandon to the breaking waves. Each cabin has an open-beamed ceiling and cozy furnishings, and is surrounded by beautiful landscaping and flowers. The cabins numbered 7 through 10 are the nicest of the lot, each with a fireplace, four-poster bed, view of the ocean, and lots of other romantic stuff. If you're on a budget, go for cabins numbered 1 through 4, which are without fireplaces but still offer that enchanting ocean view and a full helping of romance.

There are no kitchens in the cabins, because the lodge owners want you to eat at their restaurant. Like the cabins, the restaurant has a stunning view, plus a beautiful stone fireplace inside. Even if you don't eat all your meals there, be sure to have at least one breakfast outside on the restaurant's deck. You'll never drink coffee that good again, and it's not just high-quality beans that make it extraordinary.

Besides the view, what I like best about Lucia Lodge is that it's right across the highway from Lime Kiln Creek State Park, one of the newest additions to the California state park system. And what I like best about Lime Kiln is its beautiful limestone waterfall, which

A lime kiln at Lime Kiln Creek State Park

cascades with breath-taking beauty over pads of thick moss and rock. There is only one trail in the park; it runs from the campground to a set of old lime kilns that were used to make bricks at the turn of the century. A right fork off this trail takes you upstream to the waterfall.

If you want to go to the beach, don't think about beating a path from your cabin door. Lucia Bay is inaccessible from land because of its steep surrounding cliffs. But if you drive only a few miles north or south, you can access the public beaches of Los Padres National Forest. Most remarkable of these is Sand Dollar Beach to the south, and neighboring Jade Cove. One of the largest pieces of jade ever found was discovered there. Rockhounds are on the beach almost every day, trying to repeat the experience. These two beaches are not good for swimming, however, due to rip tides and extremely cold water.

Another great thing about Lucia is that it feels like, looks like, and is a part of Big Sur, but if you're coming from the south, you reach it 25 miles sooner than you reach Big Sur. On Highway 1's winding terms, that means you arrive at your vacation destination about an hour sooner than everybody heading to the main town.

Facilities, reservations, fees: There are 10 cabins at Lucia Lodge. None of the cabins have kitchens, but a restaurant is available. Reservations are recommended. Fees range from $85 to $150 per night. Pets are not permitted.

Special note: A national forest adventure pass is required for recreation in this area. See page 11 for details.

Who to contact: Lucia Lodge, Highway 1, Big Sur, CA 93920; (408) 667-2391.

Season: Open year-round.

Directions: From San Luis Obispo, drive north on U.S. 101 for 24 miles to the Highway 46 West exit near Templeton. Turn west on Highway 46 and drive 23 miles to Highway 1. Turn north on Highway 1 and drive 50 miles to Lucia Lodge on the left. (Plan on nearly two hours for those last 50 miles.)

56. GORDA SPRINGS COTTAGES
near Ventana Wilderness, off Highway 1 in Gorda

For most Southern Californians, the tiny coastside town of Gorda is far enough north that it seems like Northern California. It's not just Gorda's location (35 miles north of San Simeon), or the long drive on winding Highway 1 required to reach it. It's more that the place has a Northern California feel, like the kind of coastal town you might find in Mendocino County.

But luckily, Gorda is only a four-hour drive from Santa Barbara, or two hours from San Luis Obispo—perfect for a weekend getaway. If it's foggy, you can spend your days hiking in the inland forests. If it's sunny, you can spend your days at the beach. If neither of these activities suit your mood, you can just sit on your cabin's patio and stare at the miles of Pacific Ocean spread out before you.

Gorda Springs Cottages are located on the inland side of Highway 1, right behind the Whale Watchers Cafe and General Store. The store is the only commercial enterprise in Gorda, which means that Gorda is a place with no nightlife, no fanfare, and no noise. To all of this we say, "Hallelujah!" In place of the hubbub, you have the sound of the waves, plus beautiful wildflowers and ocean views. It's a fair trade.

You drive up a dirt driveway on the hill behind the general store, and head for one of six sweet little cabins. They vary in size from studios to two bedrooms; all have fully equipped kitchens and most have fireplaces. Flowers bloom all over the grounds, and you may be surprised to find that you have two llamas for neighbors. They like to be petted.

Most people spend their Gorda vacations at the various Los Padres National Forest public beaches in the area. Far and away the best strip of sand is Sand Dollar Beach; a short trail leads from the picnic area parking lot down to it. Sand Dollar has some of the most consistently beautiful waves on the central coast, which attract many surfers. Surf fishing is excellent here, but swimming is not recommended, due to rip tides.

If you somehow get your fill of beachcombing, whale watching, fishing, surfing, sunbathing, and observing the local elephant seals, you can turn your attentions inland and do a little hiking. At Gorda, you're in perfect position to access the nearby Ventana and Silver Peak wilderness trailheads. The Los Padres National Forest Pacific Valley Ranger Station is located 10 miles north of Gorda and can provide you with up-to-date trail information. Here are some tips to get you started: Five miles south of Gorda on Highway 1 is the start of the Soda Spring Trail; two miles further south is the start of the Salmon Creek Trail. In only a couple of miles of hiking on either trail you will see waterfalls, cascading streams, giant boulders, and big Douglas fir trees. If you choose to head north on Highway 1 instead, the Kirk Creek and Vicente Flat Trailhead can be found across from Kirk Creek Campground, six miles north of Gorda. Check out the views of the coast from the first couple miles of this path.

When you come to Gorda, make sure you bring all your vacation supplies with you, because although the general store is surprisingly well stocked with groceries, beer, and wine, they might not have your favorite brand. You can buy gas at the Gorda store, which has saved the butts of many Highway 1 travelers. If you want to do without kitchen chores while you're on vacation, Gorda's Whale Watchers Cafe serves wonderful meals three times a day.

Facilities, reservations, fees: There are six cabins at Gorda Springs, all with fully equipped kitchens. A restaurant, store, and gas are available. Reservations are recommended. Fees range from $125 to $300 per night, depending on the number of people and size of cottage. Pets are not permitted.

Special note: A national forest adventure pass is required for recreation in this area. See page 11 for details.

Who to contact: Gorda Springs Cottage Rentals, Box 1, Town of Gorda, Highway 1, Big Sur, CA 93920; (805) 927-4600.

Season: Open year-round.

Directions: From San Luis Obispo, drive north on U.S. 101 for 24 miles to the Highway 46 West exit near Templeton. Turn west on Highway 46 and drive 23 miles to Highway 1. Turn north on Highway 1 and drive 39 miles to Gorda. The cafe and cabins are on the right side of the road.

57. SPRUCE CREEK BACKPACK
Silver Peak Wilderness, off Highway 1 near Gorda

The Salmon Creek Trail is one of many paths leading into the Ventana and Silver Peak wildernesses. Like the others, it begins without fanfare on Highway 1. There's no big parking area, no easily spotted trail sign, and no hint or indication that this is the start of a path to outdoor heaven.

But if your pack is full of supplies, your water purifier is at the ready, and you know where to find the trailhead, you can take a spectacular short backpacking trip to Spruce Creek Camp on the Salmon Creek Trail. Along the way, you'll make a side-trip to Salmon Creek Falls, one of the most impressive waterfalls on the Big Sur coast, and hike through some spectacular wilderness scenery.

The waterfall is your first stop along the route, because it's only a few hundred yards from the highway. From the large parking pullout on the east side of the road, follow the Salmon Creek Trail from the south end of the guardrail. Immediately you'll see several cutoffs on the left; don't take the first one, which is right by an old wooden gate. Instead, walk up the Salmon Creek Trail for about five minutes. When you hear a waterfall loud and clear, take any of the left cutoffs and head down to the stream.

If you like, take off your pack and climb over the big boulders at the fall's base to get up high and obtain a good vantage point. Salmon Creek Falls drops more than 100 feet in a huge rush of water, with three big chutes plummeting down and joining at the bottom. A huge boulder is balanced at the top, separating the streams.

After admiring the falls, make your way back to the Salmon Creek Trail and continue hiking upstream. It's a moderate uphill climb to the junction with Spruce Creek Trail, gaining 900 feet in slightly less than two miles. The undergrowth is dense and lovely, but watch out for ubiquitous poison oak. (Wearing long pants is a good idea on this trail.) More pleasant foliage is also abundant: In the spring, you'll spot plenty of Douglas iris, shooting stars, and Indian paintbrush. In the first mile, you have good views ahead and to your left of Silver Peak, elevation 3,600 feet. On stretches of open slope, you also have lovely views of the ocean.

When you enter a dense Douglas fir grove and hear the sound of running water, you're about to arrive at the Spruce Creek Trail

Salmon Creek Falls, on the way to Spruce Creek

junction. Continue straight (and downhill) for a few hundred yards to Spruce Creek Camp, elevation 1,100 feet. It's conveniently located where Spruce Creek and Salmon Creek join forces, a mere two miles from where you left your car. There are two fire grills at the camp, and plenty of flat spaces for tents, but best of all are the dozens of clear pools under the shade of alders and maples. You'll be taking off your boots and soaking your feet in the sweet water in no time.

Facilities, reservations, fees: There are four campsites at Spruce Creek Camp. Water is available for filtering. A free campfire permit is required for overnight stays from May to November; they can be obtained at any Forest Service office. Supplies are available seven miles north in Gorda. Pets are permitted.

Special note: A national forest adventure pass is required for recreation in this area. See page 11 for details.

Who to contact: Los Padres National Forest, Monterey Ranger District, 406 South Mildred Avenue, King City, CA 93930; (408) 385-5434.

Maps for backpacking: For a map of Los Padres National Forest, send $4 to USDA-Forest Service, 630 Sansome Street, San Francisco, CA 94111. For a topographic map of the area, ask for Villa Creek from the USGS.

Season: Open year-round; beware of high water immediately following heavy rainfall.

Directions: From San Luis Obispo, drive north on U.S. 101 for 24 miles to the Highway 46 West exit near Templeton. Turn west on Highway 46 and drive 23 miles to Highway 1. Turn north on Highway 1 and drive 32 miles to the Salmon Creek Trailhead on the east side of the road, located at a hairpin turn. (It's exactly 7.6 miles south of Gorda.) Park in the large parking pullout along the road. The Salmon Creek Trail leads from the south end of the guardrail. (The distance from San Luis Obispo is approximately 65 miles; allow two hours of driving time.)

58. LAKE SAN ANTONIO
SOUTH SHORE RESORT CABINS
Lake San Antonio, off U.S. 101 near Paso Robles

It's a rare Southern California reservoir that offers more than just waterskiing, bass fishing, and power boating, but Lake San Antonio provides more. Located in the Central Coast grasslands east of San Simeon and west of U.S. 101, Lake San Antonio has 5,700 surface acres of water—enough to keep water recreationists busy all summer long. But the lake is also a major winter habitat for eagles, both bald and golden, and Eagle Watch boat tours are an excellent reason to come to Lake San Antonio in January or February.

Whatever the season, start your trip by booking a cabin rental at the lake's South Shore Resort. The South Shore is a busy place with a restaurant, grocery store, gas station, and marina—pretty much everything you might need or want. They rent one, two, and three bedroom cabins with fully stocked kitchens and great views of the lake. Don't expect log cabins, or even old, rustic-looking cabins; these are more in the line of aluminum-sided mobile homes, but they serve their purpose. The rental options are numerous: You can choose from the North Shore or South Shore, smoking or non-smoking, lake view or no lake view, and so on. If you want to save a few bucks, you can rent a self-contained RV instead of a cabin, and bring your own cooking utensils and linens.

The water sport offerings at Lake San Antonio are plentiful, including all the usual boating activities as well as fishing for striped bass, catfish, crappie, bass, and bluegill. You don't have your own boat? No problem; you can rent boats, motors, jet skis, waterskiing equipment, and fishing tackle at the South Shore Marina. Take note: San Antonio is far and away the most popular waterskiing lake on the Central Coast. If you like to take things slow, you can rent a kayak or paddle boat and just cruise around in the coves.

If eagle-watching strikes your fancy, plan your stay for a weekend in late December to early March. On Fridays, Saturdays,

the Monterey County Parks Department offers Eagle
aboard the *Eagle One*, a 56-foot tour boat. On Sundays,
a few bucks extra and have Sunday brunch aboard the
Eagle O.. vhile you scan the skies for big birds. Call (800) 310-2313
for reservations.

Mountain biking and hiking are also possible activities, but
save these for winter and spring when the temperatures are cooler.
Summertime bakes out here in the foothills, although nobody
cruising around the lake seems to mind much.

Facilities, reservations, fees: There are 16 cabins at Lake San Antonio
Resort, ranging in size from one bedroom to three bedrooms. There are
also 12 RV rentals, and hundreds of campsites for tents and RVs.
Reservations are recommended. Fees range from $55 to $195 per night;
rates are reduced from October to March. Pets are not permitted.

Who to contact: Lake San Antonio Resort, Star Route, Box 2620,
Bradley, CA 93426; (800) 310-2313 or (805) 472-2313.

Season: Open year-round; best in winter and spring for wildlife and
wildflowers, and best in summer for boating. Eagle tours run from late
December to March.

Directions: From San Luis Obispo on U.S. 101, drive north for 27 miles
to the Highway 46/Fresno/Bakersfield exit. Take that exit, then cross
over the freeway and drive west on Road G14, which becomes
Nacimiento Lake Drive. Stay on Nacimiento Lake Drive for 19 miles,
crossing over the dam at Nacimiento Lake, then bear left on Interlake
Road. Drive nine miles on Interlake Road, then turn right at the sign
for South Shore/Lake San Antonio. Follow the signs to the resort
headquarters.

---

59. CAMBRIA PINES LODGE
near San Simeon State Beach, off Highway 1 in Cambria

I had never camped in the company of peacocks before, but
then again, the cottages at Cambria Pines Lodge are a far cry from
traditional camping. After one night, I found myself getting well
accustomed to both the peacocks and the cottages' luxury.

Cambria Pines Lodge is a large resort and conference center in
the artsy, coastside town of Cambria, not far from Hearst Castle and
San Simeon. Most people know Cambria for golf, shopping, and art
galleries, or as a place to have lunch after touring William Randolph

Hearst's mega-mansion. But outdoor lovers will also find plenty to do in Cambria.

For starters, there's San Simeon State Beach, which you can reach via a five-minute drive north from your cottage. Visitors go there for hiking, beachcombing, or whale watching; the latter is best from late November to January when the whales migrate south. (In the spring when the whales return, they are usually further off shore, and harder to see.) Tidepooling can be excellent at the state beach, especially during winter minus tides.

The closest and best beach access from Cambria Pines Lodge is via Moonstone Beach Drive, which connects to Highway 1 at both of its ends. Take one Moonstone Beach turnoff or the next, then park your car at the Leffingwell Landing parking lot.

Or, if you prefer to get some exercise, you can walk to the beach. The Cambria Pines Lodge has a "trailhead" located alongside unit number 810. A long set of stairs gets your heart rate up on the first portion of the route, then you turn right on Burton Drive, left on Main Street, and cross Highway 1 to Windsor Street and the beach. It's a nice way to explore the village and gain access to the ocean at the same time.

Moonstone Beach, San Simeon State Beach

Once you reach the sand, you can try your hand at surf fishing. Barred surf perch can be caught in December and January, and walleye surf perch are available in any season. Other possibilities include corbina, spotfin, and yellowfin, especially toward late summer. For larger fish, head out on a commercial boat to catch kelp bass, Pacific mackerel and California halibut. Pier fishing is also possible off Hearst Memorial State Beach.

If you'd like to do some sightseeing, an interesting side trip is to drive north on Highway 1 for 10 miles (past San Simeon) to visit the historic lighthouse at Piedras Blancas. You can see its original Fresnel lens on display in the town of Cambria.

The cottages at Cambria Pines are duplexes, and sadly, they lack any kitchen facilities. However, they do have king-sized beds and fireplaces, and are located a few steps away from an enclosed indoor pool. For duplexes, they are surprisingly quiet and private. Many other accommodations are also available at the resort, including townhouse-style units and motel rooms. The lodge is set in 25 acres of Monterey pines, with lovely gardens and landscaping, plus those perky resident peacocks strutting their stuff.

In many places, having a cottage without a kitchen can be a real inconvenience, but I never missed it at Cambria Pines. Breakfast is included in the room rate; it's a huge restaurant buffet with pancakes, eggs, potatoes, granola, orange juice, and coffee. It's guaranteed you won't go hungry in the morning. For other meals, you can choose from a wide variety of restaurants in the town of Cambria, or eat at the lodge's restaurant.

Facilities, reservations, fees: There are 10 cottages at Cambria Pines Lodge, plus numerous townhouse-style accommodations. Reservations are recommended. Fees range from $65 to $115 per night, which includes breakfast. A restaurant is available for lunch and dinner. Pets are not permitted.

Who to contact: Cambria Pines Lodge, 2905 Burton Drive, Cambria, CA 93428; (800) 445-6868 or (805) 927-4200. Fax (805) 927-4016.

Season: Open year-round.

Directions: From San Luis Obispo at U.S. 101, take the Highway 1 exit and drive north through Morro Bay for 33 miles to Cambria. Just north of the downtown Cambria exit, take the Burton Drive exit east. Drive a quarter-mile and Cambria Pines Lodge is on your left.

60. CAYUCOS VACATION RENTALS
Cayucos State Beach, off Highway 1 near Morro Bay

The little town of Cayucos is quintessential Central California Coast, and that's why we like it so much. Located 13 miles south of Cambria, and 10 miles north of Morro Bay, Cayucos is a sleepy coastal town that hasn't been developed the way many other coastal towns have been. All recreation revolves around the ocean—surfing, beachcombing, windsurfing, swimming, kayaking, and fishing—which seems exactly the way it should be.

Two companies rent private homes in Cayucos for vacation rentals. All of the rentals are fully furnished, including linens, so all you need to bring is your clothes. There are enough grocery stores, shops, and restaurants in town so that you can get almost anything you want.

We were surprised at how many vacation homes are available with ocean views. It seems like almost everyone has one in Cayucos. But your ocean view can be from the inland side of Highway 1 or the coastal side; we recommend that you rent a house on the coastal side, so you have ready beach access without having to cross the highway. If you're going to have a beach vacation, you might as well be on oceanfront property. "Near-oceanfront" just isn't the same thing.

Most visitors rent a place in Cayucos for a few days; rates are discounted according to the number of nights you reserve. In summer, many places have a week-long minimum stay, because they are usually rented out to families taking a week's vacation.

Two state beaches in Cayucos provide long stretches of sand for all beach activities—Cayucos State Beach and Morro Strand State Beach. Besides the beach, Cayucos' premier attraction is its historic pier, which was built in 1875, and incredibly, still stands. Anglers can fish without a license from the pier, although most people just stroll along it instead, enjoying the views and the seagulls. The pier is wheelchair-accessible, and lit for night fishing.

If you feel like taking a little side trip, Morro Bay State Park is only a short drive away. You can visit its blue heron rookery natural preserve, or hike on one of the nine dome-shaped, volcanic hills or "morros" in the area (but not Morro Rock itself). You can even rent a kayak and paddle around Morro Bay. If you've never been there, another great side trip is a tour of Hearst Castle, only 20 miles to the north. Whatever else you want to say about it, it's a fascinating place.

Truthfully, all you need to know about Cayucos is the way they advertise themselves: "If you like life in the fast lane; if you like gourmet restaurants and elegant hotels, Cayucos is not for you!" Well, thanks for telling us. But we do like quiet seaside towns with long sandy beaches, so we'll be making a trip to Cayucos again soon.

Facilities, reservations, fees: There are 50-plus private homes for rent at Cayucos Vacation Rentals and Beachside Rentals. Reservations are required. Fees range from $75 to $175 per night; in summer, a week-long minimum stay is usually required. Pets are permitted in some rentals with prior approval.

Who to contact: Cayucos Vacation Rentals, 177 North Ocean Avenue, Cayucos, CA 93430; (805) 995-2322 or (800) 995-2322. Or contact Beachside Rentals, 149 Cayucos Drive, Cayucos, CA 93430; (805) 995-3680 or (800) 995-3680.

Season: Open year-round.

Directions: From San Luis Obispo at U.S. 101, take the Highway 1 exit and drive north through Morro Bay for 18 miles to Cayucos. You will need to stop at the rental office for Cayucos Vacation Rentals or Beachside Rentals; they will give you a key and directions to your vacation rental.

61. MONTANA DE ORO BACKPACK
Montana de Oro State Park, off U.S. 101 near San Luis Obispo

Every time we come here, we wonder the same thing: How can a state park this good be free of charge? We can't figure it out, but we're glad it is. Day-use at the park costs absolutely nothing, and camping is a mere seven bucks in winter, nine dollars in summer.

But instead of staying in the rather dull 50-site car campground located behind the park visitor center, spend your seven or nine bucks on a more precious experience: an easy backpacking trip to one of the park's environmental camps. There are four secluded environmental sites at the park, each requiring a hike of a half-mile to two miles one-way. They are Hazard Grove Camp and Bloody Nose Camp, located in a eucalyptus grove near some park residences, and Badger Flat and Deer Flat, located on high bluffs overlooking the ocean. Forget the first two and head right for one of the best camps: Badger Flat or Deer Flat.

What's so good about Montana de Oro State Park? Three main items: Flowers, ocean, and hiking trails. The park's name means "mountain of gold," and they aren't talking about the expensive mineral, they're talking about yellow flowers. Somewhere between February and May each year, the blooming season occurs, and the coastal park lights up with poppies, buttercups, tidytips, mustard, and all their colorful friends. This would be spectacular enough on its own, but it's made even better by that fact that the flowers grow on top of the rugged headlands that line the park's beaches. The coast is

Coastal bluffs, Montana de Oro State Park

still wild here at Montana de Oro, and a walk along its blufftops reveals steep dropoffs, rocky offshore outcrops, and colonies of sea lions.

Then there are the hiking trails. The first ones you will get acquainted with are the ones that will lead you to your chosen environmental camp. Both Badger Flat and Deer Flat are located on top of coastal bluffs, so it's an uphill walk from the park road to reach them. For Deer Flat Camp, park your car at the end of the park road, 1.5 miles past park headquarters, at the Coon Creek Trailhead. Then walk back up the park road for less than a quarter-mile, and look for a gated dirt road on your right. Hike up the dirt road to the top of the bluff (it should only take about 15 minutes), and you'll see a little outhouse, picnic table, garbage can, and a couple flat spots for tents. You won't share this site with strangers; it's all yours, and you can have as many as eight people in your party. You are surrounded by coastal scrub that is just high enough to keep some of the wind off you, but not high enough to block the incredible views of the ocean. In spring, look for blooming Indian paintbrush, monkeyflower, hooker's onions, and yellow violets.

For Badger Flat Camp, park your car in the small parking area on the east side of the road, three-quarters of a mile past park head-quarters. From there, hike up the dirt road (signed as Badger Trail). Just before the intersection with Rattlesnake Flats Trail, you'll see the camp. It has the same amenities as Deer Flat Camp, but it's less protected by brush. A small eucalyptus grove nearby provides a place you could go for wind protection, if necessary.

You can bring your camp stove with you for cooking, but no campfires are permitted. Barbecue grills are located at Spooner's Cove. Be sure to pack in plenty of water; you can get mighty thirsty looking at the ocean all day. And keep your food in your tent at night; raccoons and coyotes may show up for snacks if you don't.

Another option on the long days of summer is to have an early dinner at one of the restaurants in Los Osos or San Luis Obispo, drive over to the park, hike up the cliff, and set up camp just in time to watch the sun set around eight o'clock. Wow—the perfect date. Then wake up at dawn and check out the ocean. What, you left your binoculars in the car? No big deal, hike back down and get them. Now this is easy camping.

While you're in the park, be sure to hike the Bluffs Trail, for a great view of the park's eroded marine terraces and its offshore sea stack, Grotto Rock. The flat trail contours along the top of Montana de Oro's shale and sediment bluffs, with nonstop views of colorful rock cliffs and the big blue Pacific. If you're hankering to get down to the water's edge, head for the lovely beach at Spooner's Cove, right across from the visitor center turnoff.

If you like to climb, head for Valencia Peak, the tallest summit in the park. With a cool ocean breeze keeping you comfortable, this aerobic hike is a spectacular day-trip. If you forget to carry water, or if you hike in the heat of high noon, it can be rather unpleasant. Park near Spooner's Cove and head uphill on the inland side of the park. In two miles and with an 1,100-foot elevation gain, you arrive at the top of Valencia Peak, elevation 1,347 feet. On a clear day you can see from Point Sal in the south to Piedras Blancas in the north. Hope you brought a few sandwiches or a good book; you'll want to stay a while.

Facilities, reservations, fees: There are four hike-in campsites at Montana de Oro State Park; each site can accommodate eight people. No water is available; you must pack in bottled water. Campfires are not permitted; bring a backpacking stove. Reservations are recommended; phone Parknet at (800) 444-7275. Fees range from $7 to $9 per night. Pets are not permitted.

Who to contact: Montana de Oro State Park, Los Osos, CA 93402; (805) 528-0513 or Morro Bay State Park at (805) 772-7434. Or San Luis Obispo Coast State Parks at (805) 549-3312.

Maps for backpacking: A map of Montana de Oro State Park is available for $1 at the visitor center. For a topographic map of the area, ask for Morro Bay South from the USGS.

Season: Open year-round.

Directions: From U.S. 101 in San Luis Obispo, take the Los Osos exit and head west on Los Osos Valley Road. Drive 12 miles on Los Osos Valley Road to the Montana de Oro State Park entrance.

62. SANTA MARGARITA LAKE KOA CABINS
near Santa Margarita Lake, off Highway 58 near San Luis Obispo

I admit it: The first time I stayed in a KOA cabin, I felt a little funny. The cute little log cabins with their front-porch swings looked a lot like kids' playhouses, and there I was, trying to act like a serious outdoor writer.

Well, two nights in the cabins at KOA Santa Margarita Lake turned me into a believer. On the night it rained, I was warm and dry in my cabin with electric heat and lights. After a whole day of exploring around Santa Margarita Lake and the Santa Lucia Wilderness, I drove home to a hot shower at the KOA, clean clothes, and a barbecue dinner outside my cabin. It beat the heck out of eating freeze-dried lasagna and wearing dirty socks.

KOA Santa Margarita Lake is located only one mile from the lake, where you can rent boats, fish, and hike. In fact you can do anything at the lake except touch the water, which means no swimming, windsurfing, or waterskiing. Most people don't complain about the rules, however, because the reason they come here is to fish. Rainbow trout are stocked in winter and spring, and bass fishing is good in the summer. The lake is large—nearly 800 acres—and although it is set at a low elevation in the foothill country, it is prettier than other nearby lakes like San Antonio and Nacimiento. Tall, rocky crags form a backdrop behind the lake, giving you something to look at in a place that is otherwise as flat as a pancake.

There are six cabins at the KOA, partially shaded by canyon oaks. Each one has its own barbecue grill and picnic table out front. The camp has a small store where you can buy basic groceries and supplies. The Rinconada Store is a mile down the road, where you can buy tackle and bait.

If hiking's your bag, not fishing, an overnight stay at the KOA cabins puts you in a good position for exploring around. Take a drive

Santa Margarita Lake

down U.S. 101 to Arroyo Grande and then head east to Lopez Lake, where you can access the trails at Lopez Lake Recreation Area. The best of these are the Duna Vista and Two Waters trails. (Wildflowers are gorgeous along the lake in springtime.) Or drive beyond Lopez Lake and into the backcountry to reach the Santa Lucia Wilderness trailheads along Lopez Creek, including those leading to popular Big Falls and Little Falls. The Santa Lucia Ranger District in Santa Maria can provide you with trail information and maps.

Facilities, reservations, fees: There are six cabins at Santa Margarita KOA, plus 54 campsites for tents or RVs. Restrooms and showers are located nearby. Reservations are recommended. Cabin fees are $30 per night. Pets are permitted.

Who to contact: Santa Margarita/San Luis Obispo KOA, 4765 Santa Margarita Lake Road, Santa Margarita, CA 93453; (800) KOA-5619 or (805) 438-5618.

Season: Open year-round.

Directions: From San Luis Obispo, drive eight miles north on U.S. 101 to the Highway 58/Santa Margarita exit. Drive through the town of Santa Margarita, staying on Highway 58. Turn right and follow the signs for Santa Margarita Lake. After eight miles, you will see the KOA on the right, located one mile before you reach the lake.

63. CLAM DIGGER COTTAGES
by Pismo Pier, off U.S. 101 in Pismo Beach

There are a few places left on the California coast that haven't been turned into condominiums or chain hotels, and Clam Digger Cottages is one of them. Located in the central coast town of Pismo Beach, the Clam Digger is the perfect place to wake up to the sound of the ocean, play at the beach all day, and then return home to a barbecue on the back deck of your cottage.

The watery adventures possible in Pismo Beach are unlimited, including fishing, swimming, surfing, and just exploring the coastline. Although the town has suffered from some urbanization in the past few decades, there's still some of the old Pismo Beach left, including a long fishing pier and wide, sandy beaches. Bustling seafood restaurants and coffee shops neighbor the surf shops and fishing tackle stores, but they don't outnumber them. One surf shop is located right next to the Clam Digger; it rents surfboards, wetsuits, boogie boards, and bicycles. That should be enough to keep you busy.

All of the Clam Digger Cottages come with a serviceable kitchenette, including the basic dishes and utensils you'll need for cooking. Ours even had a coffeemaker. The weatherbeaten cottage buildings are lined up in two rows and spaced pretty close together, so don't expect a lot of privacy. Make sure you pay the few extra bucks for a cottage that is closest to the ocean—that way you can walk out of your back door first thing in the morning and go for a swim in the sea. We recommend the cottages numbered 3, 5, 7, and 20. (Numbers 1 and 2 are beachfront also, but they are on the end of a row on a side street, so they can be a little noisy.)

All of the cottages have heaters for foggy days and cool nights, which are not uncommon on the central coast. On sunny days, you'll probably use the barbecue, table, and chairs on your back deck. The rooms come equipped with televisions, which you can ignore. The only telephone is the pay phone at the motel office.

Even if you don't fish, be sure to take a walk along the 1,250-foot Pismo Pier. If you are lucky enough to time your visit for an evening with a full moon and clear skies, you can see one of the world's greatest sights—moonshine on ocean waves. I suppose it doesn't look like this every night in Pismo Beach, but it made my trip unforgettable.

Anglers can drop a line in the ocean off the edge of the pier. You might even get lucky and snag a passing halibut, but what you're most likely to catch are rockfish. And although it ain't what it used to be, you can still dig for clams in Pismo Beach. The 1990s have seen a resurgence in the clam population along the area's beaches. Don't forget your clamming shovel, and your California fishing license, of course.

Facilities, reservations, fees: There are 12 cottages at Clam Digger, all with fully equipped kitchens. Reservations are recommended. Fees range from $50 to $150 per night. Pets are permitted.

Who to contact: Clam Digger Cottages, 150 Hinds, Pismo Beach, CA 93449; (805) 773-4626.

Season: Open year-round.

Directions: From U.S. 101 in Santa Maria, drive north for 17 miles to Pismo Beach. Take the Price Street exit, drive west, then turn left on Pomeroy Street. Follow Pomeroy toward the ocean until you see the large public parking lot. Drive through the parking lot to Clam Digger Cottages.

Western Sierra

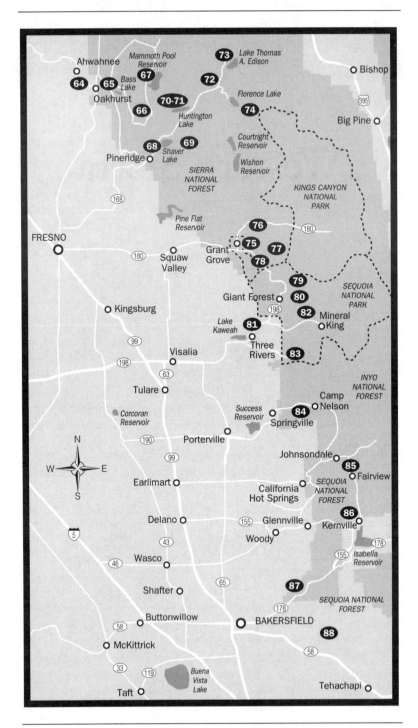

Western Sierra—map page 160

64. THE HOMESTEAD
near Sierra National Forest, off Highway 49 in Ahwahnee

Cindy Brooks and Larry Ends are the perfect kind of people to run a resort for outdoor enthusiasts, because they are outdoor lovers themselves. In 1992, they left their desk jobs and big-city life in Los Angeles and moved to Ahwahnee to open The Homestead, an equestrian-oriented resort on 160 acres. Why? Just because they love horses, and they love breathing country air.

The Homestead is not just for the horsey set, however. My hiking partner and I stayed in the cabins at The Homestead, and neither of us knows a saddle horn from a pair of saddle shoes. Cindy and Larry made us feel right at home, and set us up with plenty of hiking, mountain biking, fishing, and touring information so that we could plan the kind of trip we enjoy. With Sierra National Forest, Bass Lake, and southern Yosemite close by, there are plenty of activities to choose from.

If horses are your thing, and you like to travel with yours, you'll be all set at The Homestead. In addition to its four cabins, The Homestead also has a corral where your horse can go on vacation. We stayed in the cabin located next to the corral and above the barn. In the morning, we awoke to the soft whinnying of horses, a sound that qualifies as some of the sweetest music in the world.

Cindy and Larry will provide you with information on all the local horseback riding trails; they ride regularly and make it a point to have updated trail information.

All units at The Homestead are completely separate cabins, newly built and beautifully appointed. Each cabin, including the above-the-barn unit, has a fully equipped kitchen and a fireplace for cool nights. The cabins also have air-conditioning, which can be a real bonus in the summer at this 2,000-foot elevation.

A great place to start your exploration of the area is on the Sierra Vista National Scenic Byway, a fabulous driving loop that begins by Bass Lake on Beasore Road. Recreational opportunities at Bass Lake mostly involve boating, waterskiing, and fishing at the low-elevation reservoir. But as you drive the Scenic Byway, you'll ascend to as high as 7,300 feet, to a land of big conifers, imposing granite domes, and wide-angle vistas of the Sierra Crest and surrounding wilderness areas.

Another option is to head a few miles north on Highway 41 to Sky Ranch Road, from which you can access the Nelder Grove of Giant Sequoias and the lovely Shadow of the Giants National Recreation Trail, or the short and scenic trail to the top of Fresno Dome (wow, what a view). If you continue past Sky Ranch Road on Highway 41, you reach a trailhead for the Lewis Creek Trail (great wildflowers and two small, pretty waterfalls). Or head further north to Fish Camp and the Yosemite Mountain Sugar Pine Historical Railroad, and relive history with a ride on the narrow-gauge steam trains. A few miles beyond Fish Camp is the southern entrance to Yosemite National Park, which is filled with many more possible excursions...

Needless to say, there's a lot to do. Let Larry and Cindy at The Homestead provide you with maps and brochures, then get out there and get busy.

Facilities, reservations, fees: There are four cabins at The Homestead, all with fully equipped kitchens and fireplaces. A horse corral is available for visitors traveling with horses. Reservations are recommended. Fees are $125 per night; two-night minimum on weekends. Pets are not permitted.

Who to contact: The Homestead, 41110 Road 600, Ahwahnee, CA 93601; (209) 683-0495. Fax (209) 683-8165.

Season: Open year-round.

Directions: From Fresno, drive north on Highway 41 for 45 miles to Oakhurst. Turn northwest on Highway 49 and drive five miles to Ahwahnee. Turn left on Road 600 and drive 2.5 miles to The Homestead, on the right side of the road.

65. THE FORKS RESORT
Bass Lake, off Highway 41 near Oakhurst

Bass Lake may not be for everybody, but it's definitely for anybody who likes boating or fishing. The lake is situated at 3,500 feet in elevation in Sierra National Forest, and if that makes you think of warm summer days and waterskiing, you're thinking right.

Bass Lake is only 14 miles from the southern entrance to Yosemite National Park, but the folks who come here usually don't head for Yosemite. Instead, they while away their days on the big, pretty lake, which covers more than 1,000 acres when it is full.

Hiker on top of Fresno Dome near Bass Lake and Oakhurst

Usually it doesn't start looking empty (or ugly) until autumn. Water-skiing is the main attraction, but jet skiers, anglers, and swimmers also share the waters. The lake is so big that there seems to be room for everybody, even though the place is extremely popular on summer weekends.

Bass Lake has so much development around its edges that it can seem like a small city. There are numerous campgrounds, restaurants, and resorts, plus plenty of places to rent boats (fishing boats, canoes, patio boats, Waverunners, you name it) and buy fishing equipment if you didn't bring your own. The fishing is good, but not that great for bass, as you might expect. Instead, trout fishing is popular in winter and spring, with the Department of Fish and Game dropping in heavy plants of rainbows. In summer, people catch a little bit of everything: catfish, bluegill, bass, crappie, and occasionally trout.

There are numerous places where you can stay at the lake, but my favorite is The Forks Resort. It has cabins of varying sizes, a good general store, its own dock with fishing boat rentals, and a cafe that is the kind of place where the waitresses are all named Thelma. Okay, I'm making that part up, but the cafe looks like it's right out of the 1950s, and is "the home of the world-famous Forks Burger." I can't vouch for the burgers, but I can tell you that the milk shakes are out of this world.

The cabins at The Forks Resort are unremarkable, but they make the perfect base camp for a Bass Lake vacation. Each has a fully equipped kitchen, plus a porch with a barbecue grill, so you can cook up all those fish you catch. The one-bedroom cabins have two double beds, so you can squeeze in four people if you want, but they'll be more comfortable in a "one-bedroom suite" cabin, which has an extra room. The two-bedroom cabins can accommodate as many as six people. If you can afford it, get a "two-bedroom suite" cabin, because in addition to extra space, you also get a fireplace. Also, make sure you request a cabin with a lake view.

Facilities, reservations, fees: There are 20 cabins at The Forks Resort, ranging in size from one to two bedrooms and with fully equipped kitchens. Deluxe two-bedroom cabins are available which can accommodate as many as six people. Reservations are recommended. Fees range from $70 to $115 per night. Pets are permitted; $25 fee per stay.

Who to contact: The Forks Resort, 39150 Road 222, Bass Lake, CA 93604; (209) 642-3737.

Season: Open from late March to early October.

Directions: From Fresno, drive north on Highway 41 for 45 miles to Oakhurst, then turn east (right) on Road 426. Drive seven miles on Road 426, then turn left at the sign for Bass Lake. Drive one mile; The Forks Resort will be on your left.

---

66. BONNIE B RANCH
Sierra National Forest, off Highway 41 near Oakhurst

A lot of people hold a private fantasy about owning their own ranch... The kind of place that has a few horses grazing on the grounds, a main ranch house with extra bedrooms where your friends can stay, and maybe even a few fishing ponds sprinkled around the property.

You can daydream about having a place like this, or you can rent Bonnie B Ranch for a week and make it real. I've tried it both ways, and I can testify that the latter choice is far more satisfying.

Here's what you need to do: Gather up a group of five to eight people, including yourself. You can invite your family, your friends, or what the heck, even your boss (if you want to score some points). Tell them to pack up their fishing gear, outdoor clothes, and a week's worth of groceries. Then head to the town of North Fork, just southeast of Oakhurst and Bass Lake in Sierra National Forest, and get started on your private ranch vacation.

The reason you need a few folks to stay at Bonnie B Ranch is because you're paying to rent the entire three-bedroom ranch house, and all of the 440 acres surrounding it. That doesn't come cheap, but then again you aren't just renting a motel room or even a little cabin. Current rates at the ranch are $350 per night or $2,300 per week. At the weekly rate, a group of six people will pay about $55 each per night. For that price, they get lodging in a beautiful 3,000-square-foot ranch house, plus all the horseback riding and fishing for big bass they can stand. After we visited, I realized I had paid a lot more at plenty of other places and gotten a lot less.

Fishing is one of the highlights at Bonnie B Ranch. The ranch has five small lakes which are loaded with hand-raised bass, including some bigger than 10 pounds, and plenty of bluegill and crappie. The largest of the lakes can be fished by float tube or pram (bring your own); the rest are best suited for shorefishing.

Hikers and equestrians can choose from 16 miles of trails that have been built on the property. Spring wildflowers are breathtaking, maple and oak trees bring autumn colors, and winter snow makes the property a white wonderland. The ranch is available for rent year-round; my first choice would be spring, but all seasons are excellent.

In case you are wondering if you'll be staying in a run-down barn, here are some details on the ranch house: It's a three-bedroom, three-bath home perched on a hill, with a large living area and giant picture windows that look out over the grounds to the mountains beyond. From your living room, you can gaze at Home Lake, the largest of the ranch's ponds, or the horses grazing in the pasture below the house, or far off to the high mountains of the Sierra. In fact, the ranch house's panoramic view and big fireplace are so enchanting that it may be hard for you to leave the premises.

The ranch dates back to 1891. On the property you will find a covered bridge, historic gristmill, and plenty of stone work. Throughout its history it has been operated as a cattle ranch and a dude ranch, but most recently it has been owned and operated as a guest ranch by the local Bryant family. The Bryants keep a staff person on the premises to keep everything running smoothly.

It's unlikely you'll want to leave Bonnie B Ranch during your stay, but if you feel like taking a drive, you're situated right by the Sierra Vista Scenic Byway. Bass Lake is also close by, and southern Yosemite is a 40-minute drive.

Facilities, reservations, fees: There is a three-bedroom, three-bath ranch house with a fully equipped kitchen at Bonnie B Ranch, suitable for up to eight people. Reservations are required. Fees range from $350 per night to $2,300 per week, and include horseback riding and fishing in five private ponds. A $150 cleaning fee is charged (non-refundable), and a refundable $400 security deposit is required. Pets are not permitted.

Who to contact: Kerry Bryant, Bryant Farms/Bonnie B Ranch, 323 26th Street, Manhattan Beach, CA 90266; (310) 546-3792.

Season: Open year-round.

Directions: From Fresno, drive north on Highway 41 for 25 miles to Road 200 (North Fork Road) and turn right. Drive northeast on Road 200 for 17 miles, past the turnoff for Road 221, to the left turnoff at Bonnie B Road. (If you reach the town of North Fork, you've gone too far.) Turn left on Bonnie B Road and enter the ranch.

67. WAGNER'S MAMMOTH POOL RESORT
Mammoth Pool Reservoir, off Highway 41 near Oakhurst

I'd like to stay at the cabins at Wagner's Mammoth Pool Resort, near Mammoth Pool Reservoir. Heaven knows I've tried, but somehow the odds are always against me.

The first time I set out for Wagner's, my car broke down along the way and I never made it. The next time my car worked fine, but an early-season snowstorm hit and CalTrans closed the road. The following year I planned a trip to the area for Memorial Day weekend, but then I learned that the reservoir is closed each year from May 1 to June 16. Why? So migrating deer can swim across the lake. No kidding.

So I've never stayed at Wagner's Resort, although everybody tells me that their cabins are comfortable, their fishing advice is honest, and even their grocery store is well-stocked. In fact, it's the only place around for miles where you can get ice cream, which is a big deal around here on a summer day. The resort's owners are ranchers from way back, and nice people too; they can tell you everything there is to know about the history of the area. Apparently before the dam was built and Mammoth Pool Reservoir was created, a small town stood on the resort grounds, complete with a school and post office. The buildings are long gone, but the Wagners keep the town's stories alive.

Wagner's Resort is less than two miles from the shore of Mammoth Pool Reservoir, a five-mile-long lake created by a dam on the San Joaquin River. That's what makes the resort popular with visitors all summer—quick and easy access to all the fishing and boating activities you want.

Although the reservoir's elevation is only 3,300 feet, the scenery makes it seem higher. Mammoth Pool has steep walls that rise 2,000 feet above the water surface, and it is surrounded by a mixed

Whiskey Falls, near Mammoth Pool Reservoir

forest of Ponderosa pine, incense cedar, oaks, and chaparral. Imagine something like Hetch Hetchy Reservoir in Yosemite and you've got the basic idea.

Mammoth Pool Reservoir is perfect for outdoor recreation. The trout fishing season begins in April each year and runs till autumn, except for the weird deer-swimming closure each year in May and early June. The majority of vacationers usually don't show up until late June; then the water is shared by anglers, swimmers, waterskiers, and jet skiers. By late summer, the lake level can be drawn down substantially, which turns a pretty lake into an ugly lake. Make sure you check on the water level before you plan your trip.

Hikers can also find something good at Mammoth Pool Reservoir, at least in the early season before the summer temperatures start to bake. Skirting the west side of the reservoir, you'll find a section of the historic French Trail, which runs 75 miles from Redinger Lake near North Fork to south of Devils Postpile National Monument. The trailhead is at Logan Meadow, just past Wagner's Resort. Along the route, you get wide open views of the lake interspersed with shady conifer forest.

And remember this: If while you're hiking along the shoreline, you happen to see a deer swimming in the lake... well, you don't need to get your head examined. It can happen here.

Facilities, reservations, fees: There are 10 cabins at Wagner's Mammoth Pool Resort. A general store and RV/tent camping are available. Reservations are recommended. Fees range from $50 to $85 per night. Pets are permitted with prior approval.

Who to contact: Wagner's Mammoth Pool Resort, (209) 841-3736. (Their phone does not operate from late October to April 1.) Or Sierra National Forest, Minarets Ranger District, P.O. Box 10, North Fork, CA 93643; (209) 877-2218.

Season: Open from April to October, depending on snow conditions.

Directions: From Fresno, drive north on Highway 41 for 25 miles to Road 200 (North Fork Road) and turn right. Drive northeast on Road 200 for 18 miles to North Fork. Turn left on Road 222, then left again on Road 274 and drive approximately eight miles. On the northern shore of Bass Lake, turn right on Beasore Road. Follow Beasore Road for 17 miles to the Grizzly Road turnoff on the right, located at Jones Store. Turn right on Grizzly Road, drive 12 miles to its end at Minarets Road, then turn left on Minarets Road. Drive three miles and turn right on Mammoth Pool Road. Follow Mammoth Pool Road for three miles to Wagner's Mammoth Pool Resort.

68. SHAVER LAKE LODGE CABINS
Shaver Lake, off Highway 168 near Fresno

People who have never been to Shaver and Huntington lakes tend to think of them as being a package deal. They're both big reservoirs, both owned by Southern California Edison, and both are popular for fishing and boating. They're also located just 20 miles apart on Highway 168 in the southern Sierra. But let's get one thing straight: Those who vacation at Shaver Lake and those who vacation at Huntington Lake are unlikely to belong to the same club. That's because Shaver Lake is known for fast boats and waterskiing, and Huntington Lake is known for sailing.

There are other, lesser known differences between the lakes. Shaver Lake is sometimes drawn down by the end of the summer, while Huntington Lake rarely is. Shaver is smaller than Huntington, but the fishing is more reliable, especially in its sheltered coves. Shaver

Lake is set at 5,500 feet in elevation, while Huntington is nearly 2,000 feet higher, so Shaver is a bit warmer for swimming and water sports.

Whereas Huntington Lake is surrounded by private homes, resorts, and campgrounds, Shaver Lake has much less development along its edges. In fact, other than two Forest Service campgrounds, the only place you can spend the night at Shaver Lake is in the cabins at Shaver Lake Lodge.

When you call to make your reservation, be sure to ask for a cabin numbered between 5 and 15, preferably numbers 7, 8, 9, 11, 12, 13, and 14. These are the cabins with the lake views. Without a lake view, what's the point? Some of the higher numbered cabins are clustered too close together on the hillside, and only offer views of the other cabins. (Cabins number 5 and 6 are duplexes, so sign up for those only if you trust you'll have good neighbors. All the rest are single units; cabin number 9 is our absolute favorite.)

If you plan on setting up housekeeping, be forewarned that the cabins do not have kitchens. You get a small refrigerator and a microwave, but that's all; it's just enough to make your oatmeal and coffee in the morning. The cabins are not equipped with dishes or utensils; bring your own from home.

About half of the cabins have televisions, so if you have an opinion about that one way or another, make sure you mention it when you reserve. The only telephone is the pay phone at the lodge—thank goodness.

Keep in mind that even the lakefront cabins aren't exactly lakefront—a road separates them from the water's edge. The road gets little traffic, though, compared to the roar of Highway 168, so it shouldn't bother you too much. The road goes only to the few private homes on Shaver Point, and you can walk right across it to reach the Shaver Lake Lodge Marina and the water's edge. All kinds of boat rentals are available at the marina, including kayaks, canoes, sailboats, fishing boats, wave runners, pontoon boats, and so on. You should be able to find something to suit your speed. If all the boats are rented out, Sierra Marina at Shaver Lake is up the road a mile.

Shaver Lake's cabins sit right next to the lodge restaurant, which features an extensive menu for lunch and dinner. (You're on your own for breakfast, but there are plenty of restaurants in the town of Shaver Lake, just five minutes away. Plus there's always that microwave in your cabin.) The restaurant's food is very well prepared, priced fairly, and served in mountain-sized portions. Dinner entrées include prime rib, pork chops, halibut, and chicken breast, as well as more casual food like hamburgers and salads. In summer, lots of people sit outside on the restaurant's big deck overlooking the lake and linger over long meals.

Shaver Lake Lodge is also open in wintertime. Downhill skiers stay in the cabins and drive 15 miles up Highway 168 to Sierra Summit Ski Area. Cross-country skiers and snowmobilers need drive only eight miles up Highway 168 to Tamarack Winter Sports Area. Miles of snow-covered trails exists for all kinds of winter sports enthusiasts.

If you'd like to stay at Shaver Lake but want to avoid the crowds, just show up in the off-season (late September or October), especially during the week. In addition to the autumn peace and quiet, if you bring your own linens and towels you get a discounted, off-season rate on your cabin rental.

Facilities, reservations, fees: There are 20 cabins at Shaver Lake Lodge, ranging in size from studios to two bedrooms. Most have microwaves and small refrigerators; none have full kitchens. A restaurant and small store are available. Boat rentals are available. Reservations are recommended. Fees range from $60 to $90 per night. Pets are not permitted.

Who to contact: Shaver Lake Lodge, 44185 Highway 168, Shaver Lake, CA 93664; (209) 841-3326.

Season: Open year-round.

Directions: From Fresno, drive north on Highway 41 for six miles to the Highway 168/Clovis turnoff. Turn east on Highway 168 and drive 47 miles to the town of Shaver Lake. Continue two miles past the town; the resort is on the right side of the road.

69. DINKEY CREEK CHALETS
Sierra National Forest, off Highway 168 near Shaver Lake

If you've been hearing about the Dinkey Lakes Wilderness your whole life, but somehow have never quite managed to make the trip, here's the perfect way to do it without joining the hordes of backpackers who infiltrate the area every summer. Book a stay at the Dinkey Creek Chalets, and then spend a few days exploring this year-round outdoor recreation area.

The Dinkey Creek Chalets are managed under a special use permit from the U.S. Forest Service. They are located directly on

Sierra National Forest land, about a 20-minute drive east of the town of Shaver Lake and a 20-minute drive southwest of the Dinkey Lakes Wilderness. The chalets were built in the 1990s, so they are modern in style with fully equipped kitchens and baths, wood-burning stoves, and satellite TV. Each one is nestled in the conifers, with a redwood deck out front that is perfect for barbecuing and dining *al fresco* in summer. You don't even need to worry about packing all your food for your vacation; almost

Dinkey Lakes Wilderness

anything you can think of can be purchased in the town of Shaver Lake, 13 miles away. Several restaurants are also available there.

The chalets are located within a few hundred feet of Dinkey Creek and its historic wooden trestle bridge. The bridge is not only picturesque, it's also the only free-span redwood bridge in California. Wild azaleas and ferns bloom along the creek's edges.

The beauty continues as you head for the Dinkey Lakes Wilderness, a short drive away via Rock Creek Road and Forest Service Road 9S10. (Be prepared for two miles of rough road at the end.) Once you're out of the car, you immediately cross a creek and head into the wilderness area. A perfect day-hike is the seven-mile loop to First Dinkey Lake. At 1.3 miles, take the right fork for the start of the loop, then start visiting one lake after another: Mystery, Swede, South, and First Dinkey. From First Dinkey Lake you can loop back to the parking lot, or backtrack a short distance toward South Lake and continue on to Second Dinkey Lake, Island Lake, Rock Lake, and so on. The trail is remarkably flat, so you can cover a surprising amount of ground in a few hours.

In winter, cross-country skiing, snowmobiling, and snowshoeing are all possible right outside the door of your chalet. Downhill skiers can drive up the highway to Sierra Summit Ski Resort, about 40 minutes away.

Facilities, reservations, fees: There are five cabins at Dinkey Creek Chalets, each large enough to accommodate up to six people. Each chalet has a fully equipped kitchen. Reservations are recommended. Fees range from $75 to $100 per night; weekly rates are discounted. Pets are permitted.

Who to contact: Dinkey Creek Chalets, 53861 Dinkey Creek Road, Shaver Lake, CA 93664; (209) 841-3435 or (209) 855-3998.

Season: Open year-round.

Directions: From Fresno, drive north on Highway 41 for six miles to the Highway 168/Clovis turnoff. Turn east on Highway 168 and drive 47 miles to the town of Shaver Lake. Turn right on Dinkey Creek Road and drive 13 miles. The resort is on the right side of the road.

70. LAKESHORE RESORT
Huntington Lake, off Highway 168 near Fresno

Of all the big lakes in Sierra National Forest that are open for recreation, Huntington Lake is the most versatile of the lot. While lakes like Shaver and Bass are primarily for waterskiers and fast boats, and lakes like Edison and Florence are primarily for fishermen, Huntington Lake manages to make room for all kinds of recreationists, including those who just want to sit by the lake's edge and while away the hours. Although sailing is Huntington's big claim to fame, you'll find plenty of people fishing, boating, camping, hiking, picnicking, and sunbathing as well. The lake is big—five miles long and a half-mile wide—so it almost never seems too crowded, even on summer weekends.

The cabins at Lakeshore Resort are about as versatile as the lake itself. There's a grand total of 27 cabins at the resort, with no two exactly alike, so you're bound to find one to suit your style of vacationing. We stayed in one of the lower-priced cabins, which had a queen bed in a large main room, a big eat-in kitchen, and a separate bathroom. It was cheerful and cozy, and it seemed huge compared to many cabins we've rented. All of Lakeshore Resort's cabins are located right behind the Lakeshore restaurant, store, and saloon, and they're just a short walk from the lake. Most are widely spaced along the hillside, so you don't feel like you're right on top of your neighbors.

Lakeshore Resort is open year-round. In summer, you can go hiking, boating, fishing, or waterskiing, and in winter you can go snowmobiling, snowshoeing, and downhill or cross-country skiing. Only 10 minutes away from your cabin is Sierra Summit Ski Area where you can tackle the slopes of China Peak.

In summertime, serious hikers won't want to miss the chance to "bag" Kaiser Peak, via a 10-mile round-trip trail that leads from D & F Pack Station. Not-so-ambitious hikers can walk the beautiful easy trails to Rancheria Falls or Indian Pools, or take a pleasant walk along the edge of Huntington Lake. A moderate six-mile round-trip hike leads to Twin Lakes and beyond to George Lake, via the Potter Pass Trail that begins on Kaiser Pass Road. The view from Potter Pass makes the trip worthwhile even if you don't go all the way to the pretty alpine lakes. (George Lake is another 1.5 miles beyond the upper Twin Lake, resulting in a nine-mile round-trip to visit all three lakes.)

When you arrive at Huntington Lake, stop in at the Forest Service's Eastwood Visitor Center at the intersection of Highway 168 and Kaiser Pass Road for updated trail information and permits.

Huntington Lake is at 7,000 feet in elevation, and some people find that hiking in these mountains is a bit too strenuous. Luckily

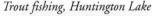
Trout fishing, Huntington Lake

anybody can access the wilderness on horseback, and the sure-footed steeds at neighboring D & F Pack Station can escort you on two-hour trail rides, half-day rides, or longer fishing and pack trips. Phone (209) 893-3220 for rates and information.

Many visitors opt to leave the landlubbers behind and spend all their vacation time on Huntington Lake. If you don't have your own boat, you can rent one at Rancheria Cove Marina, less than a quarter-mile from your cabin. They have small fishing skiffs, large patio boats, skiing boats, various noisy personal water craft, and peaceful canoes and kayaks. Trout fishing is decent from the shoreline but better while trolling; lots of people circle around tiny Big Creek Cove or just work their way up and down the long edges of the lake. Every few days someone catches a kokanee salmon, but most of the time you catch small planted trout. I wish I could say that I caught any kind of fish, even a minnow, but I was the only person in our boat who went home empty-handed.

To sum up: A vacation at Lakeshore Resort means a stay in a spacious, cozy cabin, plus a chance at great hiking, decent fishing, all kinds of water sports, and skiing in wintertime. And it's open year-round. Gee, this place has everything we like in a cabin vacation. About the only complaint we have is their discriminatory policy about pets: Dogs are okay, but no cats. Plenty of felines would be irate about this if they knew.

Facilities, reservations, fees: There are 27 cabins at Lakeshore Resort, most with fully equipped kitchens, plus 20 RV spaces. A general store, restaurant, and saloon are available. Reservations are recommended. Fees range from $50 to $120 per night. Pets are permitted in some cabins with prior permission.

Who to contact: Lakeshore Resort, P.O. Box 197, Lakeshore, CA 93634; (209) 893-3193. Fax (209) 893-2193.

Season: Open year-round.

Directions: From Fresno, drive north on Highway 41 for six miles to the Highway 168/Clovis turnoff. Turn east on Highway 168 and drive 70 miles, past Shaver Lake and Sierra Summit Ski Area, to the left turn for Huntington Lake. Bear left on Huntington Lake Road and drive one mile. Lakeshore Resort is on the right side of the road.

71. HUNTINGTON LAKE RESORT
Huntington Lake, off Highway 168 near Fresno

Most cabins are rustic, plain, serviceable. Most cabins don't even try to be anything but what they are—cabins. The cabins at Huntington Lake Resort are the exception. They're adorable. They're cute. They have a green and white gingerbread paint job on the outside, and a homey sweetness on the inside. When you drive up, you take one look and say, "Oh, how sweet," and then you keep saying it.

Unlike the other cabin resorts on big Huntington Lake, these cabins are set at the lake's far west end, near Huntington's big dam at 7,000 feet in elevation. They're across the road from the lake, but up high on the hillside, so most of the cabins have at least partial lake views. Even though this section of Huntington Lake Road is not plowed in winter, the resort stays open all year for visitors who are willing to snowmobile or ski in four miles. The county road is excellent for cross-country skiing; numerous groomed trails in the area are also available for skiing and snowmobiling.

Since you're staying at the lake's west end, you're in perfect position for a few summertime day-trips. One of the best is driving up scenic Forest Service Road 8S32 for 4.5 miles to Mushroom Rock

Mushroom Rock Vista, Sierra National Forest near Huntington Lake

Vista and Black Point Trail. The two destinations are nearly across the road from each other, and both are easy walks that anyone can enjoy. You drive to within 100 yards of Mushroom Rock Vista, which delivers exactly what its name promises—a big rock that looks oddly like a mushroom. Beyond the rock is the vista, a long-distance view of the forested slopes of the San Joaquin River Canyon and Shaver Lake. Far beyond, you can see the foothill country.

Black Point Trail requires a little more physical effort, but it's only a one-mile round-trip with a 500-foot elevation gain to a spectacular overlook of Huntington Lake, Shaver Lake, Kaiser Ridge, and the San Joaquin River Canyon. To reach Black Point Trail, continue on Road 8S32 for a quarter-mile past the turnoff for Mushroom Rock Vista, then turn right on Road 8S32F and drive a quarter-mile to the trailhead.

Hikers interested in more of a challenge can walk the Coarse-grass Meadow Trail along Home Creek directly from their cabin, or drive to nearby Upper Billy Creek Campground to walk the eight-mile Lower Kaiser Loop Trail. Both trails offer lovely views and beautiful cascading streams, as well as stunning wildflowers.

Anglers and sailors can rent a boat from the Huntington Lake Resort Marina, the lake's "west end" marina, less than a quarter-mile away. The marina provides sailboat and fishing boat rentals, plus fishing tackle and supplies, and a no-nonsense snack shop and cafe. (Note that plenty of people don't bother with a boat; instead they fish from shore or from the lake's dam. The usual catch is small stocked trout, plus occasional kokanee salmon.) Home Creek, which flows right next to the resort's cabins, is also a fair trout stream.

However you choose to spend your days, you get to end each one by returning home to your sweet green-and-white shuttered cabin at Huntington Lake Resort. There, you can cook your catch of the day in your kitchen or on the barbecue by your front door, and eat it outside on your patio. Then it's time to pull out your guitar and sing a few songs to the sunset.

Facilities, reservations, fees: There are 10 cabins at Huntington Lake Resort, ranging in sizes to accommodate two to eight people, most with fully equipped kitchens. Reservations are recommended. Fees range from $50 to $90 per night. Pets are permitted with prior approval; $5 fee per day.

Who to contact: Huntington Lake Resort, P.O. Box 257, Lakeshore, CA 93634; (209) 893-3226.

Season: Open year-round, but from November to May, the road to the resort is not plowed. During the snow season, you must cross-country ski or snowmobile four miles from the parking area. The resort owners will bring in your luggage and gear by sled.

Directions: From Fresno, drive north on Highway 41 for six miles to the Highway 168/Clovis turnoff. Turn east on Highway 168 and drive 70 miles, past Shaver Lake and Sierra Summit Ski Area, to the left turn for Huntington Lake. Bear left on Huntington Lake Road and drive five miles to the west end of the lake. Huntington Lake Resort is on the right side of the road.

72. MONO HOT SPRINGS RESORT
Sierra National Forest, off Kaiser Pass Road near Huntington Lake

Mono Hot Springs Resort is a place where it seems like time has stood still. The road to reach it is long, narrow, and winding, with no gas stations or services along the way. You can't find a public telephone within 20 miles of the resort, and electricity is available only when they turn on the generator. Even so, you only have power if you've paid extra for Mono Hot Springs' "modern" cabins. If you stay in their "rustic" cabins, it's kerosene and flashlights after dark.

Here's what my visit to Mono Hot Springs was like: I got an early start driving from Huntington Lake, because it was raining and I knew I had to get up and over 9,200-foot Kaiser Pass. The 18-mile drive from the lake took me well over an hour, partly because of the narrow, slow-going road, but mostly because I had to stop and put chains on my Toyota, then drive at a slow crawl through rapidly deepening snow. (This was during the first week of October, when sunny weather had been predicted.)

After 18 miles of no other cars, no commercial enterprises, no signs of civilization, no anything except trees and snow, I was surprised to come upon the resort's large cluster of stone and wood cabins, plus a store, restaurant, and hot springs bathhouse. So this is where everyone was hiding.

I got my key and headed for my low-budget "rustic" cabin, which consisted of just two rooms—a bedroom and a kitchen/dining area, both about as minimalist as you can imagine. The "kitchen" had only a table and chairs, plus an icebox (yes, the kind you put ice in, not a real refrigerator), and a wood stove. The latter unfortunately bore this sign: "Do not use wood stove; it's ornamental." That meant

Rustic cabin at Mono Hot Springs

I'd have to cook outside over a campfire, which was no small feat given the rain/sleet/snow that was coming down.

Luckily the resort restaurant was open, with a small cozy dining room and a roaring fire in the hearth. Mono's Indian Camp Fine Food Cafe, as it's called, serves buffalo steaks and buffalo burgers in addition to the regular kind, and even offers a few veggie dishes. I opted for a stack of pancakes and hot coffee, plus some good conversation with the cafe's cook and some other vacationers. The restaurant is a friendly, casual place.

Given that the weather was not great for hiking, I decided to spend a few hours in the hot springs bathhouse. Mono Hot Springs Resort's *raison d'être* is its natural warm mineral waters. A sign outside the bathhouse informs you of how many parts per million of carbonates, bicarbonates, chloride, sulfates, and such are in the water. The bathhouse has six private bathing tubs, each in its own little room, where you can soak away all your cares for just a couple of bucks. The tubs vary from old-fashioned clawfoot to modern fiberglass, but all of them are rustic-looking. Don't expect their enamel to be sparkling white. The baths stay open every day until 8 p.m.

If you prefer to bathe *al fresco*, there's a small outdoor mineral pool that's just big enough for two or three people. Those who want full pampering can hire the services of the resort masseuse, who will massage your aching limbs for a reasonable fee.

Speaking of pampering, be sure to reserve one of the six modern cabins instead of the "rustic" ones, unless you really want to rough it. The modern cabins are built of native cobblestone and come with bathrooms and full kitchens, plus electricity. Some even have their own showers. The rustic wood cabins cost half as much, but they may be a tad too rustic for some people. In addition to no electricity or heat, they have no cooking facilities except a fire pit (outside), and no bathrooms. You share a nearby outhouse-style toilet and must pay for showers or baths at the bathhouse. The rustic cabins are about as close to camping as staying in a cabin can be.

Assuming the weather is better on your trip than it was on mine, you'll want to take advantage of all the great outdoor adventures possible in the area. Hikers can set out from the resort and walk to Doris and Tule lakes, both popular for swimming and fishing for trout and bass. Doris Lake is only one mile from the cabins, so even small children can make the trip. Other trails into the John Muir and Ansel Adams wildernesses are available within a few miles at Edison Lake and Florence Lake.

A pack station is located six miles from the resort and provides hour-long rides, full-day rides, and longer pack trips. Stream fishing is excellent in Mono Creek, Bear Creek, and the South Fork of the San Joaquin River (all within hiking distance) and lake fishing is first-rate in Edison and Florence lakes. Boat rentals are available at both lakes.

Facilities, reservations, fees: There are 15 cabins at Mono Hot Springs Resort, ranging in size from studios to two bedrooms. The modern cabins have fully equipped kitchens and bathrooms. The rustic cabins do not have kitchens or bathrooms. Some cabins have beds but no linens; bring your sleeping bag and pillow. A restaurant, general store, and post office are available. Access to hot springs tubs and showers is provided for a $4 fee. Reservations are recommended. Fees range from $30 to $65 per night. Pets are permitted; $4 fee per night.

Who to contact: From November 1 to May 15, contact Mono Hot Springs Resort, P.O. Box 215, Lakeshore, CA 93634; (209) 325-1710. From May 15 to November 1, contact Mono Hot Springs Resort, General Delivery, Mono Hot Springs, CA 93642; (209) 325-1710.

Season: Open May 15 to November 1.

Directions: From Highway 168 at the eastern edge of Huntington Lake, turn right on Kaiser Pass Road and drive 17 miles (narrow and winding) to a fork in the road. Bear left for Mono Hot Springs and Edison Lake, drive 1.6 miles and turn left again. You'll reach the resort in a quarter-mile. (Trailers and motor homes are not recommended on Kaiser Pass Road.)

73. VERMILION VALLEY RESORT
Lake Thomas A. Edison, off Kaiser Pass Road near Huntington Lake

Let's get it straight: Before you make the trip to Vermilion Valley Resort at Lake Thomas A. Edison, make sure you are fully prepared. The place is awesome, but it's also 40-plus miles from the nearest decent-sized town (Shaver Lake), and those aren't miles that you want to drive more than one time per vacation. First off, you need to cover 20 winding miles from Shaver Lake to Huntington Lake, then another 18 curving miles over 9,200-foot Kaiser Pass to Mono Hot Springs, then a final five twisting miles to Vermilion Valley Resort at Lake Thomas A. Edison.

When you reach the place, you find that it isn't exactly the Hilton, but it has all the basics. Vermilion Valley Resort's cabins are tent cabins, which are basically just big tents with wood floors and twin bunk beds. They have no heat, no kitchen facilities, and no electricity. Make sure you bring your sleeping bags and flashlights. If this proves to be too rustic for you, you can stay in one of the resort's four motel rooms with kitchenettes. It's wise to reserve early, though; the rooms are popular.

If you get tired of cooking meals on your camp stove or over a campfire, you can eat at the resort restaurant, which is really just a cafe attached to the general store. It has an open kitchen, a few tables and chairs, trophy trout mounted on the walls, and some of the nicest people in the universe who happen to work there.

During my first meal, I met a French people who were hiking the Pacific Crest Trail with two llamas and their 16-month-old baby, and an older couple from the San Francisco Bay Area who vacation at Vermilion Valley Resort every year. Out here, nobody bothers much with formalities, so friendships were formed in mere seconds.

Breakfast is the resort cafe's big claim to fame, comprised of big stacks of buttermilk pancakes, eggs, sausage, bacon, and just about everything you'd expect. Lunch and dinner are mostly burgers and sandwiches, but the cook usually comes up with some kind of special for dinner. It was *carne asada* on the night we were there.

Edison Lake is a big trout producer, so the conversation at all meals usually revolves around who's catching what with which tackle. If you fish Edison Lake, you most likely will catch trout. The only problem is that when you catch the big one, you'll want to call home and tell everybody, but there's no public telephone within 20 miles. Luckily the resort owner is a big-hearted guy who will let you use his cellular phone for $2 a minute.

What you need to know about Edison Lake is that the water level fluctuates like the stock of Apple Computer. Up, down, up, down. It's not the most beautiful lake you've ever seen when it's drawn down, although it's a stunner when it's full, backed by the rugged 12,000-foot peaks of the high Sierra. The lake is at 7,700 feet in elevation.

Hikers can access the Pacific Crest Trail from Edison Lake, either by hiking the Mono Creek Trail along the north edge of the lake or taking the ferry across the lake. Those seeking an excellent day-hike should take the Devil's Bathtub Trail north from Vermilion Valley Resort. It's five miles one-way to the Devil's Bathtub, a rocky, beautiful alpine lake. Or hike the Mono Creek Trail south from Edison Lake to Mono Hot Springs Resort, stopping to admire beautiful Mono Meadow and Doris Lake along the way. You can even take a dip in the hot springs when you arrive at the resort (see story on page 177).

Facilities, reservations, fees: There are 10 tent cabins at Vermilion Valley Resort, plus four motel rooms with kitchenettes. A cafe, general store, boat launch, and boat rentals are available. Reservations are recommended. Fees range from $35 to $70 per night. Pets are permitted.

Tent cabins at Vermilion Valley Resort, Thomas A. Edison Lake

Who to contact: Vermilion Valley Resort, P.O. Box 258, Lakeshore, CA 93634; (209) 259-4000 or (209) 855-6558.

Season: Open May 15 to November 1.

Directions: From Highway 168 at the eastern edge of Huntington Lake, turn right on Kaiser Pass Road and drive 17 miles (narrow and winding) to a fork in the road. Bear left for Mono Hot Springs and Edison Lake and drive 6.5 miles to Vermilion Valley Resort. (Trailers and motor homes are not recommended on Kaiser Pass Road.)

---

74. MUIR TRAIL RANCH
John Muir Wilderness, off Kaiser Pass Road near Florence Lake

If you have a big family, or like to vacation with a group of friends, you are in the perfect position for a fantasy-level High Sierra vacation at your own private mountain ranch. Where? In the John Muir Wilderness. How? By renting the Muir Trail Ranch for a week. Want to know more? Keep reading.

First, let's talk location. The Muir Trail Ranch is on 200 acres of private land near Florence Lake in Sierra National Forest, completely surrounded by the John Muir Wilderness. Getting to the ranch requires driving from Fresno to Huntington Lake, then taking narrow and winding Kaiser Pass Road to Florence Lake, then taking the water taxi across the lake, then hiking or horsepacking five miles from the taxi drop-off point to Muir Trail Ranch. Sounds remote? Sounds hard to get to? It is, and that's one reason why it's so good.

Next, let's talk money. The minimum rental period for the ranch is one week, and that will cost you $7,500. What?!? Yes, it sounds expensive, but that rate is for as many as 15 people, which works out to $500 per person for a week, or about 70 bucks a night. Fifteen people will not overcrowd the ranch; in fact, you'll be housed with room to spare in eight log cabins and four tent cabins. The tent cabins are equipped with electric lights and outlets; the log cabins even have wash basins and toilets. Now we're talking luxury.

In addition to exclusive use of the cabins and the surrounding beautiful land, you also have access to the ranch's big kitchen and dining room for preparing all your meals. You'll have to pack in all of your groceries for the week. If meal planning and cooking sounds like too much trouble, you can hire a catering company to handle everything for you. Just tell them what you like to eat.

So what do you do during your week-long stay at your own private ranch in the Sierra? Well, up here at 7,700 feet in elevation, the wildflowers are pretty, fly fishing in the San Joaquin River is excellent, photography opportunities abound, and hiking trails wind deep into the John Muir Wilderness. Bring your fishing license; you'll want to go stream fishing as well as angling in surrounding alpine lakes. Thirty horses are available at the ranch, and they are almost always willing to hike to a pretty lake with you. (Except on Sundays, when the horses have the day off.)

A few staff members live and work at the ranch. They take care of basic facility maintenance, generating electricity, and keeping the horses fed and happy. They also run a small ranch store with fishing supplies and other vacation necessities, and they will guide you on horseback trips into the wilderness. Both day-trips and overnight pack trips are possible. Otherwise, you're basically on your own for your entire vacation.

One of Muir Trail Ranch's greatest features is its two enclosed hot springs, which everyone uses for bathing purposes as well as pure hedonistic pleasure. One bath is about 105 degrees Fahrenheit; the other is a "cooler" 98 degrees. If it's too hot outside for taking a hot bath, you can always go jump in the San Joaquin River, located about 100 feet away from the tent cabins.

When you make your way to Muir Trail Ranch, plan on taking nearly four hours to cover the 90 miles from Fresno to Florence Lake, even though the road is paved all the way. To say that the last 20 miles are narrow and winding is a huge understatement. Once you reach Florence Lake, you can opt to hike in all the way to Muir Trail Ranch, a 10-mile trip, or take the water taxi across the lake and hike the remaining five miles. People who aren't in good enough condition for the hike, or who are carrying a lot of gear with them, can ride in on horses. Lots of people choose to pack their belongings in on horses, then hike in themselves.

Facilities, reservations, fees: There are eight log cabins at Muir Trail Ranch, plus four tent cabins. Reservations are required. The fee is $7,500 for 15 people for one week. Each additional person is $500 for one week; the maximum number of people is 20. Horses are available for $50 per day. Pets are not permitted.

Who to contact: From October to mid-June, contact Muir Trail Ranch at P.O. Box 269, Ahwahnee, CA 93601-0269; (209) 966-3195. From mid-June to late September, contact the ranch at P.O. Box 176, Lakeshore, CA 93634-0176 (no phone).

Season: Open June to September.

Directions: From Highway 168 at the eastern edge of Huntington Lake, turn right on Kaiser Pass Road and drive 17 miles (narrow and winding) to a fork in the road. Bear right for Florence Lake and drive six miles to the lake and store. From there, you will either hike to Muir Trail Ranch, ride a horse, or take the water taxi across the lake and hike the remaining distance. (Note that trailers and motor homes are not recommended on Kaiser Pass Road.)

---

75. GRANT GROVE CABINS
Kings Canyon National Park, off Highway 180 in Grant Grove

When the cabins at Giant Forest in Sequoia National Park closed in 1997, there were a lot of unhappy campers. People were disappointed that they would never again be able to rent a cabin amid a grove of the most amazing trees on earth, the Giant Sequoias.

The Giant Forest cabins had always been the most popular lodging in Sequoia and Kings Canyon National Parks. Where else could you open up your front door and reach out and touch a Giant Sequoia? Unfortunately, all those adoring visitors were impacting the health of the ancient trees, and the park wisely decided that it was time to tear down the cabins and give the old Sequoias a rest.

But if you think there is no place left in the national parks where you can stay in a rustic cabin and partake of the whole Sequoia and Kings Canyon experience, think again. The cabins at Grant Grove Village may not have Giant Sequoias growing right alongside them, but the big trees are not far away. In fact, the General Grant Tree, the third largest tree in the entire world, is located less than a mile from the Grant Grove cabins. Old General Grant can provide you with a Giant Sequoia fix any time you need one.

Here's the scoop on the Grant Grove cabins: There are nine regular cabins with electricity, propane heat, carpeting, and private baths. These are the best and most popular of the lodgings; reserve them as far in advance as possible. There are also 23 rustic semi-housekeeping cabins without private baths, but with propane heat. The rustic cabins have wood-burning stoves, kerosene lamps, and a patio with a picnic table for outdoor cooking. If you can get along without your own bathroom, these are a pretty good option. (Restroom and shower facilities are located nearby.)

Sunset Trail in Grant Grove, Kings Canyon National Park

Remember to bring all your own outdoor cooking utensils and dishes, or plan to eat in the restaurant at Grant Grove. None of the cabins have kitchens or any kind of indoor cooking facilities. The restaurant at Grant Grove is basically a large coffee shop, but the food is passable and affordable, with a fairly broad selection to choose from.

Grant Grove also has 19 tent cabins, with wood-burning stoves and kerosene lamps. These look a lot like barracks from the outside, especially because there are no trees or plants around them, and they are spaced far too close together. If it was up to me, I'd stay in my own tent in one of the park's car campgrounds before I'd stay in one of the tent cabins.

The cabins at Grant Grove are open year-round, and it's hard to say which is the best season for a visit. If you like conifers covered in snow and cross-country skiing, plan on a winter trip. Some of the prettiest cross-country trails imaginable are around Grant Grove and Giant Forest, where you can see the cinnamon-colored Giant Sequoias crowned in snow. Ski and snowshoe rentals as well as several snow play areas are available at Grant Grove and south toward Lodgepole. Rangers lead guided snowshoe walks that are easy enough for beginners, and 75 miles of marked cross-country trails can be found in the parks.

If you visit Grant Grove after the snow has melted or before it falls, you have a myriad of hiking options possible from your cabin's front door. You could start with the 2.5-mile Sunset Trail, which leads from Sunset Campground downhill to two pretty waterfalls on Sequoia Creek, then continues to Sequoia Lake. It's a given that you'll take the short walk to the General Grant Tree, but for more Sequoia sightseeing, add on the 1.5-mile North Grove Loop. Don't miss the Panoramic Point and Park Ridge Trail, which begins two miles from the cabins. The trail offers far-reaching views and a visit to an operating fire lookout tower.

Many more trailheads can be accessed by driving north or south into Sequoia National Forest, or taking Highway 180 to its end at Cedar Grove in Kings Canyon National Park. The Grant Grove Visitor Center is a few steps away from the Grant Grove cabins, so you have easy access to all the park and trail information you want.

Facilities, reservations, fees: There are nine cabins at Grant Grove with private baths, propane heat, and electricity. There are also 23 rustic semi-housekeeping cabins without baths or electricity but with propane heat, and there are 19 tent cabins. For the rustic and tent cabins, restroom and shower facilities are located nearby. There are no cooking facilities except for outside barbecues at the semi-housekeeping cabins. A restaurant, store, post office, and visitor center are available. Reservations are recommended. Fees range from $35 to $80 per night. Pets are not permitted. There is a $10 entrance fee at Sequoia and Kings Canyon National Parks, good for seven days.

Who to contact: Guest Services, Reservations Department, P.O. Box 789, Three Rivers, CA 93271; (209) 561-3314. Fax (209) 561-3135.

Season: Open year-round.

Directions: From Fresno, drive east on Highway 180 for 55 miles to the Big Stump Entrance Station at Kings Canyon National Park. Continue 1.5 miles and turn left for Grant Grove. Drive 1.5 miles to Grant Grove Village. Check in at the registration office; the cabins are located behind the office, store, and restaurant.

76. KINGS CANYON LODGE CABINS
Sequoia National Forest, off Highway 180 in Kings Canyon

There's nothing terribly special about the cabins at Kings Canyon Lodge—no fireplaces, no extra amenities, and darn little in the way of decorative charm—but oh boy, have they got a great location. That's because they're found along Highway 180, the only road that runs deep into the spectacular canyon of Kings Canyon National Park.

The lodge is located in a small section of national forest land that bisects the national park. When you're there, you would logically assume you're in the park, because you paid a national park entrance fee to get there, and you drove past several Kings Canyon National Park signs. But the way the political map reads, you're in Sequoia National Forest.

Driving east on Highway 180, you know the lodge is coming up soon when you see the hand-painted road sign that says "Caution: Ice Cream Ahead." Since there is little else on this highway from the park entrance station at Grant Grove to the "End of the Road" at Cedar Grove, 30 winding miles later, plenty of people slam on their brakes for some ice cream. The lucky ones have booked a cabin at the lodge and can spend the night in the peace of the canyon, far from the busy national park campgrounds.

Here's what you need to know about Kings Canyon Lodge: Only a few of the rustic, woodframe cabins have kitchens. Try to reserve one that does. If yours doesn't, be prepared to eat at the lodge's grill or drive some miles for food. The grill serves little else besides hamburgers, but luckily the restaurant at Grant Grove (14 miles away) and the snack bar at Cedar Grove (18 miles away) have more extensive menus.

It's a good idea to have cash with you when you enter Kings Canyon, or to plan on using your credit cards extensively. There are no automated teller machines within many miles. You can start to feel a little silly using your VISA card to buy a three-dollar sandwich.

Kings Canyon Lodge is set at a deep curve in the highway, near a towering waterfall that cascades down the steep canyon wall behind it. The lodge presents a remarkably picturesque snapshot, with its rustic buildings and old-fashioned gas pumps out front. Kings Canyon Lodge's claim to fame, besides its ice cream, is that they have the "country's oldest gravity fed gas pumps." What matters to most travelers is that you can usually use them for a fill-up. That's if the gas truck has been by lately.

The South Fork Kings River is across the highway from the lodge, and the closest and best access to it is via the Yucca Point Trail. It's a steep downhill path that leads to excellent wild trout fishing early in the year and swimming later in the summer, when the river calms down. Boyden Cave is just down the road about six miles,

Trail to Mist Falls, Kings Canyon National Park

and for a few bucks you can go on a ranger-led tour of a fascinating limestone cavern. If you don't want to take the tour, at least hike the Windy Cliffs Trail that leads from the cave entrance. You'll get marvelous views of the Kings River Canyon and Highway 180 far below you, as well as the towering granite walls of the canyon.

Many visitors stop at the picnic area at Grizzly Falls, a beautiful 80-foot waterfall right by the road that rushes into the Kings River. It's a nice break on your way to Cedar Grove and the "End of the Road," where Highway 180 stops and the wilderness begins. Trailheads are plentiful in the Cedar Grove area, including the popular eight-mile round-trip to Mist Falls. If you don't mind climbing, you can take several steep trails to scenic lookouts, including those to Hotel Creek Overlook and Lookout Peak.

Hikers who want to take it easy should walk the short paved path to Roaring River Falls, and the incredibly scenic 1.5-mile Zumwalt Meadow Loop. Plenty of anglers try their luck in the South Fork Kings River from along this path.

Facilities, reservations, fees: There are 10 cabins at Kings Canyon Lodge, some with kitchens. A cafe and bar are available, as well as gasoline. Reservations are recommended. Fees range from $60 to $90 per night. Pets are not permitted. There is a $10 entrance fee at Sequoia and Kings Canyon National Parks, good for seven days; you will need to pay this fee even though the lodge is located in national forest land.

Who to contact: Kings Canyon Lodge, P.O. Box 820, 67751 Highway 180, Kings Canyon National Park, CA 93633; (209) 335-2405. (The phone is not answered in the off-season.)

Season: Open April through October.

Directions: From Fresno, drive east on Highway 180 for 55 miles to the Big Stump Entrance Station at Kings Canyon National Park. Continue 1.5 miles and turn left for Grant Grove and Cedar Grove. Drive 15 miles on Highway 180 to Kings Canyon Lodge on the right.

77. WEAVER LAKE BACKPACK
Jennie Lakes Wilderness, off Highway 180
near Kings Canyon National Park

Do you adore Kings Canyon and Sequoia National Parks? Of course; who doesn't? Do you ever find yourself wishing you could camp in the parks, but have the whole place to yourself and not be bothered by hundreds of other people who want the same thing you do?

Okay, here's your chance. Weaver Lake is not quite in Kings Canyon and Sequoia National Parks; it's just over the boundary line in Sequoia National Forest, but only the legislators and bureaucrats could tell the difference. The scenery is the same—awesome. The drive to reach the trailhead requires entering Kings Canyon National Park at the Big Stump entrance station, then driving out of the park and into the national forest. After a final short stretch on a dirt road, you leave your car at the edge of the beautiful Jennie Lakes Wilderness, a 10,000-acre wonderland of meadows, conifer forests, lakes, and streams, then hike in to Weaver Lake.

You have two choices regarding how to make the trip. Most people choose the easier option, which is a two-mile hike from Fox Meadow, a few miles beyond the Forest Service campground at Big Meadows. If you don't want to get to Weaver Lake that fast, but would rather take a longer hike (or if you don't want to drive your car on a dirt road), you can leave your car at the trailhead just west of Big Meadows and hike in 3.5 miles to the lake. Take your pick. Either way, sooner or later you'll wind up at the edge of Weaver Lake, choosing from several excellent campsites near the water's edge.

Starting from the Fox Meadow Trailhead, the path is well signed all the way, and passes through a mix of conifer forests and meadows.

In the spring, you'll see plenty of wildflowers in bloom. At seven-tenths of a mile, take the left fork for Weaver Lake, climbing up into granite country. At just over two miles, you'll reach the shallow but pretty lake at 8,700 feet in elevation. The brave immediately strip down to their underwear and go swimming. The smart head for the far side of the lake to take their pick from the half-dozen campsites.

With your overnight permit from the Hume Lake Ranger District, you are permitted to have a campfire if you like, and spend a couple of nights at the lake. Don't forget your water purification system so you can filter water for drinking, or else plan to do a lot of standing around watching your water boil. Bring your fishing rod; you might be able to catch some trout for dinner, but don't plan on fish being your only source of food. Shallow Weaver Lake has seen a fair amount of angling pressure over the years.

Mostly, you should plan on hiking, swimming, and gazing at the lake, and forgetting all about civilization for a few days.

Facilities, reservations, fees: There are several primitive campsites at Weaver Lake. There is no fee for camping, but you must pay the Sequoia National Park entrance fee ($10) to access the trailhead. Water is available for filtering. A free campfire permit is required; they are available from the Hume Lake Ranger District on Highway 180 or the Sequoia National Forest office in Porterville. Pets are permitted.

Who to contact: Sequoia National Forest, Hume Lake Ranger District, 35860 East Kings Canyon Road, Dunlap, CA 93621; (209) 338-2251 or fax (209) 338-2131.

Maps for backpacking: For a map of Sequoia National Forest, send $4 to USDA-Forest Service, 630 Sansome Street, San Francisco, CA 94111. A detailed map of the Sequoia/Kings Canyon area, including Weaver Lake, is available for a fee from Tom Harrison Cartography at (415) 456-7940 or Trails Illustrated at (800) 962-1643. For a topographic map of the area, ask for Muir Grove from the USGS.

Season: Open June to September.

Directions: From Fresno, drive east on Highway 180 for 55 miles to the Big Stump Entrance Station at Kings Canyon National Park. Continue 1.5 miles and turn right on the Generals Highway, heading for Sequoia National Park. Drive seven miles and turn left on Forest Road 14S11, signed for Big Meadows. Drive four miles to the Big Meadows Campground, then continue past it, turn right, and follow the signs for four miles to Fox Meadow and the Weaver Lake Trailhead. The last 1.5 miles are unpaved.

78. MONTECITO SEQUOIA LODGE
Sequoia National Forest, off Highway 198 near Kings Canyon National Park

🚶🚶 🐟 ⚓ 🐎 🚤 🏃 ⑨

Montecito Sequoia Lodge is located in Sequoia National Forest, on a narrow strip of Forest Service land that separates two national parks: Kings Canyon and Sequoia. Understandably, not everybody sees the distinction between Sequoia National Park and Sequoia National Forest, but what makes it important is this: Since the lodge is located on Forest Service land, not national park land, the owners have a lot more freedom to run their business as a full-service concession. For visitors, this means that you get all the benefits of close proximity to Kings Canyon and Sequoia national parks, plus all the benefits of a large-scale resort with far more amenities than you could find in the parks.

Keep in mind that Montecito Sequoia Lodge is not for everybody. The place is run like a High Sierra Club Med, with a heavy emphasis on organized activities, especially for families. If you like to be left alone to do your own thing, you might find the place too obtrusive. But if you're looking for a way to keep you and your kids busy, active, and happy in the outdoors, you're in luck. In fact, with all the activities here for children, you might actually get some time alone with your spouse.

The lodge is located at 7,500 feet in elevation along the Generals Highway, and bills itself as a "family vacation camp." That means in addition to all the great outdoor adventures possible in the national forest and national park land surrounding Montecito Sequoia, there is also plenty to do right at the resort. Organized activities include tennis, archery, basketball, volleyball, canoeing, waterskiing, horseback riding, swimming, and cross-country skiing in winter.

The lodge is reached via a long driveway off the main highway, so as you pull in, you feel like you are heading to your own private vacation retreat in the middle of the national forest. At the end of the driveway, you are greeted by the sight of a pretty little lake, a big lodge, and several cabins beyond it. The setting is perfect, especially with the imposing peaks of the Great Western Divide towering in the background.

Many people like the simple payment options at Montecito Sequoia Lodge. You can rent a cabin on the "bed, dinner, and breakfast" plan, so your meals are paid for in addition to your accommodations. Or you can rent a cabin on the "family activities plan," which means your activities, meals, and accommodations are covered, all for one price. Forget just renting a cabin and going your own way for meals; that's not an option here.

Neither the 13 cabins nor any of the lodge accommodations have kitchens; you're expected to eat your meals in the lodge dining room. Not that this is a bad idea. Montecito Sequoia has developed a reputation for healthy, California cuisine-style food, served buffet style. We liked the fact that one entrée at dinner is always vegetarian, and we liked eating outside on the huge deck overlooking high, snow-covered peaks.

The cabins at Montecito Sequoia Lodge house two to eight people. Each has a king or queen bed, two or three bunk beds, a wood-burning stove, and electricity. For bathrooms and showers, you must walk to the nearby bathhouses. (If you want your own bathroom, you'll have to stay in one of the lodge rooms, not a cabin.) Bedding is provided for the cabin's king or queen bed; bring sleeping bags for the bunks. Also bring your own towels; none are provided.

In the winter, visitors come to Montecito Sequoia to take advantage of excellent cross-country skiing and snowshoeing. Nearly 100 miles of groomed and backcountry trails lead from the lodge into surrounding national forest land; vistas are extraordinary in every direction. If you don't have your own cross-country equipment, you can rent everything you need. Full lesson packages are also available for all levels of skiers. You can choose between a Sunday through Friday weekly ski package, or a two-day weekender package, or a discounted midweek ski package. All packages include lodging, meals, and a trail pass. Weather permitting, ice skating is also available on the lodge's small lake.

Facilities, reservations, fees: There are 13 cabins at Montecito Sequoia Lodge, plus 30 lodge rooms. The cabins do not have private baths; a central bathhouse is available. Reservations are required. Fees range from $49 to $79 per person per night, and include meals. In summer, a complete vacation package is available that includes accommodations, meals, and all activities. Pets are not permitted. There is a $10 entrance fee at Sequoia and Kings Canyon National Parks, good for seven days.

Who to contact: Montecito Sequoia Lodge, P.O. Box 858, Grant Grove, Kings Canyon National Park, CA 93633; (209) 565-3388. Fax (209) 565-3223. For reservations, write to 1485 Redwood Drive, Los Altos, CA 94024; (800) 227-9900 or (650) 967-8612.

On top of Buena Vista Peak, near Montecito Sequoia Lodge

Season: Open year-round.

Directions: From Fresno, drive east on Highway 180 for 55 miles to the Big Stump Entrance Station at Kings Canyon National Park. Continue 1.5 miles and turn right on the Generals Highway, heading for Sequoia National Park. Drive eight miles to the right turnoff for Montecito Sequoia Lodge. Turn right and drive a half-mile to the lodge.

79. PEAR LAKE SKI HUT
Sequoia National Park, off Highway 198 near Lodgepole

Attention all cross-country skiers and snowshoers: On your mark, get set, get going to Sequoia National Park's Pear Lake Ski Hut.

But first, understand that to reach the ski hut and spend a few days, you need to do two things: First, secure a reservation with the Sequoia Natural History Association, and second, be in good enough shape so that you can cross-country ski or snowshoe six miles, much of it uphill. The total elevation gain is 2,000 feet from the trailhead at Wolverton Ski Area to the ski hut north of Pear Lake, so it's not advisable for novice skiers or snowshoers. But with a few days of training and good aerobic conditioning, even intermediates can make the trip, especially if they start early in the day and take their time.

The ski hut (really a cabin) is open to public use from mid-December to mid-April each year. You must have a reservation to stay there, and to get one you must make a written request by mid-November. A lottery is held, and dates are assigned accordingly. Usually everybody gets a reservation, although not always on the precise dates they want. Holiday weekends are the hardest to reserve; weekdays are easy. In fact, when I phoned in late February, long after the lottery was held, I was told that there were still some weekday reservations available, although all weekends were booked up. The moral: If you really want to go to Pear Lake Ski Hut, just be flexible; you'll get the chance.

The cabin houses 10 people in bunk beds; most people go with a group of friends so they have the whole place to themselves. If your group is smaller than 10 people, you can still reserve the ski hut, but you will probably share it with another group. No matter, you'll quickly make friends. If you don't, you can settle your differences with a good snowball fight.

If you've seen or stayed at the Ostrander Ski Hut at Glacier Point in Yosemite National Park, you'll find that the Pear Lake Ski Hut is similar in style and facilities, but a little smaller and more remote. It's also harder to ski to. Whereas at Glacier Point you may see other people out skiing for the day, at Pear Lake you are likely to see no one but the folks you came with. The Pear Lake "hut" is an impressive stone building with huge wooden rafters that serves as a backcountry ranger station in the summer months. It is heated by a wood pellet stove. Propane cooking stoves and lanterns are provided, as well as all cooking and eating utensils, and a composting toilet.

The trail to reach the lake is a spectacular day-hike in summer, and an equally spectacular ski or snowshoe trip in winter. With your gear loaded on your back, you set out on the Lakes Trail from Wolverton Ski Area at 7,200 feet, heading east along Wolverton Creek. Taking a left fork at nearly two miles out, you start your serious climb up to the lake country. The apex of your ascent is at a spot called "The Hump" at 9,400 feet. I guarantee you'll be out of breath here; the route is steep and the air is thin.

In the summer, most day-hikers avoid "The Hump" by taking a longer, alternate trail over "The Watchtower," a giant hunk of granite with spectacular views and steep dropoffs. When snow falls, that alternate route is closed, but you can see the Watchtower's rocky pinnacle from further down the trail.

After "The Hump," you have less than three miles of trail to cover. This is the prettiest stretch for skiers, and it's mostly downhill. You'll glide along the icy shores of Heather Lake, Emerald Lake, and Aster Lake. When you reach Pear Lake Ski Hut six miles out, you are less than a half-mile from the shores of large Pear Lake.

If you've never cross-country skied or snowshoed to a camp, ski hut, or cabin before, the Sequoia Natural History Association makes your trip easier by sending you a suggested packing list. The list includes all the winter clothing and skiing equipment you might expect, plus some important essentials like a sleeping bag (bunks are provided but no bedding), propane fuel and matches (for the propane stoves and lanterns), enough food for your stay plus extras for emergencies, and water purification equipment. You must filter or boil all your water.

The Association also insists that campers carry survival equipment, just in case an avalanche, white-out, or other snow emergency should occur. This includes a tent or bivy sack, backpacking stove and fuel, whistle, pocket knife, flashlight, waterproof matches, map and compass, and so on. Other suggested equipment includes sunscreen, a water bottle, sunglasses, ski goggles, and binoculars. Remember that with a winter-season camping trip, there is much more to be prepared for than in summer.

Facilities, reservations, fees: There is one ski hut at Pear Lake with 10 bunk beds; a maximum of 10 people are allowed at one time. Propane cooking facilities and utensils are provided. Reservations are required. The fee is $15 per person per night. Pets are not permitted. Ski rentals and supplies are available at the Wolverton Ski Area. There is a $10 entrance fee at Sequoia and Kings Canyon National Parks, good for seven days.

Who to contact: Sequoia Natural History Association, HCR 89, Box 10, Three Rivers, CA 93271-9792; (209) 565-3759.

Maps for skiing/backpacking: Park maps are available for free at the entrance stations. A more detailed map is available for a fee from Tom Harrison Cartography at (415) 456-7940 or Trails Illustrated at (800) 962-1643. For a topographic map of the area, ask for Lodgepole from the USGS.

Season: Open from mid-December to mid-April.

Directions: From Visalia, drive east on Highway 198 for 40 miles, through the town of Three Rivers, to the Ash Mountain Entrance Station at Sequoia National Park. Continue 20 miles on the Generals Highway, past Giant Forest, to the Wolverton Ski Area turnoff on the right side of the road. The trail to Peak Lake begins at the far edge of the parking lot.

80. BEARPAW HIGH SIERRA CAMP
Sequoia National Park, off Highway 198 near Giant Forest

I'd like to tell you about Bearpaw High Sierra Camp, but then again, I really don't want more people to know about it. It's already too darn hard to get reservations to stay there. Why is Bearpaw High Sierra Camp so popular? Because it provides an incredibly luxurious camping experience in one of the most scenic spots in all of the Golden State.

Here's the deal: Bearpaw High Sierra Camp, elevation 7,800 feet, is accessible by trail out of Giant Forest in Sequoia National Park. You hike an incredibly easy 11.5 miles (it's nearly flat), through some of the most gorgeous high-country scenery you can possibly imagine. When you arrive at Bearpaw Meadow, you are spoiled by the opulence of tent cabins with clean beds, linens, and bedding, plus showers and homestyle meals. Not only that, but you are treated to incredible vistas of the Great Western Divide's snowy peaks in every direction.

You don't have to carry a heavy backpack. You don't have to plan out your meals in advance, carefully measuring out 1.3 ounces of this, 2.4 ounces of that, 1.5 ounces of this, and so on. You don't have to pack a camp stove or pots and pans. You don't even have to carry a tent. All you need are your clothes, and whatever personal items you want to bring—cameras, books, a day pack, fishing equipment, etc.

Your ticket to Bearpaw High Sierra Camp is the stunning High Sierra Trail, a popular trans-Sierra route that eventually leads all the way to Mount Whitney. In this section, the path travels along the north rim of the Middle Fork Kaweah River Canyon, and it offers views, views, views all the way. Most people start the trip early in the day, so they can take their time and shoot off a ton of film on the hike in to camp. While 11.5 miles may sound like a long hike, remember than you don't have to carry much, and that there is a mere 1,000-foot elevation gain along the trail.

If you start early, you'll beat some of the midday heat (much of the trail is exposed and sunny), and arrive at Bearpaw with plenty of energy and daylight left. The last mile of trail is even more extraordinary than the first 10 miles—some describe it as "fantasy in rock." At Bearpaw Meadow, the campground is perched on the edge of a granite gorge.

Once in camp, you can spend a day hiking the eight-mile round-trip to Upper and Lower Hamilton Lakes on a spectacular rocky ledge trail. The lakes are set in a glacially carved basin at the bottom of 13,000-foot peaks. Many other excellent day hikes are available in the area; the staff members at Bearpaw can point you on your way.

One of the nicest things about the camp is that it is only big enough for 12 people, plus the two staff members who work there. Every camper is likely to become your dear friend in about two minutes; it seems that only really nice people go to Bearpaw High Sierra Camp.

So how do you get a reservation for this high-country paradise? It isn't easy. On January 2nd of every year, the park service starts taking telephone reservations for the following summer at Bearpaw. Within a couple of hours, every date for the next season is booked.

If you're not one of the lucky ones to get through on January 2nd, it can seem disappointing—but it doesn't have to be. That's because although tons of people make reservations for Bearpaw, lots of them never show up. The reservation office keeps a waiting list, and as people drop out, the wait-listers get in. When I phoned in mid-February, the waiting list already had 40 people on it, but the reservationist assured me that I had about a 95 percent chance of getting to go to Bearpaw anyway. Since they have a 30-day cancellation policy, you are usually phoned at least 30 days in advance to see if you want to fill an empty space at the camp.

Vista from the High Sierra Trail to Bearpaw Meadow High Sierra Camp

Even if being on the waiting list doesn't pan out for you, you still have a chance. You can go to Sequoia National Park on your vacation anyway, maybe planning to car camp at one of the park campgrounds, then keep phoning the reservation office each day while you're there. People drop their Bearpaw reservations even as late as the last minute, so if you're willing to be spontaneous, you may still get to go.

If all this sounds like too much trouble, you have one final option: You can get a reservation and an overnight permit to stay at the Bearpaw Meadow Backpacker's Camp, which is near the High Sierra Camp. You get to hike the same beautiful 11.5-mile trail to your camp, you get the same views of the Great Western Divide, and you have all the same activity options once you're in the Bearpaw area. What you don't get are meals, showers, and sleeping provisions.

There's no getting around it. If you go to the backpacker's camp instead of the High Sierra Camp, you go the old-fashioned way, which means measuring 1.3 ounces this and 2.5 ounces of that, and loading up a heavy backpack. It's your decision.

Facilities, reservations, fees: The Bearpaw High Sierra Camp can accommodate 12 people at a time in tent cabins. Reservations and a permit are required; phone (209) 335-5500 as early as January 2 for the following summer. The fee is $125 per person per night, which includes breakfast and dinner. Lunches are for sale at the camp for an extra fee. Double occupancy in tents is required. Pets are not permitted. There is a $10 entrance fee at Sequoia and Kings Canyon National Parks, good for seven days. A free wilderness permit is required for overnight stays; it is provided as part of your High Sierra Camp reservation.

To stay at the backpackers' campground at Bearpaw Meadow instead of the High Sierra Camp, you must obtain a wilderness permit in advance by mail or fax; phone (209) 565-3708 for more information. You may fax or mail your permit request for the following summer any time after March 1; a $10 fee is required to secure your permit reservation.

Who to contact: Bearpaw Meadow High Sierra Camp Reservations, (209) 335-5500; fax (209) 335-2498. Or Sequoia and Kings Canyon National Parks, Three Rivers, CA 93271-9700; (209) 565-3134 or fax (209) 565-3730.

Maps for backpacking: Park maps are available for free at the entrance stations. A more detailed map is available for a fee from Tom Harrison Cartography at (415) 456-7940 or Trails Illustrated at (800) 962-1643. For a topographic map of the area, ask for Lodgepole from the USGS.

Season: Open from late June to early September.

Directions: From Visalia, drive east on Highway 198 for 40 miles, through the town of Three Rivers, to the Ash Mountain Entrance Station at Sequoia National Park. Continue 16 miles on the Generals Highway to the Giant Forest area. Turn right on Crescent Meadow Road and drive 3.5 miles to the Crescent Meadow parking area. The High Sierra Trail begins near the edge of Crescent Meadow.

---

81. SEQUOIA VILLAGE INN CABINS
near Sequoia National Park, off Highway 198 in Three Rivers

The cabins at Sequoia Village Inn have the three essentials for a perfect easy camping vacation: Location, location, location. Situated at the edge of Sequoia National Park, they are ideally positioned for you to make day-trips into the remote southern areas of the national park at Mineral King and South Fork, as well as the less remote central areas of the park at Potwisha and Giant Forest.

Right across the road from Sequoia Village Inn is where the Marble Fork and the East Fork of the Kaweah River tumble together. Especially in the spring when the river level is high, you can hear nothing but the sweet music of rolling water. In summer, when the temperature heats up in Three Rivers, the sound of the Kaweah is always refreshing.

As if that wasn't enough, the people who run Sequoia Village Inn have gone out of their way to make the place really nice, with well-constructed buildings, private patios and verandas, and lovely gardens. The inn has five cottages, two larger chalets, and one suite. The cottages are all slightly different, but all have full kitchens and most have views of either the Kaweah River or the mountains. They feature special touches like verandas, clawfoot tubs, four-poster beds, and unique tilework. The large chalets are two stories high and have three bedrooms, with beautiful mountain views, fireplaces, full kitchens, and room for up to nine people. A swimming pool and hot tub are located on the premises.

With a one-minute drive from your cottage, you can be at the Ash Mountain entrance station to Sequoia National Park. From there, your first stop in winter and spring should be Potwisha Campground, where you can pick up the trail that leads to Marble Falls on the Marble Fork of the Kaweah River. Even in summer, this waterfall cascades beautifully over large boulders, but the route can

---

On top of Moro Rock, Sequoia National Park

be hot because of the low elevation. March, April, and May are the best months to visit, when the foothill wildflowers bloom and the air is comfortably cool.

From the same campground, you can take a five-mile loop hike to see Monache Indian historical sites, including some pictographs painted on the side of Hospital Rock. Along the route, there are many pools where you can take a dip in the Middle Fork Kaweah River, providing the current is not too strong.

If you visit Sequoia National Park in summer and want to reach higher elevations and cool mountain air, just continue up Highway 198 for another 12 winding miles from Potwisha until you reach the Giant Forest area of the park. Be sure to walk the 380 stairsteps to the top of Moro Rock—it's not just a tourist attraction; it provides beautiful views. Then take a hike on any of a multitude of trails: Sunset Rock, Crescent Meadow, or the Huckleberry and Hazelwood Loop. Up here at 6,000 feet you're in the land of big Sequoias and granite and marble outcrops, an extreme contrast from the foothill country where your cabin is. Be sure to say hello to the biggest Sequoia of them all, the General Sherman Tree, in Giant Forest.

A longer drive from Sequoia Village Inn can take you into spectacular Mineral King in southern Sequoia National Park. It's 25 curving miles from the start of Mineral King Road in Three Rivers to the end of the road in Mineral King Valley, but if you get an early start on the drive and leave yourself all day to hike and explore, it's totally worth it. Many trails of varying difficulty lead from this scenic valley; see the following story for more information.

Facilities, reservations, fees: There are five cottages, two three-bedroom chalets, and one small suite at Sequoia Village Inn. All have fully equipped kitchens; the suite has a refrigerator and microwave only. Reservations are recommended. Fees range from $79 to $160 per night. Pets are permitted.

Who to contact: Sequoia Village Inn, 45971 Sierra Drive, P.O. Box 1014, Three Rivers, CA 93271; (209) 561-3652.

Season: Open year-round, best in springtime.

Directions: From Visalia, drive east on Highway 198 for 40 miles, through the town of Three Rivers. Six miles past Three Rivers, you'll see Sequoia Village Inn on the left. If you reach the Ash Mountain entrance station to Sequoia National Park, you've gone a half-mile too far.

82. SILVER CITY RESORT
Sequoia National Park, off Highway 198 in Mineral King

Silver City Resort in Mineral King is one of those fantasy-level outdoor vacation spots where after you visit once, you keep going back year after year. Not only that, but it's the kind of place that you keep thinking about, all winter long, while the Southern Sierra is shut down by deep snow. Like a long-lost lover, you just can't seem to get Silver City off your mind.

First of all, the resort is located in the beautiful Mineral King Valley in the southern section of Sequoia National Park, one of the most visually stunning places in all of California. Mineral King is accessible by only one road, and it's a long and winding one that starts in the town of Three Rivers and ends 25 miles later in this valley. That means that people don't discover Mineral King on their way to someplace else; they either know about it and make a special trip, or they don't.

Silver City Resort holds a special honor in Mineral King because it's the only commercial enterprise there, except for two national park campgrounds. The resort's general store and cafe are the meeting place for most everybody in the valley. A few lucky people own summer homes in Mineral King, but except for them and a few dozen campers, you won't see hordes of people. The road in is too long and slow for day visitors, and there are few places for overnighters to stay.

You will see backpackers heading for the trailheads in Mineral King Valley, then disappearing into the wilderness. A week or so later they'll turn up at the Silver City restaurant, desperately looking for any food that isn't freeze-dried.

If you've got a cabin reservation at Silver City Resort, you don't need to go backpacking, but you will definitely want to sample some of the gorgeous trails in Mineral King. Hikers looking for an easy stroll should start walking by the pack station at the end of Mineral King Road, following the Farewell Gap Trail along the East Fork Kaweah River. Here the river is really just a stream, and plenty of people cast a line into it as they walk, hoping to catch a trout or two. A lovely grove of aspens can be found only one mile up the trail from the pack station. Another pleasant easy hike is the Cold Springs Nature Trail out of Cold Springs Campground. Both paths offer fabulous views of Sawtooth Peak, Mineral Peak, and Rainbow Mountain, and parallel a babbling section of the Kaweah River. Hike either trail at sunset and you'll have plenty of memories to fuel your off-season fantasies about returning to Mineral King Valley.

Hikers who want more of a challenge can choose between several trails to spectacular high alpine lakes, including the Eagle Lake Trail (6.8 miles round-trip), Mosquito Lakes Trail (7.4 miles round-trip), Monarch Lakes Trail (8.4 miles round-trip), and Crystal Lake Trail (10 miles round-trip). All paths begin at the end of the road in Mineral King Valley, a mere five miles from Silver City Resort. Of these trails, Mosquito Lakes is the easiest—it has the last elevation gain—and Crystal Lake is the most challenging. Which destination is the prettiest? For me, it's a toss-up between Eagle Lake and Monarch Lakes, but it's best if you decide for yourself. All of the lakes are located above 10,000 feet in elevation, so expect classic high-country scenery, with plenty of stark granite and blue, blue water.

After so much hiking around, you'll be glad to know that one of the most surprising things about Silver City Resort is how good their cafe food is. It's simple fare—eggs and pancakes for breakfast, burgers and sandwiches for lunch and dinner—but it's not fried to death and it tastes remarkably fresh and delicious. They even serve veggie burgers—a rarity in the mountains—and you can get a half-decent salad. Best of all, the food is cheap, which comes as another surprise. They could charge whatever the heck they want out here and people would pay it anyway.

The resort serves its full menu Thursday through Monday. On Tuesday and Wednesday, they offer only beverages and their homemade pies, so if you're staying over midweek, make sure you bring provisions to cook in your cabin's kitchen or outside on the barbecue. The variety of pies is surprising—apple, marionberry, chocolate-walnut, blueberry, and so on—but eventually you'll need to eat something else. Be sure to check out the great black and white photos on the cafe's walls of Mineral King at the turn of the century.

The cabins at Silver City Resort come in a wide range of sizes and configurations, from an incredibly tiny one-room cottage (no kitchen, no bath, no electricity, and truly the smallest cabin we've ever stayed in) to large three-bedroom chalets with full kitchens, full bathrooms with showers, propane lamps, and wood stoves. I would recommend any of the cabins, with the possible exception of the one-room cottages, which are rather dark and cramped inside. For a few bucks more you can rent a one- or two-bedroom cabin, and have your own kitchen, although probably not your own bathroom. Some of the two-bedroom cabins have their own toilets, but for showers you must proceed to the central shower and restroom buildings.

For all of the cabins, you're instructed to bring flashlights, lanterns, ice, food, sleeping bags, and linens. (Some cabins have linens, but if you bring your own, you can save five bucks a night.)

One of the great Silver City traditions is "Thanksgiving dinner," which is served on the last Saturday evening that the resort is open, usually in mid-September. For nine bucks, visitors get the biggest,

Lower Monarch Lake, Mineral King, Sequoia National Park

most filling Thanksgiving dinner they can imagine, with all the required side dishes and a multitude of pies for dessert. Plus extra helpings if you please. A few folks come up from Three Rivers and Visalia just to attend the dinner, as do many of the private cabin owners in Mineral King Valley. The restaurant holds three or four seatings throughout the evening, so all the Silver City cabin guests and outside visitors get a chance to feast. At each seating, there is much gaiety and good conversation among folks who were strangers only minutes before.

Sound like fun? You betcha. Just remember, once you go for the first time, you'll be hooked. All year long, you'll be thinking about when you can make your next trip to Mineral King and Silver City Resort...

Facilities, reservations, fees: There are 11 cabins at Silver City Resort, ranging in size from studios to two bedrooms, most with fully equipped kitchens. Some cabins have private bathrooms; a central restroom and shower area is also available. There are also three larger chalets, each with three bedrooms, fully equipped kitchens, and private bathrooms, for groups of up to 8 people. A restaurant and general store are available. Reservations are recommended. Fees range from $50 to $200 per night. Pets are not permitted. There is a $10 entrance fee at Sequoia and Kings Canyon National Parks, good for seven days.

Who to contact: Silver City Resort, P.O. Box 56, Three Rivers, CA 93271; (209) 561-3223 in summer or (209) 734-4109 in winter.

Season: Open from Memorial Day through end of September.

Directions: From Visalia, drive east on Highway 198 for 38 miles to Mineral King Road, 2.5 miles east of Three Rivers. (If you reach the Ash Mountain Entrance Station, you've gone too far.) Turn right on Mineral King Road and drive 25 miles to Silver City Resort on the left side of the road.

83. LADYBUG BACKPACK
Sequoia National Park, off Highway 198 in South Fork

The South Fork area is the forgotten region of Sequoia National Park. Accessible only by a 13-mile dead-end road out of Three Rivers, South Fork is the place to go when you just want to get away from it all. Solitude in a national park? You can find it here. Solitude in a campground? You can get it by hiking away from the South Fork drive-in camp and heading to the small backpacker's camp on the Ladybug Trail.

The elevation is low—only 3,600 feet—so the area is accessible year-round. There may be no finer winter walk than a hike on the Ladybug Trail out of South Fork. Even on Labor Day weekend, we hiked in solitude on the Ladybug Trail, and when we arrived at Ladybug Campground, 1.7 easy miles later, nobody was camped there. It was a hot day, but we had our very own trail camp in Sequoia National Park, right next to a chain of clear, cold pools for wading and fishing.

The trail and camp share the same name—Ladybug—because the little brick-red beetles predominate. Thousands of them nest by the South Fork Kaweah River in winter, but you can find at least a few hundred at any time of the year. We didn't see any of the little guys until we sat down next to the creek; then we noticed they were all around us, on every rock and blade of grass. I even found a rare yellow one. If you grow weary of counting ladybugs, there are also plenty of butterflies to survey.

The Ladybug Trail starts from the far end of the South Fork Campground, where a sign states that Ladybug Camp is 1.7 miles, Cedar Creek is 3.2 miles, Whiskey Log Camp is 4.0 miles, and the trail dead-ends at 5.1 miles. A few hundred feet from the camp, the route crosses the South Fork Kaweah River on the Clough Cave Footbridge.

The hike leads through dry foothill country, but with a surprising amount of shade from canyon oaks and bay trees. The route is only slightly uphill, so the 1.7 miles to your campsite can be easily covered in less than an hour. You travel parallel to the river for the entire trip, with occasional views of tree-covered ridges to the south, and increasingly wider views of the entire canyon as you climb.

When you reach the camp at elevation 4,400 feet, you'll find only a few primitive campsites between the trail and the river, in a flat clearing beneath shady incense cedars. The conifers along the river here provide a welcome contrast to the grasslands along the trail. If when you arrive, you find that other people are already camping here, you have the option to continue on the trail for another 2.3 miles to Whiskey Log Camp.

But most likely you'll stay right here, because Ladybug is a little-used gem of a camp. It's not just the lovely cedars lining the edge of the stream and towering over your campsite, or the sweet, clear river where you can filter your water and take refreshing baths. One of the

South Fork Kaweah River at Ladybug Camp

camp's great secrets is that just downstream of it, a perfect 25-foot waterfall drops over rocks and ferns. You have to scramble a little to reach it, but there's an obvious route. The waterfall is tucked into a rocky corner in the river gorge, so the only way to see it well is to position yourself at its base. It's a lovely, sheltered spot, perfect for prayer or quiet contemplation.

If you decide to camp at Ladybug, remember to bring a filter for pumping your drinking water and your backpacking stove for cooking. If you are thinking about catching fish for dinner, forget it. The rules are catch-and-release only from downstream of the Clough Cave Footbridge to an elevation of 7,600 feet. But for catch-and-release angling, or just for a picnic, head upstream of Ladybug Camp, beyond where the trail switchbacks away from the river. There's a marvelous stretch of stream with pristine pools, rounded boulders, and ferns growing in huge clumps, making little rock-and-waterfall gardens.

If it's cool enough when you visit that you start hankering for sunshine, just continue on the Ladybug Trail toward Whiskey Log Camp for a short distance. The trail climbs up and out of the shade to a sunny south-facing slope, loaded with grassland wildflowers.

There's one more positive and one more negative to consider regarding Ladybug Camp. The positive: You don't have to pay a park entrance fee to visit the South Fork section of Sequoia National Park, and there is no fee for camping at Ladybug Camp. The negative: There's poison oak all over the place because of the low elevation. The trail and the camp are usually cleared of it, but be wary if you venture off-trail.

Facilities, reservations, fees: There are six campsites at Ladybug Camp. Water is available for filtering. Campfires are permitted. There is no fee for camping or day-use at the South Fork section of Sequoia National Park, but if you are going to other park regions, there is a $10 entrance fee, good for seven days. A free wilderness permit is required for overnight stays. They are available on a first-come, first-served basis from any ranger station, or in advance by mail or fax. Phone (209) 565-3708 for wilderness permit information. Pets are not permitted.

Who to contact: Sequoia and Kings Canyon National Parks, Three Rivers, CA 93271-9700; (209) 565-3134.

Maps for backpacking: Park maps are available for free at the entrance stations. A more detailed map is available for a fee from Tom Harrison Cartography at (415) 456-7940 or Trails Illustrated at (800) 962-1643. For a topographic map of the area, ask for Dennison Peak from the USGS.

Season: Open year-round.

Directions: From Visalia, drive east on Highway 198 for 35 miles to one mile west of Three Rivers. Turn right on South Fork Drive and drive 12.8 miles to South Fork Campground. (At nine miles, the road turns to dirt.) Day-use parking is available just inside the campground entrance. Walk to the far side of the campground to the Ladybug Trailhead.

---

84. CAMP NELSON CABINS
Sequoia National Forest, off Highway 190 near Camp Nelson

If you've never been there, it's hard to imagine how beautiful southern Tulare County is. I don't mean the section that you see while driving on Highway 99 around Visalia; I mean the part that's east of there, where the elevation starts to climb, the temperatures drop, and the trees grow really enormous.

The northeast part of Tulare County is encased within the border of Sequoia and Kings Canyon National Parks, so the beauty of that area is expected. But the scenery doesn't stop at the park boundary line; it keeps going all the way to the southeast end of Tulare County through miles of national forest land. This is one of the few places in California where just driving your car feels like a scintillating outdoor experience. Everywhere you look, the views are awesome.

Accessing the area takes some effort; the main road to Sequoia National Forest south of the national parks is winding Highway 190 out of Porterville and Springville. The better the scenery gets, the more twisty the road gets, so prepare to drive slow and take your Dramamine. Your destination is the town of Camp Nelson at 5,000 feet in elevation, where a company called Mountain Real Estate will rent you a cabin to serve as your base camp.

Each of Mountain Real Estate's cabins is someone's private home—they're vacation retreats that don't get used much by their owners, so they rent them out. The cabins vary in size and amenities, but all of them have fully equipped kitchens, plus fireplaces or wood-burning stoves. Most of them have all the necessary bedding and towels, and many have laundry facilities, televisions, and VCRs. All you need to pack are your clothes and your groceries.

With Camp Nelson as your base, your nearby outdoor options include the Golden Trout Wilderness to the north, and a multitude of trailheads to the south along Highway 190 between Camp Nelson and Johnsondale. The first trailhead I'd hit is the one for the Needles Lookout, a couple miles from Quaking Aspen Campground. After an easy and beautiful 2.5-mile hike, you reach the historic Needles fire lookout tower and can check out the stupendous views of the Kern River Basin, Lloyd Meadow, and the Golden Trout Wilderness.

View from the Needles Lookout Trail

Next, head for the peak of 9,300-foot Slate Mountain, accessible via the Summit Trailhead on Forest Service Road 21S78. It's a longer and harder trip than the easy hike to the Needles Lookout, but the views are even more impressive. You'll be able to see the granite spires of the Needles and Olancha Peak as you hike to Slate Mountain's summit.

Closer to home, make sure to pay a visit to the Amos Alonzo Stagg Tree, the sixth largest Giant Sequoia in the world at 243 feet tall and 29 feet in diameter. The tree can be seen by taking a short walk from the parking area at Alder Drive in Camp Nelson. (Alder Drive is best accessed via Redwood Drive, 2.5 miles east of Camp Nelson on Highway 190.)

As if there wasn't enough to do in Sequoia National Forest, there's another spectacular chunk of public land available nearby for exploration: Mountain Home Demonstration State Forest and Balch County Park. These two adjacent parks are reached by driving west on Highway 190 toward Springville, turning right (north) on Balch Park Road (Road 239), then turning right again on Bear Creek Road (Road 220). After a winding and scenic 14 miles, you arrive at park headquarters. Pick up a map, then head for the Adam and Eve Loop Trail or the Redwood Crossing Trail. Both offer Giant Sequoias, clean mountain air, and crystal clear streams.

Facilities, reservations, fees: There are 11 cabin rentals available from Mountain Real Estate, ranging in size from one to three bedrooms, all with kitchen facilities. Reservations are required. Fees range from $70 to $110 per night. Pets are permitted in some cabins.

Who to contact: Mountain Real Estate, P.O. Box 95, Camp Nelson, CA 93208; (209) 542-2822 or (209) 542-0812.

Season: Open year-round.

Directions: From Porterville, drive east on Highway 190 for 30 miles to Camp Nelson and the Pierpoint Springs Resort on the right. Mountain Real Estate is located adjacent to Pierpoint Springs Resort; they will give you your keys and directions to your cabin.

85. ROADS END RESORT
Kern River, off Highway 178 near Kernville

When you hear about a place with a name like Roads End Resort, it makes you want to pack up the car and go straight there. Well, go ahead. This place is as good as its name, especially if you like the idea of a cabin right alongside the Wild and Scenic Kern River.

If you've never been to the outdoor paradise north of Kernville and Lake Isabella in Sequoia National Forest, your first visit will be a stunner. Much of the lowland terrain near the Kern River is chaparral and oaks—not much different than say, San Diego. But drive a few miles up the road and suddenly you're in a land of lush meadows and

Giant Sequoias. Yup, they have it all here.

The Kern River is best known for river rafting and fishing, and you can do both if you visit Roads End Resort in springtime or early summer. As the season wears on and the river quiets down, your activities might change to innertubing and swimming, but nobody complains.

On my first trip to Roads End, I was a bit confused by the fact that the road doesn't end here; in fact it keeps going all the way until it joins up with Highway 190 and heads out to Porterville. When the resort was built in 1922, this really was the end of the road, but times have changed. Roads End Resort was originally a pack station for taking hunters into the high country at Big Meadow and Cannell Meadow, which are now accessible by automobile.

Although Roads End's cabins are antiques, they have been well cared for. Each one is painted dark green on the outside and is lined with knotty pine and plenty of charm on the inside. Most have fireplaces and fully equipped kitchens. (One cabin has only a microwave and refrigerator; it's a small cabin for just two people.) Half the cabins are directly on the river; the other half are across the road, a few steps away. Fear not: After nightfall, there is very little auto traffic, so you won't be bothered by road noise.

Although most people visit Roads End for its easy access to the Kern River, you can also use it as a base camp for some very special day hiking and exploring. The number of trails and trailheads located within a few miles of the resort is a bit intimidating. Here are my favorites: The North Fork Kern River Trail (especially in springtime for wildflower viewing), the Packsaddle Cave Trail (bring your flashlight and peek inside a limestone cavern), the Trail of 100 Giants on the Western Divide Highway (an easy stroll around impressive Giant Sequoias), and any of the multitude of trails in the high country off Sherman Pass Road.

Geez, I get all excited just thinking about it. Talk to the nice folks at Roads End Resort for updated trail information, or stop in at the Sequoia National Forest Visitor Center in nearby Kernville.

Roads End Resort is open year-round, and one of the best times to visit is in spring, before the summer temperatures heat up. Winter can also be lovely, with little or no snow at the resort but deep snow only a few miles away in the high country.

Facilities, reservations, fees: There are six cabins at Roads End Resort, most with fully equipped kitchens. A general store and campground are available. Reservations are recommended. Fees range from $65 to $80 per night with a two-night minimum. Pets are not permitted.

Who to contact: Roads End Resort, Star Route 1, P.O. Box 98, Kernville, CA 93238; (760) 376-6562.

Season: Open year-round, best in springtime.

Directions: From Kernville on the north end of Lake Isabella, drive 19 miles north on Sierra Way/Road 99. Roads End Resort is located three-quarters of a mile north of the small settlement of Fairview.

86. WHISPERING PINES LODGE CABINS
Kern River, off Highway 178 near Kernville

If the name "Whispering Pines" doesn't make you want to jump out of your chair and drive to Kernville right away, try this phrase on for size: "bed and breakfast cottages and bungalows on the Kern River."

That's the Wild and Scenic Kern River, and a cabin vacation along its edges is one of the best ways to celebrate springtime in Central California. Rafters and kayakers, rejoice—this is your kind of place, but you'll have to share it with plenty of hikers, windsurfers, mountain bikers, anglers, and just about every other kind of outdoor recreationist.

Each cottage or bungalow at Whispering Pines has a river view, a fireplace, and a king-sized bed. Several have full kitchens; those that don't have refrigerators and coffeemakers. Everything is carefully decorated and kept up. The cottages also have HBO and telephones, but we'll overlook that little flaw.

Breakfast is included in the price of your cabin, and it's more than your basic Danish and coffee. You head to the resort's dining room each morning for gourmet coffee, homemade breads and muffins, quiches, and fresh fruits. The owners have obviously gone to some trouble to make things nice; they even hand out the local newspaper to guests, but you can ignore it if you want.

River trips are offered on the Upper Kern River for every level of ability. Numerous companies in town can get you set up with the kind of trip and equipment you want. If the Kern doesn't completely captivate your every moment, Kernville also boasts a close proximity to Lake Isabella. Isabella is one of the largest bodies of water in Southern California, with a capacity of 11,000 surface acres of water.

(The average for the year is usually about 8,000 surface acres.) It is a popular lake for windsurfing and waterskiing, although plenty of people fish there, mostly for bass. Trout fishermen usually stick to flyfishing on the Kern River, although the Department of Fish and Game plants some rainbow trout in Isabella.

Kernville is surrounded on three sides by Sequoia National Forest land; numerous hiking trailheads lead from Sierra Way. The Cannell Meadow National Recreation Trail begins less than a mile from Whispering Pines; it is a nine-mile trail that leads from the foothills at 2,800 feet in elevation to Cannell Meadow at 7,500 feet. In spring, the lower stretches of this trail are lovely; in summer, you'll want to start at the upper end or you'll bake in the heat. To reach the lower trailhead, drive north on Sierra Way for three-quarters of a mile; you'll see the trail sign on the right side of the road; park near the horse corrals.

Twenty miles north on Sierra Way you'll find the turnoff for Sherman Pass Road to Big Meadow and Horse Meadow; you can take this road to access the upper end of the Cannell Meadow Trail or dozens of other spectacular paths. A few favorites: the Sherman Peak Trail, Salmon Creek Trail, and Manter Meadow Loop.

South Creek Falls on Sierra Way near Kernville

A shorter drive to Wofford Heights and then up Highway 155 takes you into the richly forested Greenhorn Mountains. The area offers a myriad of hiking trails in summer and cross-country skiing trails in winter. Hikers shouldn't miss two easy but lovely trails: the Unal Trail and the Sunday Peak Trail. In the winter, cross-country skiers can glide to their hearts' content at Shirley Meadows Ski Area.

Facilities, reservations, fees: There are 17 cabins at Whispering Pines Lodge, some with fully equipped kitchens. Reservations are recommended. Fees range from $99 to $129 per night for two people, including breakfast. Additional persons are $15 per night. Pets are not permitted.

Who to contact: Whispering Pines Lodge, 13745 Sierra Way, Route 1, Box 41, Kernville, CA 93238; (760) 376-3733.

Season: Open year-round; best in winter and spring.

Directions: From Kernville on the north end of Lake Isabella, drive north on Sierra Way/Road 99 for a half-mile to Whispering Pines Lodge.

87. OAK FLAT LOOKOUT TOWER
Sequoia National Forest, off Highway 178 near Bakersfield

Have you ever taken a hike or a drive to a forest fire lookout tower, perched high on a mountaintop amid miles of wild country? As you gazed at the panorama spread out before you, did you find yourself dreaming of getting a job as a lookout, and living alone in your mountain tower with nothing but scenery, silence, and solitude?

For those of you with lookout scout envy, I know the perfect place to go camping. It's the Oak Flat Lookout Tower in the Green-horn Mountains near Bakersfield, and yes, it's open for public use. This is how you arrange to spend a night or two there: First, apply for a permit with the Greenhorn Ranger District of Sequoia National Forest, either by mail, fax, or in person. Permits are issued on a first-come, first-served basis to anyone 18 years or older, so the qualifications aren't too tough. You must pay a $25 fee per night, which goes directly to maintaining the lookout tower.

Once you've got your permit and reservation, start packing. Remember to pack light because everything must be hauled up to the tower, which means climbing 40 steep stairs or using a small, manual basket pulley system. The heaviest thing you carry should be bottled water, as none is available at the tower. Plan on one gallon per person per day.

Pack your sleeping bags or some kind of bedding, and your favorite pillow. (There are two small beds inside.) Flashlights and candles are a good idea, plus plenty of matches for lighting the propane appliances, which include an overhead light, heater, oven, and refrigerator. Bring firewood if you want to have a campfire outside. Most important of all, take along plenty of trash bags for hauling out your trash at the end of your trip.

Got your warm clothes for windy nights? Shorts and T-shirts for hot summer days? Hiking boots? Plenty of good food, plus cooking and eating utensils? Toilet paper for the outhouse? Okay. You're ready. The rangers at the Greenhorn District will provide you with a key for the lookout road gate and the tower. In winter, snow, rain, or ice can make the road impassable except for four-wheel-drive vehicles, but most of the year a passenger car is fine. Remember that you are 15 miles from the nearest pay phone or services, so if you have a need to stay in touch with the outside world, bring along a cellular phone.

The Oak Flat Lookout Tower is at 4,910 feet in elevation, overlooking the Kern River. It was built in 1934 and was used to detect fires until 1984. Since you're staying in a historic building perched on a mountaintop high above a river, it's easy to figure out what to do while you're there: Sit and admire the view.

If you want to complement your trip by visiting a fire lookout that's still in operation, drive to the Breckenridge Lookout, also on the Greenhorn Ranger District of Sequoia National Forest. On clear days you can see all the way to Mount Whitney.

Facilities, reservations, fees: The Oak Flat Lookout Tower can accommodate up to four people. Propane cooking facilities are provided. Reservations and a permit are required. The fee is $25 per night. Pets are permitted.

Who to contact: Greenhorn Ranger District, Sequoia National Forest, 3801 Pegasus Drive, Bakersfield, CA 93308; (805) 391-6088.

Season: Open year-round, best in winter or spring.

Directions: From Bakersfield, drive east on Highway 178 for 12 miles to Rancheria Road. Drive 15 miles north on Rancheria Road (gravel) to Forest Service Road 27S20. Turn right and drive one-tenth of a mile.

88. RANKIN RANCH
Walker Basin, off Highway 58 near Caliente

Listen up, pardner, while I tell y'all about Rankin Ranch, deep in the Tehachapi Mountains, way out there in the town of Caliente. What? You say you never heard of the place? Now don't get all excited and fall off your horse... Just keep readin' and I'll let you in on the secret...

Rankin Ranch is a touch of the old California, a leftover from the time of cowboys, cattle ranching, hay rides, and horseshoes. It is situated at 3,500 feet in elevation in the Walker Basin, roughly midway between Bakersfield and Tehachapi on Highway 58. The land surrounding Rankin Ranch is a classic high mountain valley, with a mix of wide open meadows and forest. If this sounds to you like a good place to saddle up and ride into the sunset, you're right.

A man named Walker Rankin founded the original cattle ranch on this land in 1863, and the place has stayed in the family ever since. It is one of the oldest and largest family-owned ranches in California; various members of the Rankin family still live on the 31,000 acres and raise Herefords.

Rankin family members have also used their land to build a successful "guest ranch" business—a vacation resort for people who want to play Cowboy or Cowgirl for a while. For 33 years, vacationers have been coming to Rankin Ranch to ride horses, fish, hike, and live the ranch life for a few days. The place is especially popular with families; the owners maintain a long and varied list of scheduled activities for children.

You have to enjoy group activities and lots of friendly people to have a good time at Rankin Ranch. Misanthropes and those who prefer to go solo will feel out of place here, because the emphasis is on making friends. In fact, one of Rankin Ranch's specialties is planning family reunions and other large-group special occasions; they can accommodate a total of 40 people at one time.

The ranch has 12 duplex-style cabins that are on the modern side, with carpeting and wood paneling. Big families can rent both sides of a duplex and open the adjoining doors, so the place becomes one extra-large cabin. Your fee for a night at the ranch includes three big meals in the ranch dining room and all the horseback riding you can stand, plus a myriad of other ranch activities: tennis, trout fishing in little Julia Lake, horseshoe tournaments, bingo, swimming, volleyball, hay rides, and so on. You pay nothing extra for anything, including the organized children's programs, so you know in advance exactly what your vacation will cost.

The best season to visit may be springtime, before school is out and the prime vacation season starts, when Rankin Ranch offers its lowest rates of the year. Not only can a spring visit save you a few bucks, but you also get a chance to see the Walker Basin's spectacular wildflower display. From late March to May, the mountain slopes and high meadows come alive with lupine, poppies, thistle, baby blue-eyes, deep red owl's clover, and Indian paintbrush. It's truly a sight to behold.

Even if you've never been on a horse before, you'll have a good time at Rankin Ranch. Here's a tip for beginners: Don't go out and buy a pair of cowboy boots before your trip to the ranch. Plenty of real cowboys wear any old shoes with low heels, and you should, too. Sturdy jeans or pants are a necessity, and if you wear a hat, make sure it ties around your neck or fits securely, so it won't blow off and scare your horse. The ranch offers free riding instruction, and each horse is carefully selected for the abilities of each rider. Before long, even novices are riding out of the corral to check on the cattle or help bale the hay.

Now that you know all about it, you can saddle up and get yourself to Rankin Ranch. Hey, what's the rush? You're still a young whipper-snapper; you've got time to make the trip before all your cows head back to the barn.

Facilities, reservations, fees: There are 12 cabins at Rankin Ranch; none have kitchen facilities. Fees range from $125 to $150 per person per night, and include three full meals a day and horseback riding privileges. Children under 12 stay for reduced rates. Reservations are required. Pets are not permitted.

Who to contact: Rankin Ranch, P.O. Box 36, Caliente, CA 93518; (805) 867-2511.

Season: Open from the week before Easter to the end of November.

Directions: From Interstate 5, just before the Interstate 5/Highway 99 split north of Grapevine, take the Lake Isabella, Lamont, Arvin exit. Drive 15 miles north on Wheeler Ridge Road, then turn right (east) on Highway 223 (Bear Mountain Boulevard) and drive 16 miles. At the Highway 223 junction with Highway 58, drive east for one mile and take the Caliente cutoff. Drive through Caliente (past the post office), continuing 2.5 miles until the road forks. Take the left fork up the hill; it's nine miles to Rankin Ranch from the fork.

Eastern Sierra
& Death Valley

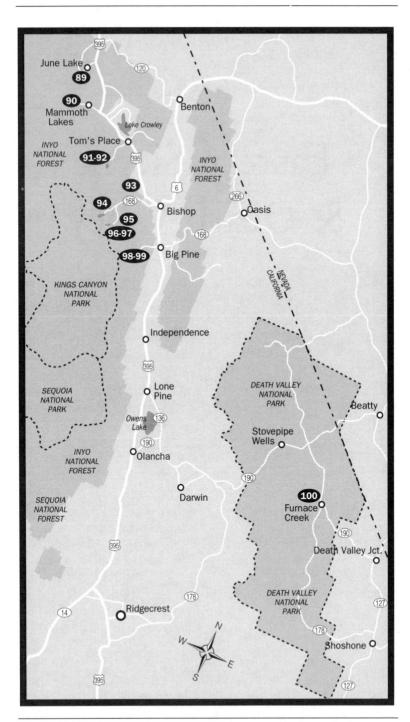

June Lake

89

90
Mammoth
Lakes

Benton

Lake Crowley

Tom's Place

INYO
NATIONAL
FOREST

91-92

INYO
NATIONAL
FOREST

93

6

94

168

266

95

Bishop

Oasis

96-97

98-99

Big Pine

168

KINGS CANYON
NATIONAL
PARK

Independence

395

DEATH VALLEY
NATIONAL
PARK

Beatty

SEQUOIA
NATIONAL
PARK

Lone
Pine

Owens
Lake

136

Stovepipe
Wells

INYO
NATIONAL
FOREST

190

Olancha

SEQUOIA
NATIONAL
FOREST

Darwin

100
Furnace
Creek

190

190

Death Valley Jct.

395

127

DEATH VALLEY
NATIONAL
PARK

14

178

Ridgecrest

N

W   E

S

178

Shoshone

395

127

NEVADA
CALIFORNIA

89. BIG ROCK RESORT
June Lake, off U.S. 395 near Mammoth Lakes

When Southern Californians think of going on a serious skiing or snowboarding trip, they bypass all their local ski areas and load up their sport utility vehicles for the long drive to Mammoth. There's nothing wrong with the ski resorts in the nearby San Gabriel and San Bernardino Mountains; they just aren't the Eastern Sierra.

The majority of those SUVs head for the glamour runs on Mammoth Mountain and the town of Mammoth Lake's popular hotels, restaurants, and nightlife. But there's a less visited recreation area, just 30 miles to the north, in the town of June Lake. If you want to have a skiing vacation in a place that doesn't feel like a transplanted Los Angeles, give June Lake a try.

At June Mountain Ski Area, you'll find less crowds and cheaper lift tickets. You'll have snowmobiling, sledding, snowshoeing, and cross-country skiing options. And best of all, you'll be sharing a quiet, winter wonderland vacation with your loved ones in a lakeside cabin at Big Rock Resort.

As it turns out, the cabins at Big Rock are a perfect destination in any season. They're perched on the shoreline of large June Lake, the prettiest lake along the June Lake Loop, the main access road. In summer, visitors take advantage of excellent trout fishing, a myriad of Inyo National Forest hiking trails, sailing and boating on the lake, and biking the spectacular June Lake Loop. The resort offers motor-boat and paddle boat rentals, or cabin guests can bring their own boat and launch it for free.

For hikers, a trailhead is located practically across the street from Big Rock Resort, by the June Lake Firehouse. From there, you can hike five miles through flower-filled Yost Meadows and the June Mountain Ski Area to Yost Lake. Or, if you prefer to get your butt kicked by a steep climb, drive two miles down Highway 158 toward Silver Lake to access the Yost Creek Trailhead. The trail leads to both Yost Lake and Fern Lake, but the right fork to Fern Lake has a killer last mile. The left fork to Yost Lake is longer but more moderate.

In winter, the snow is the thing at June Lake, with 2,500 vertical feet of skiing available on June Mountain, just 1.5 miles from Big Rock's cabins. Many snowboarders insist that the boarding is better here than at neighboring Mammoth Mountain. One thing is for certain: The lines at the chair lifts are a lot shorter.

The cabins at Big Rock Resort have everything you need for either a winter or summer vacation. They come in sizes from one to three bedrooms, accommodating anywhere from two to 10 people. Their kitchens are fully equipped, so all you need to do is buy your groceries in the village of June Lake, which is right next door. Some cabins have microwaves and many have fireplaces, so be sure to request the amenities you want when you make your reservation. One word of caution: The two-bedroom cabins are duplex-style, so if you're looking for peace and quiet, these may not be the best choice. If you want guaranteed privacy, rent a one-bedroom or three-bedroom cabin, and no one will share your exterior walls.

Facilities, reservations, fees: There are eight cabins at Big Rock Resort, ranging in size from one to three bedrooms, all with fully equipped kitchens. The two-bedroom cabins are duplexes. A restaurant and boat rentals are available. Reservations are recommended. Fees range from $70 to $140 per night. Pets are permitted with advance permission and a $50 deposit.

Season: Open year-round.

Who to contact: Big Rock Resort, P.O. Box 126, 1 Big Rock Road, June Lake, CA 93529; (800) 769-9831 or (760) 648-7717. Fax (760) 648-1067.

Directions: From U.S. 395 at the Highway 203/Mammoth Lakes turnoff, drive 15 miles north on U.S. 395 to Highway 158 at June Lake Junction, the southern turnoff for the June Lake Loop. Turn left on Highway 158 and drive 2.5 miles to Big Rock Road on the right. Turn right and drive to the resort.

MORE CABIN RENTALS IN JUNE LAKE:

•Reverse Creek Lodge, Route 3, P.O. Box 2, June Lake, CA 93529; (760) 648-7535 or (800) 762-6440.

•Fern Creek Lodge, Route 3, P.O. Box 7, June Lake, CA 93529; (760) 648-7722.

•Silver Lake Resort, P.O. Box 17, June Lake, CA 93529; (760) 648-7525.

•The Four Seasons, Route 3, P.O. Box 8-B, June Lake, CA 93529; (760) 648-7476.

•Gull Lake Lodge, P.O. Box 25, June Lake, CA 93529; (760) 648-7516.

•June Lake Pines Cottages, P.O. Box 97, June Lake, CA 93529; (760) 648-7522 or (800) 481-3637.

90. TAMARACK LODGE RESORT
Twin Lakes, off U.S. 395 in Mammoth Lakes

One of the best lakes you can drive to in the Mammoth Lakes area is Twin Lakes, where a large, hourglass shaped body of water is continually replenished by the rushing cascade of 250-foot Twin Falls. The water is also continually replenished by the Department of Fish and Game, who keep Twin Lakes filled with rainbow trout all summer long.

Twin Lakes was once two separate lakes, which are now adjoined by a marshy area and a bridge. The lake is set in a cliff-lined granite bowl and is a favorite spot of flyfishermen and scenery-lovers, for the simple reason that it's gorgeous. With a place as fine as this, wouldn't it be great to spend a few days there? That's what we thought, so we booked ourselves a stay at Tamarack Lodge Resort, which has 25 cabins spaced around its six-acre grounds by the shore of Twin Lakes.

Unlike the majority of the lodging options at Mammoth Lakes, which are mostly bland condominiums and motels, the Tamarack Lodge is a classic 1924 mountain resort, with a big stone fireplace and log-lined walls. Alas, the resort's cabins have only partial views of the Twin Lakes, but you'll get over it when you realize you can walk a few steps to the water's edge and get any view you want.

Tamarack Lodge Resort is located a couple of miles outside of the main drag in Mammoth Lakes, so you're far enough away from the hustle and bustle of the town, but

Twin Lakes and 250-foot Twin Falls

you can still have access to it if you so desire.

The list of outdoor activities in Mammoth Lakes is long enough to fill an entire book. Here are some of the highlights: Skiing and snowboarding at Mammoth Mountain Ski Resort. Cross-country skiing right from your cabin door. Trout fishing in Twin Lakes, as well as the other lakes along Lake Mary Road—Lake Mary, Lake Mamie, and Lake George. Swimming in Horseshoe Lake. Mountain biking in summer, when Mammoth Mountain Ski Resort transforms itself into a mountain bike park.

And hiking, hiking, hiking. The best trails that are close to Tamarack Lodge are the short hikes to Panorama Dome and Sky Meadows. The Panorama Dome Trail begins off Lake Mary Road, just past the turnoff to Twin Lakes. It's an easy half-mile hike to the top of a rocky dome with stunning summit views. The Sky Meadows Trail begins at Coldwater Campground, traces a short and easy path to rocky Emerald Lake, then continues to Sky Meadows, where the summer wildflowers will intoxicate you.

From nearby Lake George, you can hike to Barrett and T.J. Lakes, or Crystal Lake and the Mammoth Crest. At Horseshoe Lake, you can walk the easy path around the lake's perimeter, or take the side trail to McLeod Lake. And while you're in Mammoth Lakes, you must take a day-trip to Devils Postpile National Monument. You can hike to the columnar basalt formation called the Devils Postpile, plus view spectacular Rainbow Falls and Lower Falls. Trails continue from the Devils Postpile into the Ansel Adams and John Muir wildernesses, so you won't run out of things to do.

Facilities, reservations, fees: There are 25 cabins at Tamarack Lodge Resort, ranging in size from studios to three bedrooms, all with fully equipped kitchens. Twelve motel-style rooms are also available. A restaurant is available. Reservations are recommended. Fees range from $70 to $300 per night. Pets are not permitted.

Season: Open year-round.

Who to contact: Tamarack Lodge, P.O. Box 69, Mammoth Lakes, CA 93546; (760) 934-2442 or (800) 237-6879.

Directions: From U.S. 395 at Mammoth Lakes, take the Highway 203 turnoff and drive west for four miles, through the town of Mammoth Lakes, to the intersection of Highway 203/Minaret Road and Lake Mary Road. Continue straight on Lake Mary Road for 2.2 miles, then bear right on Twin Lakes Road and follow it for a half-mile to the Tamarack Lodge Resort.

MORE CABIN RENTALS IN MAMMOTH LAKES:

•Zwart House, P.O. Box 174, Mammoth Lakes, CA 93546; (760) 934-2217.

•Crystal Crag Lodge, P.O. Box 88, Mammoth Lakes, CA 93546; (760) 934-2436.

•Convict Lake Resort, Route 1, Box 204, Mammoth Lakes, CA 93546; (760) 934-3800 or (800) 992-2260.

•Pine Cliff Resort, P.O. Box 2, Mammoth Lakes, CA 93546; (760) 934-2447.

•Edelweiss Lodge, P.O. Box 658, Mammoth Lakes, CA 93546; (760) 934-2445.

91. ROCK CREEK LODGE
Inyo National Forest, off U.S. 395 near Tom's Place

From November to May each year, this is what you need to know: Rock Creek Lodge is the only resort in spectacular Rock Creek Canyon that is open year-round. Plenty of folks are grateful for those extra months in wintertime, because here at 9,373 feet in elevation, midway between Bishop and Mammoth Lakes, cross-country skiers are in snowy heaven.

Rock Creek Lodge was founded in the 1920s as one of the first ski resorts in America. Although summer season is busy at Rock Creek Lodge, with hordes of visitors showing up for the plentiful fishing and hiking adventures of the Eastern Sierra, the winter season has always been and still remains Rock Creek Lodge's special niche.

Here's how a winter visit to Rock Creek Lodge works: First, you confirm your cabin reservation, then you drive to the town of Tom's Place on U.S. 395. Drive partway down Rock Creek Road to the East Fork Parking Area, a California Sno-Park site. At a prearranged time, the lodge's snowmobile will meet you and shuttle you in the last two miles to your cabin. (Rock Creek Road is not plowed past East Fork in winter; the only access to the resort is via snowmobile.) From the moment you arrive, you can strap on your skis and glide wherever you wish.

Even if you've never cross-country skied before, you won't feel left out in the cold. Rock Creek Lodge is an excellent place for novices: full equipment rentals and lessons are available. You won't be

---

Wood piles at a cabin at Rock Creek Lodge

a novice for long. Experienced skiers can go off on their own, perhaps even opting to stay at the lodge's backcountry hut at Mosquito Flat. You cross-country ski in, carrying only your food and sleeping bag. Rock Creek Lodge keeps the hut stocked with wood, fuel, stoves, cooking utensils, and chairs. Six people can spend a cozy few days and nights there, skiing and snowshoeing to their hearts' content.

Since you won't be going anywhere once the snowmobile has left you at Rock Creek Lodge, the resort is fully equipped. A beautiful log cabin serves as the restaurant. Inside are long wooden tables where you sit, eat excellent meals, and meet all your neighbors. It's impossible not to make friends during your stay. Only breakfast and dinner are served; for lunch you're on your own. (Groceries are available at the lodge's small store.) In winter, dinners and breakfasts are included in the price of your cabin. You don't choose from a menu; instead you eat whatever they are serving that night. During our visit, it was lasagna on Saturday, teriyaki chicken on Sunday, enchiladas on Monday, and so on. Maybe it was enhanced by the cold air and the exercise, but everything tasted incredibly good.

The lodge has both "modern" and "rustic" cabins. "Modern" means they have their own showers; "rustic" means you must walk to a separate building for hot water plumbing. All cabins have kitchenettes. The cabins are well spaced, with plenty of breathing room between them. For either type of cabin, you need to bring your own sleeping bag and towels (pillows and pillowcases are provided). A flashlight is also a good idea, especially if you are staying in the rustic cabins and need to make an after-dark trip to the showers.

It's hard to pin down what is the best part of a winter trip to Rock Creek Lodge, but after debating it for a while, we settled on this: The best part is that because the road is closed, there are no cars visible anywhere in this snowy wonderland. Civilization? You'll quickly forget all about it.

Facilities, reservations, fees: There are 13 cabins at Rock Creek Lodge, all with cold running water and seven with full bathrooms and showers. A common shower house is available. All cabins have kitchenettes. A restaurant and general store are also available. Reservations are required. Winter fees range from $70 to $105 per night per person, including breakfast and dinner; children under 12 stay for reduced rates. A ski-in wilderness hut is available for $25 per night per person. Summer fees range from $65 to $125 per night; summer rates for cabins are based on double occupancy and do not include meals. Pets are permitted in summer only; $10 fee per night.

Who to contact: Rock Creek Lodge, Route 1, Box 12, Mammoth Lakes, CA 93546; (760) 935-4170. Fax (760) 935-4172.

Season: Open year-round.

Directions: From Bishop, drive 24 miles north on U.S. 395 to the Rock Creek turnoff near Tom's Place. Turn west on Rock Creek Road and drive eight miles to Rock Creek Lodge on the left. In winter, you will drive only six miles and park at the East Fork parking lot. A snowmobile will meet you at the parking lot and shuttle you the final two miles to the lodge.

92. ROCK CREEK LAKES RESORT
Inyo National Forest, off U.S. 395 near Tom's Place

If you can get a cabin at Rock Creek Lakes Resort, you must have been born under a lucky star. The resort is located right across the road from Rock Creek Lake in gorgeous Rock Creek Canyon, and gosh darn it, the place is booked up almost all the time. Many people vacation here year after year; they keep the same week every summer on permanent reservation.

However, if you can live spontaneously, you have a chance. Rock Creek Lakes Resort keeps a waiting list for cancellations, and if you are willing to pack up and go on short notice, you'll get your cabin. We tried the waiting-list technique last summer, and we were called two different times for two different weeks. Another option is to visit on weekdays only, not weekends, especially before or after the main summer season. Or plan your trip a year in advance: If you can't get a reservation for this summer, make one for next summer.

Why is Rock Creek Lakes Resort so popular? Two reasons: fishing and hiking. For starters, you can walk from your cabin to the boat dock at Rock Creek Lake and then fish your heart out all week long. Small boats are rented at the lake, with trolling motors only. Many people just float around in rubber rafts and kayaks or fish from the shore. Angling prospects are good; the lake is stocked all summer with rainbow trout.

If you want to head for other waters, the Owens River, Crowley Lake, McGee Creek, and Hot Creek are only a short drive away. And if a big lunker pulls your rod out of your hands and into the water, don't lose heart: You can rent a rod for $7 a day at the Rock Creek Lakes Resort Store. You say you don't want to work while you're on vacation? They'll even wind your line on your reel for you, for a fee.

If hiking interests you as much as, or more than, fishing, the Rock Creek Lakes Resort is ideally located for access to the many trailheads of Rock Creek Canyon. Most trails lead into the John Muir Wilderness, a dramatic landscape of 13,000-foot peaks, permanent snow fields, and gem-like lakes. The Hilton and Davis lakes trailhead

Overlooking the Little Lakes Valley from the Mono Pass Trail

is a quarter-mile from the turnoff to the cabins; you could walk to the trailhead and then hike four miles to the Hilton Lakes or five miles to Davis Lake. Or, drive one mile to the Mosquito Flat trailhead at the end of Rock Creek Road, then set off on the mostly flat trail through Little Lakes Valley. The trail is gorgeous and easily accessible; you can hike for as long or short a distance as you like. You'll see dozens of small lakes, one after another about every half-mile.

More ambitious hikers can begin at Mosquito Flat and follow the Mono Pass Trail to Ruby Lake and beyond, heading steeply uphill to scenic, 12,400-foot Mono Pass. The trailhead at Mosquito Flat is at 10,300 feet, one of the highest trailhead elevations in California, which means you enter the high country by automobile, rather than having to climb forever to get there. That's convenient, because you don't have a lot of free time: There are more trails and more destinations in Rock Creek Canyon than you could possibly cover in a single week.

If you are given a choice of cabins when you make your reservation at Rock Creek Lakes Resort, ask for one of the higher numbered ones. All of the cabins are secluded and in the trees, but numbers 1, 2, and 3 are the closest together. The cabins are on the modern side compared to others in the area, painted a cheerful red and fully furnished with kitchens, bathrooms, linens, and everything you need for your stay except food. Buy your groceries in Bishop or Mammoth.

The resort has a small lunch counter which is renowned for its homemade pies and soups. You can get a burger or a sandwich, too, but the list of pies is longer than the list of main courses. Their soups are outrageously good, as are their breakfasts. You're on your own for making dinner, but if you simply refuse to cook, go to the lunch counter before they close at 6:30 p.m., and select your dinner from the lunch menu.

Make sure you bring any specialty food items you desire with you on your trip. The resort store sells minimal groceries, but not enough for you to be able to prepare exciting menus for a whole week. They do sell firewood and ice, as well as fishing supplies and tackle. If you want to take fish home with you, they will clean and freeze them for a small fee.

Facilities, reservations, fees: There are 10 cabins at Rock Creek Lakes Resort, ranging in size from one to three bedrooms. All have fully equipped kitchens. A lunch counter and general store are available. Reservations are required. Fees range from $80 to $200 per night. Pets are not permitted.

Who to contact: Rock Creek Lakes Resort, P.O. Box 727, Bishop, CA 93515; (760) 935-4311. Fax (760) 935-9101.

Season: Open May to October.

Directions: From Bishop, drive 24 miles north on U.S. 395 to the Rock Creek turnoff near Tom's Place. Turn west on Rock Creek Road and drive nine miles to Rock Creek Lakes Resort on the right.

93. PARADISE RESORT
Lower Rock Creek, off U.S. 395 near Bishop

A stay at Paradise Resort is a different kind of vacation experience than others in the Eastern Sierra, and you should know the difference before you plan your trip. First, be aware that although this is still part of the Eastern Sierra, Paradise Resort is set along Lower Rock Creek in the arid, desert-like Owens Valley, quite a few miles from the nearest set of high mountain peaks. So if you're looking for dramatic Sierra vistas or a trail to an alpine lake leading from your cabin doorstep, this is not the place for it.

On the other hand, if fishing is your bag, you've come to the right place. Right outside your cabin door is what they call "family-style fishing," which means you can drop a line in Lower Rock Creek and hope that something with fins swims by. Lower Rock Creek is regularly stocked with trout, so your chances are pretty good, especially early in the year. More experienced anglers head for any of the numerous lakes and streams in the area, including Lake Sabrina, North Lake, South Lake, Rock Creek Lake, Crowley Lake, and the Owens River.

Hikers can drive to the nearby John Muir Wilderness trailheads in Rock Creek Canyon (see story on Rock Creek Lakes Resort on page 225) or try out the Lower Rock Creek Trail. A section of it runs right by Paradise Resort, and it is highly recommended for both hikers and mountain bikers, especially in the early summer when wildflowers are blooming. Other great side trips include a drive up U.S. 395 to the Hot Creek Geothermal Area, where you can soak in natural hot springs, or take Highway 168 east out of Bishop to visit the White Mountains and the Ancient Bristlecone Pine Forest. Hike the Methuselah Trail and take a look at the gnarled bristlecone pines, the oldest living trees on earth.

Paradise Resort's cabins are spaced close together along the river, with a few RVs sprinkled in among them. They're nothing fancy, to say the least. They have one or two bedrooms, a serviceable kitchen and bathroom, and a small front porch where you can sit outside and listen to the creek gurgle. There are no views, except of the other cabins, and of something which seems like a mirage in the dry Owens Valley—a large expanse of green lawn, with Lower Rock Creek coursing through the middle of it. At first, we mistook it for a golf course, but the owners of Paradise Resort call it a "picnic-and-play meadow." After the spring wetness dries up, they keep it green by running a sprinkler system.

If you don't catch any fish, you'll probably pay a visit to Paradise Resort's restaurant, which serves far more than the usual lodge fare of burgers, chili, and fries. The menu includes Alaskan snow crab (reportedly flown in fresh), and various gourmet cuts of beef, as well as a good selection of wine. This is camping? Sure, why not? But, if a more rustic meal appeals to you, you can always use the barbecue grill outside of your Paradise cabin to cook up some blackened hot dogs and a few roasted marshmallows. It's up to you.

Facilities, reservations, fees: There are 16 cabins at Paradise Resort, ranging in size from one to two bedrooms. All have fully equipped kitchens. RV sites are also available. Reservations are recommended. Fees range from $45 to $105 per night, with a two-night minimum stay. Pets are permitted; $10 fee per stay.

Who to contact: Paradise Resort, Route 2, Bishop, CA 93514; (760) 387-2370.

Season: Open year-round.

Directions: From Bishop, drive north on U.S. 395 for 12 miles to the turnoff for Paradise/Lower Rock Creek Road/Gorge Road. Turn left (west), then turn right immediately and drive two miles north on Lower Rock Creek Road to the resort.

94. CARDINAL VILLAGE RESORT
Inyo National Forest, off U.S. 395 near Bishop

The cabins at Cardinal Village Resort are completely different from the other cabins in Bishop Creek Canyon. Whereas the rest are much like fish camps, just places to store your stuff while you spend all day adventuring in the outdoors, historic Cardinal Village Resort is a destination in itself.

The resort is a part of an old mining claim. Its buildings date back to the turn of the century, when miners lived here and worked the Cardinal Gold Mine, just a few hundred yards away. The original town of Cardinal Village boasted a post office, store, schoolhouse, and about 100 cabins. Of those buildings, 13 of them still stand, and can be rented for your vacation.

Each building has been beautifully restored, so effectively that their exteriors look like a movie set. Each cabin is named after a lake in Bishop Creek Canyon, including Loch Leven, Lamarck, and Moonlight. Our favorites are Emerald and Baboon; they're at the far edge of the resort on the road to the Cardinal Mine.

Cardinal Village is set in a grove of aspens along Bishop Creek, where you can try your luck at trout fishing. If that proves too difficult, the resort also has Cardinal Pond, a small natural pond. Because it is stocked with trout weekly in the summer, it is popular with novice anglers.

In the summer, many visitors rent horses at Cardinal Village and take trail rides. An easy excursion on foot is to hike up the old road to the Cardinal Mine. Little remains of the mine except the building foundations and the head frame of the main shaft, but it's interesting to close your eyes and imagine the old days. Many other hiking and fishing opportunities are available in Bishop Creek Canyon, the closest of which are those at Sabrina Lake and North Lake. Sabrina Lake has a full-service boat landing with rental boats and excellent fishing for rainbow, brown, and brook trout. Much smaller North Lake is reserved for shore anglers and those in float tubes and rafts. Both lakes have an incredibly beautiful backdrop of high, snowy mountain peaks, lodgepole pines, and quaking aspens.

Hikers should be sure to follow the Piute Pass Trail from North Lake Campground that leads to Loch Leven Lake, Piute Lake, and then spectacular Piute Pass. The scenic pass is six miles out, but even if you don't make it that far, you'll be happy just to visit either of the two lakes at 2.3 and 3.5 miles out. Alternatively, you can hike from the Lake Sabrina trailhead, and head to photogenic Blue Lake in three miles, or George Lake in three miles via a left fork in the trail. All of these lakes are at greater than 10,000 feet in elevation, so the surrounding scenery is classic Sierra high country. Hike and be awed.

Each cabin at Cardinal Village has a fully equipped kitchen, and although you should bring most of your groceries with you, you can pick up a few things at the resort's general store. Breakfast and lunch are served daily in the resort cafe, and every Saturday night they hold

Lake Sabrina from the Sabrina Basin Trail

an old-West-style steak barbecue. You're on your own for dinners other evenings of the week.

Be aware that Cardinal Village is also the headquarters of Youth With a Mission, a large Christian youth group. You don't have to be any special religion to stay here, however; nor will you have any doctrine pushed on you. The main evidence of the resort's religious affiliation is that they don't sell any alcohol at the general store, so if you want a beer you'll have to bring it with you or buy it at the Lake Sabrina Boat Landing. The resort does have an interdenominational worship service every Sunday morning, and everyone is welcome. We were told that there are always a few in attendance who whisper prayers about big brown trout.

Facilities, reservations, fees: There are nine cabins at Cardinal Village Resort, all with fully equipped kitchens. A cafe and general store are also available. Reservations are recommended. Fees range from $80 to $130 per night, with a two-night minimum stay. One cabin can accommodate up to 16 people; the fee is $220 per night. Pets are not permitted.

Who to contact: Cardinal Village Resort, Route 1, Box A-3, Bishop, CA 93514; (760) 873-4789.

Season: Open May to October.

Directions: From Bishop on U.S. 395, turn west on Highway 168/West Line Street. Drive 17 miles on Highway 168 to Cardinal Village Resort. (Do not bear left at the South Lake fork; continue straight ahead.)

95. BISHOP CREEK LODGE
Inyo National Forest, off U.S. 395 near Bishop

The lodge dining room pretty much says it all about the cabins at Bishop Creek. There's a wagon wheel suspended from the ceiling, fishing lures hanging everywhere like Christmas ornaments, and a chainsaw-carved wooden cowboy propped up in the corner, dressed in somebody's sunglasses and handkerchief. Hunting and fishing trophies cover every wall of the room—the heads of several long-departed deer, an antelope, a moose, an elk; and the lifelike bodies of a few big trout.

Bishop Creek Lodge makes no pretenses: It's a fish camp, a base for people heading to South Lake or Sabrina Lake to catch trout all day, and then maybe play cards or sit by the campfire in the evening. Situated at the lofty elevation of 8,300 feet, the place also attracts hikers who want to traipse the myriad of spectacular trails in the Bishop Creek Canyon and John Muir Wilderness, but don't want to spend their nights in a tent.

When you arrive at Bishop Creek Lodge, the manager will give you your cabin key and tell you to have fun, and those are all the necessary introductions. After that, you're on your own, which is just fine with most visitors. The cabins were built by pioneers in 1928, and are typical rustic fish-camp style, but they are clean and cozy. Each cabin comes with a kitchen and bathroom, plus electricity and heat. The kitchens are fully stocked with everything you need for cooking except the food. Because supplies are minimal at the cabin store, you should buy your groceries in Bishop on the drive in to the canyon. (Either that or eat Power Bait for dinner.)

If you don't want to cook, you can eat at Bishop Creek Lodge's cafe and saloon. The menu is limited—hamburgers and a few sandwiches served all day, and steak and chicken for dinner. There's usually also a "special" at dinner, but if you ask what it is, like we did, you may be told "Chicken Something." It can be difficult to get more details; just take your chances and order it. The food is pretty good; the service is delightfully informal.

A downer for some early-morning types is that hot breakfasts are not served at the lodge, and the "continental" breakfast isn't served until 8 a.m., which is late for most serious anglers. But cereals, muffins, juice, and coffee come free with your cabin; you serve yourself in the lodge dining room. Then it's time to go exploring.

The most popular activity is fishing along the shoreline or from a rented boat at South Lake, just five miles up the road, or at Sabrina Lake, just 10 miles away. Both lakes are known for their trophy brown trout. Plenty of anglers also fish the many miles of rushing Bishop Creek, either the North, Middle, or South forks. Bring your flyfishing gear.

Hikers head for the spectacular John Muir Wilderness. A trailhead is located five miles away near the South Lake boat ramp (try the gorgeous six-mile loop hike to Ruwau, Bull, and Chocolate lakes, or the shorter out-and-back trip to Long Lake). Another trailhead is found two miles from Bishop Creek Lodge at the Bishop Creek Bridge (try the more difficult seven-mile round-trip to the four Tyee Lakes). Or head over to the trailheads by Sabrina Lake, where you can hike the popular Sabrina Basin Trail to Blue Lake, a photographer's and swimmer's delight. Remember that all of these trailheads are at 9,000-plus feet in elevation, so give yourself some time to get acclimated to the thin air before you race up the mountainside.

When you reserve your cabin at Bishop Creek Lodge, be forewarned that they are not all created equal. Cabins numbered 1, 2, and 8, plus the ones called Brown Trout and Honeymoon, are right on the road. Although it isn't a major highway, it can be a little noisy in the early morning, when cars and trucks speed up the road to the lake. If there are only two of you, cabin number 6 is the best bet. It is up on a hill, slightly away from the other cabins and farthest from the road.

Facilities, reservations, fees: There are 13 cabins at Bishop Creek Lodge, which can accommodate two to eight people each. All have fully equipped kitchens. A cafe, saloon, and general store are also available. Reservations are recommended. Fees range from $65 to $180 per night, with a two-night minimum stay. A continental breakfast is included. Pets are permitted; $10 fee per night.

Who to contact: Bishop Creek Lodge, Route 1, South Lake Road, Bishop, CA 93514; (760) 873-4484.

Season: Open from May to October, depending on snow conditions.

Directions: From Bishop on U.S. 395, turn west on Highway 168/West Line Street. Drive 14 miles on Highway 168 to the South Lake turnoff. Turn left and drive 2.5 miles to Bishop Creek Lodge.

96. PARCHERS RESORT
Inyo National Forest, off U.S. 395 near Bishop

If you like your mountain cabin to be just a little more modern, a little less rustic, and a little more peaceful than what you find at Bishop Creek Lodge, Parchers Resort may be the perfect place for you. Parchers is owned and operated by the same folks, but this resort is newer and a little more posh than 70-year-old Bishop Creek.

Tucked in between two streams—Bishop Creek and Green Creek—and set among lodgepole pines and aspens, the cabins at Parchers Resort are pleasantly secluded and partially hidden from the road. The cabins come in two styles: standard and rustic. The standard cabins are more modern and house as many as four people. Each one has a fully equipped kitchenette and small dining area, a separate bedroom with a queen or double bed, and a living area with a couple of extra twin beds for your uncles and aunts. The rustic cabins also house up to four people, but if it's just the two of you and you want to save some money, you can rent a two-person rustic cabin with no kitchen. They're half the price of the other cabins, but then again, they're not as luxurious.

Parchers Resort has another big thing going for it: It's located only 1.2 miles from big, beautiful South Lake. The lake has a fully stocked marina with aluminum boats for rent, where they boast of having some of the finest boating opportunities in the eastern Sierra. I'm not sure what they mean by "finest," but I promise that if you show up in October when the quaking aspens wear their full autumn colors, you'll have the most scenic boating of your life. The lake is set at 9,750 feet in elevation, and it's well stocked with rainbow and brown trout.

Hikers have access to numerous trails (see the hiking information in the story on Bishop Creek Lodge, page 232.) My personal favorite is the six-mile round-trip to the five Treasure Lakes. The route begins at South Lake on the Bishop Pass Trail, but after an initial climb of nearly a mile, you bear right on the Treasure Lakes Trail and leave much of the trail traffic behind. Most hikers, backpackers, and pack animals continue straight for Long Lake, Bishop Pass, or the Chocolate Lakes Loop, but you get your own private pathway that leads only to the Treasure Lakes. The first two lakes are easily accessible by trail; the remaining three require some

One of several lakes along the Bishop Pass Trail

route-finding. Many people stop at the first Treasure Lake and are satisfied; it's a sparkling gem surrounded by jagged peaks.

After a day of hiking and fishing, you might not have energy left for cooking, so you can eat at the Parchers' South Fork Restaurant. Dinner is the main event at the South Fork; in fact it's the most well-prepared grub you can find anywhere in Bishop Creek Canyon. Plenty of backpackers come off the Bishop Pass Trail after a week in the wilderness and head straight for the restaurant; most of them have already decided what they will order five miles back at Bishop Pass.

A continental breakfast is included in the price of your cabin; lunch is not available at the restaurant. You can always drive down the road to the cafe at Bishop Creek Lodge.

Facilities, reservations, fees: There are 10 cabins at Parchers Resort, most with fully equipped kitchens. A restaurant and general store are also available. Reservations are recommended. Fees range from $60 to $130 per night with a two-night minimum reservation. Pets are not permitted.

Who to contact: Parchers Resort, Route 1, South Lake Road, Bishop, CA 93514; (760) 873-4177.

Season: Open from May to October, depending on snow conditions.

Directions: From Bishop on U.S. 395, turn west on Highway 168/West Line Street. Drive 14 miles on Highway 168 to the South Lake turnoff. Turn left and drive six miles to Parchers Resort on the left.

97. LONG LAKE & BULL LAKE BACKPACK
John Muir Wilderness, off U.S. 395 near Bishop

Lakes, lakes, lakes everywhere. That's how it is on the Bishop Pass Trail, where in the space of five miles you can access Long Lake, Spearhead Lake, Saddlerock Lake, Bishop Lake, and so on. But if you're looking for an easy backpacking trip, the kind you can take your kids on and get them permanently hooked on the outdoors, you need only hike two miles on the Bishop Pass Trail and set up camp at either Long Lake or Bull Lake. Then spend a few days hiking, fishing, and exploring the area, and you'll soon find you have some young outdoor addicts on your hands.

Here's a tip to make your trip easier: Because backpackers must park one mile back from the trailhead at South Lake (you must leave your car east of Parchers Resort if you are staying overnight), you should drop off your companions at South Lake with all your gear, then go park the car and walk back while they wait for you. They can while away a half-hour fishing in Bishop Creek or dropping a line in South Lake, and everyone will be in good spirits when you start hiking.

The trail begins on the south side of the day-use parking lot, and you head uphill along the eastern shore of South Lake. The views begin almost immediately, particularly of Mount Thompson and Mount Goode. Take the left fork at three-quarters of a mile, heading for Long Lake and Bishop Pass. The majority of the climb is now over. Continue straight until you reach the junction with the trail to Bull Lake and Chocolate Lakes at 1.5 miles. It's decision time: Will you set up camp at Bull Lake or continue straight for Long Lake? Long Lake is much larger, but Bull Lake is less visited, round, and beautiful, so take your pick. Bull Lake is only a quarter-mile to your left; Long Lake is a half-mile straight ahead.

Whichever way you go, you'll wind up at a spectacular lake at more than 10,000 feet in elevation, with plenty of good campsites located near the water's edge. Luckily the two lakes are connected via a terrific loop trail, so no matter which lake you stay at, you can visit the other, plus several more. The trail is called the Chocolate Lakes Loop, and can be hiked in either direction. From Long Lake, you hike to the lake's far end, then take the steep uphill cutoff on the left. The trail is signed for Ruwau Lake, a half-mile away. From Ruwau

Lake, it's another half-mile to the two Chocolate Lakes, set below Chocolate Peak, and then another half-mile to Bull Lake.

Note that the trail is rather indistinct in places, and it's often more like a route than a real trail, especially between Ruwau Lake and the Chocolate Lakes. If you are hiking the entire loop, make sure you've brought a good map. If you have young children with you, it might be best to confine your travels to more moderate paths. For example, if you are

Camper on the edge of Long Lake

staying at Bull Lake, just hike to the Chocolate Lakes to the northeast or to Long Lake to the southwest. Both are less than a mile away. If you are staying at Long Lake, hike to Bull Lake and then to the Chocolate Lakes, or continue south on the Bishop Pass Trail to Spearhead Lake and big Saddlerock Lake.

Let's put it this way: There are so many lakes to visit, and every one is so exquisite, you simply can't go wrong.

Facilities, reservations, fees: There are numerous primitive campsites at Bull Lake and Long Lake. Water is available for filtering. Campfires are not permitted; bring a backpacking stove. A free wilderness permit is required for overnight stays; quotas are in effect from the last Friday in June to September 15. Permits are available in advance by mail, phone, or fax for this time period for a $3 fee. Mail permit requests to Wilderness Reservations, P.O. Box 430, Big Pine, CA 93513. Phone (888) 374-3773 or fax (760) 938-1137. There is no fee for camping. Pets are permitted.

Who to contact: Inyo National Forest, White Mountain Ranger District, 798 North Main Street, Bishop, CA 93514; (760) 873-2500 or fax (760) 873-2563.

Maps for backpacking: For a map of Inyo National Forest, send $4 to USDA-Forest Service, 630 Sansome Street, San Francisco, CA 94111. For a topographic map of the area, ask for Mount Thompson from the USGS.

Season: Open May to October.

Directions: From Bishop on U.S. 395, turn west on Highway 168/West Line Street. Drive 14 miles on Highway 168 to the South Lake turnoff. Turn left and drive six miles to Parchers Resort. Backpackers must park along South Lake Road in the signed spaces east of Parchers Resort; the trailhead parking area at the end of the road at South Lake is reserved for day-use.

98. GLACIER LODGE
Inyo National Forest, off U.S. 395 near Big Pine

If I had to pick my favorite lodge with cabins in the southern Sierra, I'd have one heck of a dilemma. It could be an impossible task, because I'm so crazy about them all. But I know that Glacier Lodge in Big Pine Canyon would make the top three, because it's got everything: a stunning location, cozy cabins, a top-notch restaurant, and really nice people who run the place.

I first visited Glacier Lodge in the early summer, when the wildflowers were blooming and the waterfalls were falling hard in Big Pine Canyon. You like scenery? You're in luck. You like hiking and fishing? You just won the lottery. The cabins are backed right up against the mountains, just before the land becomes the John Muir Wilderness. You can fish in Big Pine Creek, or if you have young kids with you, you can get them started in angling at the small stocked pond right in front of the lodge.

Glacier Lodge's cabins are rustic and adorable, and they come with all the critical luxuries: Bathrooms, showers, electricity, and tiny kitchens. The kitchens are nothing to brag about, but you can cook your meals in them if you like. If you don't want to cook, you can eat your meals at the Glacier Lodge restaurant. The breakfast menu includes items like the Day-Hikers Special, Backpackers Deluxe, and Switchback Omelette. Dinner is surprisingly gourmet, including a full wine list and entrées like venison, filet mignon, salmon, shrimp, and scallops, in addition to more plebeian foods like chicken, vegeterian dishes, and hamburgers. The restaurant is not open for lunch, but you can buy a few groceries at the lodge store to fill your daypack.

Speaking of daypacks, don't miss the hiking in Big Pine Canyon. You can take an easy walk to First and Second Falls on the North Fork Trail starting right from the lodge. Remember that the trailhead elevation is 8,000 feet, so even a relatively easy hike can leave you huffing and puffing on your first day in the high country.

Hikers who want a longer trip can head beyond the falls to the Big Pine Lakes. The lakes have terribly unimaginative names—First Lake, Second Lake, Third Lake, and so on—so be sure to give them better monikers when you arrive. Look for a stone cabin built by movie actor Lon Chaney near Cienega Mirth, 2.5 miles out. The cabin is now being used as a backcountry ranger residence. If you take the left fork in the trail, you'll reach First Lake at four miles from the lodge. If you have the time and energy, try to hike as far as Third Lake, five miles from the lodge and at 10,400 feet in elevation. It has a beautiful milky turquoise color caused by water flowing directly from Palisade Glacier, the southernmost glacier in the United States. The silt from the glacier is so fine that it does not settle out in the water, and this produces a vivid, cloudy, blue-green color in the lake.

Hard-core mountaineers can make the trek all the way to Palisade Glacier, 8.5 miles from the lodge and at 12,400 feet in elevation. It's a long, hard hike, and when you near the glacier, you need climbing equipment and skills. Most people are happy if they can get close enough to get a good look at it. The Palisade Crest is considered to have some of the finest alpine climbing in all of California, but it's not for the inexperienced.

Hiking the South Fork Big Pine Creek Trail is also an option, but the route is more obscure and difficult than the North Fork Trail. It gets much less foot traffic, which makes it an appealing choice on summer weekends. You can hike to Willow Lake in four miles, or Brainard Lake in five miles. The last mile to Brainard Lake has a 1,000-foot elevation gain, so be prepared to pay for your pleasure.

It used to be that you could only visit Big Pine Canyon and Glacier Lodge in summer and fall, but at the end of 1996 they decided to plow the road in winter and keep the lodge open year-round. It was so successful that when new owners bought the place in the fall of 1997, they decided to continue the custom. We say hooray for that.

Facilities, reservations, fees: There are 12 cabins at Glacier Lodge, all with fully equipped kitchens. A trailer park with shower facilities, lodge rooms, a restaurant, and a general store are also available. Reservations are recommended. Fees range from $70 to $100 per night. Pets are permitted with a $15 fee per stay.

Who to contact: Glacier Lodge, P.O. Box 370, Big Pine, CA 93513; (760) 938-2837.

Season: Open year-round.

Directions: From Big Pine on U.S. 395, turn west on Crocker Street and drive 10.5 miles to the end of the road and Glacier Lodge. (The road becomes Glacier Lodge Road.)

99. FIRST FALLS WALK-IN CAMP
Inyo National Forest, off U.S. 395 near Big Pine

Want a perfect beginner-level backpacking trip where you camp on top of a waterfall? Sign up here for the trip to First Falls Walk-in Camp, just 10 miles off U.S. 395 in Big Pine.

The trip begins at the Big Pine Canyon trailhead near Glacier Lodge, elevation 7,800 feet. Park at the backpacker's parking lot a half-mile from the end of the road, but don't take the backpacker's trail. Although it passes near the First Falls Walk-in Camp, it's not the prettiest or the easiest way to hike there. Instead, walk down the paved road for a half-mile to a gated dirt road near Glacier Lodge and

Big Pine Canyon near Glacier Lodge and First Falls Walk-in Camp

a day-use parking area. Go around the gate, then follow the dirt road past some summer homes. In minutes you cross a bridge over First Falls, a noisy, 200-foot white-water cascade. Bear right on a narrower trail and start switchbacking uphill, paralleling the cascade. As you climb, you get awesome views into Big Pine Canyon's South Fork. It takes a dozen or more tight curves in the trail to climb above the waterfall, and your body will feel the elevation if you aren't accli-mated, or if your pack is heavy.

At the top of the falls, cross another bridge over the creek, then take a hard right onto a gated dirt road, heading 100 yards into the campground. Total distance from your car? About a mile and a half, with a 500-foot elevation gain.

The campground has all the basics: stream water for filtering, pit toilets, picnic tables, and fire grills. There is no garbage service, so you must pack out all that you pack in. It's a pretty spot, surrounded by pines for wind protection but with good views if you peek between the branches. Although you're right above the waterfall, you can't see it from your perch. You'll sleep well, listening to the sound of Big Pine Creek streaming by, and the wind in the trees. Because you're a good distance off the main trail, you won't be disturbed by early-morning hikers and anglers heading into the canyon.

Of course, when you're awake and ready to hike, you can be on the North Fork Trail in a matter of seconds. Following the trail into the North Fork of Big Pine Canyon, you'll soon come across Second Falls, a larger, more impressive cascade than First Falls, less than one mile away and clearly visible from the trail. Since the route is set along the canyon bottom, you have lovely views of the tall surround-ing canyon walls, occasional lodgepole pines, and many mountain wildflowers. (You can also take an upper trail from the camp, but the route along the canyon bottom is prettier.)

The trail climbs up and over Second Falls, following a well-graded route to Cienega Mirth at 2.5 miles from camp. Wildflowers are excellent at the swampy, spring-fed mirth. If you choose to continue, you reach First Lake at four miles, then bear left and reach Second Lake at 4.3 miles. By Second Lake, you've climbed to over 10,000 feet. The first three lakes along the North Fork Trail all show the distinctive greenish turquoise color of glacial lakes, because their waters are fed by the melting of nearby Palisade Glacier.

If you aren't spending your days hiking in Big Pine Canyon, then you're probably spending them fishing. There are countless waters to fish from opening day at the end of April until closing day at the end of October. Five breeds of trout are plentiful in the canyon: golden, cutthroat, rainbow, brown, and brook. The closest fishing access is anywhere along Big Pine Creek; anglers' trails run alongside it for miles. The Department of Fish and Game keeps the creek well stocked with rainbow trout all summer, especially near the drive-in campgrounds.

Facilities, reservations, fees: There are six campsites at First Falls Walk-in Camp, available on a first-come, first-served basis. Water is available for filtering. Campfires are permitted. There is no fee for camping. Pets are permitted.

Who to contact: Inyo National Forest, White Mountain Ranger District, 798 North Main Street, Bishop, CA 93514; (760) 873-2500 or fax (760) 873-2563.

Maps for backpacking: For a map of Inyo National Forest, send $4 to USDA-Forest Service, 630 Sansome Street, San Francisco, CA 94111. For a topographic map of the area, ask for Coyote Flat from the USGS.

Season: Open May to October.

Directions: From Bishop, drive 15 miles south on U.S. 395 to Big Pine. Turn right (west) on Crocker Street, which becomes Glacier Lodge Road, and drive 10 miles to the Big Pine Canyon Trailhead on the right, a half-mile before the end of the road. Backpackers must park at this overnight parking lot, not in the day-use parking area by Glacier Lodge.

---

100. FURNACE CREEK RANCH
Death Valley National Park, off Highway 190 in Furnace Creek

The Furnace Creek Ranch is everything the Furnace Creek Inn is not. The Furnace Creek Inn stands for elegance. The Furnace Creek Ranch stands for economy. The Furnace Creek Inn defines service. The Furnace Creek Ranch defines serviceable.

But if you're on a budget, and you want to have the best Death Valley vacation possible without having to stay in a cheap motel in Pahrump, Nevada, the cabins at Furnace Creek Ranch might fill the bill. Located just one mile from the national park's Furnace Creek Visitor Center (and just one mile from the ritzy and historic Furnace Creek Inn), the cabins at Furnace Creek Ranch are perfectly situated for touring all the highlights of the park.

When you first pull into Furnace Creek Ranch, you may be

surprised to find that it's an entire little village, somewhat like Curry Village in Yosemite National Park. Once the crew quarters for the Borax Mining Company, Furnace Creek Ranch now has a post office, general store, three restaurants, a motel and cabins, a golf course, horseback riding facilities, a saloon, and of course, the Borax Museum. We even found a laundromat in which to wash our dirty hiking clothes.

Red Cathedral in Golden Canyon

The ranch's claim to fame, besides its Borax mining history, is that it has "the world's lowest golf course" at elevation minus 178 feet. We were more interested in seeing the sights in Death Valley, so each day we ate an early breakfast at the ranch cafe, then headed out. Since the distances are so great in Death Valley, it takes a couple days of driving, hiking, and exploring to feel like you've seen the park. Be prepared to put some serious miles on your automobile.

One excellent day-trip is to head up north to Scotty's Castle (60 miles from Furnace Creek) and take the tour of this fascinating desert mansion that was built in the 1930s. Afterwards, drive a few miles further to the rim of Ubehebe Crater, and either hike down into its depths or follow the trail along its edge until you reach two smaller volcanic craters.

The ambitious can drive another 40 miles further west to see the Eureka Sand Dunes, the tallest sand dunes in California at 680 feet. The drive is hell—a bumpy dirt road all the way—but the sand dunes are worth seeing. You can climb to the top and take fabulous photographs. Another day can be spent closer to the Furnace Creek area, visiting Golden Canyon, Mosaic Canyon, the Keane Wonder Mine, and Salt Creek. Yet another day can be spent driving south in the park to visit Badwater, Wildrose Peak and the Charcoal Kilns. There's a ton to see, but there are many miles between each sight.

By the time we made it back to Furnace Creek Ranch at the end of each day, we were glad to have a clean, tidy cabin to return to, with a hot shower and soft beds. The cabins are side-by-side duplexes, fairly modern and pedestrian in appearance, but adequate. We found them to be quiet and peaceful, considering how close they are situated to each other, but we were disappointed that they did not have kitchens or even kitchenettes. We ate in the ranch cafe, which was less expensive than the neighboring steakhouse, but still overpriced.

A warning: The Furnace Creek Ranch cabins have telephones and TVs, complete with pay-per-view movies and Nintendo, which gives them a motel-like ambience. Just do your best to ignore the beasts.

Facilities, reservations, fees: There are 24 duplex cabins at Furnace Creek Ranch, plus numerous motel rooms. None of the accommodations have kitchens. Campgrounds with RV and tent sites are also available. Reservations are recommended. Fees range from $80 to $120 per night. Pets are not permitted.

Who to contact: Furnace Creek Ranch, P.O. Box 1, Death Valley, CA 92328; (760) 786-2345. Fax (760) 786-2307.

Season: Open year-round, best from November to May. Summer is extremely hot.

Directions: From Barstow, drive east on Interstate 15 for 60 miles to Baker and Highway 127. Turn north on Highway 127 and drive 80 miles to Death Valley Junction. Turn west (left) on Highway 190 and drive 30 miles, past the Furnace Creek Inn, to the Furnace Creek Ranch on the left side of the road. (You can also enter Death Valley from U.S. 395 south of Lone Pine. Take Highway 190 east from Olancha for 80 miles, past Stovepipe Wells Village, then turn right and drive 14 miles to Furnace Creek Ranch.)

INDEX

Ann Marie Brown is an outdoors writer and fitness instructor who lives in Marin County, California. She is the author of six guidebooks with Foghorn Press:

Easy Camping in Southern California
Easy Hiking in Southern California
California Waterfalls
California Hiking (with Tom Stienstra)
Easy Hiking in Northern California
Easy Biking in Northern California

FOGHORN ⚓ OUTDOORS

Founded in 1985, Foghorn Press has quickly become one of the country's premier publishers of outdoor recreation guidebooks. Through its unique Books Building Community program, Foghorn Press supports community environmental issues, such as park, trail, and water ecosystem preservation.

Foghorn Press books are available throughout the United States in bookstores and some outdoor retailers. If you cannot find the title you are looking for, visit Foghorn's Web site at www.foghorn.com or call 1-800-FOGHORN.

The Complete Guide Series

- *Easy Hiking in Southern California* (256 pp) $12.95
- *Easy Camping in Northern California* (240 pp) $12.95
- *Easy Hiking in Northern California* (240 pp) $12.95
- *Easy Biking in Northern California* (224 pp) $12.95
- *Washington Fishing* (480 pp) $20.95—New 2nd edition
- *Pacific Northwest Camping* (656 pp) $20.95—New 6th edition
- *Pacific Northwest Hiking* (648 pp) $20.95—New 2nd edition
- *California Camping* (768 pp) $20.95—New 10th anniversary edition
- *California Hiking* (688 pp) $20.95—New 3rd edition
- *California Waterfalls* (408 pp) $17.95
- *California Fishing* (768 pp) $20.95—New 4th edition
- *California Golf* (864 pp) $20.95—New 7th edition
- *California Beaches* (640 pp) $19.95
- *California Boating and Water Sports* (608 pp) $19.95
- *California In-Line Skating* (480 pp) $19.95
- *Tahoe* (678 pp) $20.95—New 2nd edition
- *Utah and Nevada Camping* (384 pp) $18.95
- *Southwest Camping* (544 pp) $17.95
- *Baja Camping* (288 pp) $14.95—New 2nd edition

The National Outdoors Series

- *America's Secret Recreation Areas—Your Recreation Guide to the Bureau of Land Management's Wild Lands of the West* (640 pp) $17.95
- *America's Wilderness—The Complete Guide to More Than 600 National Wilderness Areas* (592 pp) $19.95
- *The Camper's Companion—The Pack-Along Guide for Better Outdoor Trips* (464 pp) $15.95
- *Wild Places: 20 Journeys Into the North American Outdoors* (305 pp) $15.95

A book's page length and availability are subject to change.

For more information, call 1-800-FOGHORN,
e-mail: foghorn@well.com, or write to:
Foghorn Press, 340 Bodega Avenue, Petaluma, CA 94952